PRACTICAL MANAGEMENT CONSULTANCY

PRACTICAL MANAGEMENT CONSULTANCY

Third Edition

Calvert Markham

Accountancy Books
Gloucester House
399 Silbury Boulevard
Central Milton Keynes
MK9 2HL
Tel: 01908 248000

ISBN 1 85355 727 7

British Library Cataloguing-in-Publication Data
A catalogue record for this book is available from the British Library.

2767/2

Coventry University

PO 9901055I
21619G

Typeset by Type Study, Scarborough
Printed and bound in Great Britain by Creative Print and Design Wales, Ebbw Vale, Gwent

Contents

Foreword by Barry Curnow, IMC

As President of the Institute of Management Consultants (IMC) I am delighted to write this *Foreword* for the new edition of *Practical Management Consultancy*. I have known Calvert Markham for many years and he is a long-serving member of the IMC Council. As Chairman of the IMC Professional Development Committee he was responsible for the writing and publication of the IMC training modules which provide the contemporary standard for approved courses in management from entry level through to Continuing Professional Development for experienced Certified Management Consultants. Since IMC is the body that awards the Certified Management Consultant qualification in the UK, previous editions of this book have already served as invaluable *aides-mémoire* for those studying within the profession prior to interview with the IMC Membership Review Board. It is also required reading on the growing number of postgraduate level degree and diploma courses in British universities approved by the IMC under its education policy.

The IMC is keen to further discussion, debate and understanding of the changing role and increasing relevance of consulting ability as part of general management and as a life-skill as we approach the millennium. Calvert Markham's book offers a unique insight into the processes and implications of consulting as well as a valuable introduction to its methodologies and techniques. The role of the management consultant will be exceptionally challenging over the next few years and this new edition is timely as we prepare ourselves, the consulting profession and our clients for the many changes we face in the run up to the new millennium and beyond.

As management consultants we must transfer know-how to our clients and through solving problems and learning jointly with them, encourage them to be both practical and commercially successful in running businesses imaginatively and creatively. We must also encourage organisations to see change as positive rather than negative and help them to promote growth through change based on opportunities rather than focusing only on the related threats and resistance to such changes.

Practical Management Consultancy is much more than a systematic guide for those within the business management and advisory professions or those studying for them because this book conveys a clear understanding and explanation of each step of consulting activity and also gives an understanding of the principles of why client organisations behave as they do, thereby suggesting where, when and in what ways a particular consultative action or intervention might be considered appropriate. Calvert emphasises the importance of the consultant developing such an understanding of client behaviour and cautions that client engagements need to be understood and client relationships managed in the wider context of a comprehension of the business and policy environment of the client system. With such a perspective consultancy work is much more likely to be not only practical but also comprehensible to client employees and effective for the client business.

Barry Curnow
President, Institute of Management Consultants 1996/7
Principal, Maresfield Curnow School of Management Consulting

Hampstead, London
6 January 1997

Foreword by Rod Hill, CIMA

I am pleased to welcome this third edition of Calvert Markham's comprehensive guide to establishing, marketing and operating a successful consultancy practice.

The specialised role of consultant can be difficult to move into but this book eases the process considerably. It demystifies the profession by providing a clear picture of the role of the consultant, what can and cannot be achieved and how that role can be effectively practised. The issues facing the sole practitioner or practice partner are dealt with realistically, supported by frank and revealing anecdotes from the writer's long experience as a practising consultant.

Newcomers to the profession will obtain many valuable insights into areas of perceived difficulty and the sections on the conduct of assignments, marketing and making presentations are particularly informative and reassuring. In addition the book will prove a useful reference manual for more experienced practitioners for whom the concise expositions of the latest thinking and practice in the areas of change management and the art of rational persuasion will be especially illuminating.

I therefore commend this book to all aspiring and practising management consultants.

Rod Hill   1996/97
CIMA President

Acknowledgements

This book is based on my personal experience as a management consultant over rather more than the last 20 years, working with and observing many consultants and consultancy practices in the UK. Many of them are represented in the examples I have included, but names and circumstances have been changed to protect the guilty.

My thanks must go to the many participants in courses on consulting skills that I have led, who have helped to clarify the ideas herein, as well as those freinds in consultancy who have commented on this and previous editions of the book. Barry Curnow deserves a special mention in this respect; during his busy year of office he has not only contributed a foreword in his capacity as President of the Institute of Management Consultants, but has also made many helpful suggestions for inclusion in this edition.

Finally, my thanks to my wife Carole and son Charles for their support and forbearance during the writing and revisions of this book.

CM   December 1996

Introduction

'Consultancy' is delivering specialist skills in a client environment. The critical word in this definition is 'client', implying a relationship wherein an outsider makes their knowledge and experience available to an organisation. This is in contrast to – say – a line manager, who is delivering skills in an employed environment; the delivery process is different in each case. And the delivery process of consultancy is of increasing importance to all. Not only are lawyers, accountants and other professionals, as well as those with 'consultant' in their job title, engaged in consultancy, according to the definition above; nowadays, staff functions have to increasingly engage with their internal colleagues in a consultancy fashion. In all cases where consultancy skills are needed, clients (however defined) have a choice about whether to engage a specialist, and whether to take that specialist's advice.

Over the last 50 years, management skills have been studied, codified and taught, as a necessary requirement for working in an employed environment. For the future, we can expect consultancy skills to be added as a necessary complement. Although this book is directed particularly at management consultants, much of the content is applicable to the other constituencies mentioned above.

There have also been many changes in the world of management consultancy since this book was first published (as *Practical Consulting*) in 1987. Big consultancies have got bigger, and are taking on larger projects; there are new entrants, such as some of the large IT companies; and the whole consultancy market has grown.

Even so, the basic principles of engaging in consultancy remain the same, and it is these that this book addresses.

Firstly, there are the commercial imperatives. Whether they are sole practitioners or members of a firm, consultants must be profitably engaged and this affects how they organise their work as well as influencing fee rates. They have to sell and market their services to their clients, which requires skills other than technical knowledge.

Next, engagements are usually on a project basis. Consultants need to be able to operate projects effectively and to do this within the constraints of a client-consultant relationship.

Lastly, there are some important practical skills consultants must have:

- they must be able to identify and collect the data required to inform the judgements they have to make;
- most consulting projects involve change, so they must be able to carry out their work in a way which enables the changes required to be carried out successfully;
- they must be able to communicate well, orally and in writing.

These important, distinctive requirements of a consultant have determined the contents of this book and although there are a number of common examples running through it, each chapter can stand alone. There are cross-references to topics covered in other chapters and at the start of each chapter I have tried to depict the essence of what it contains.

Chapter **1** deals with the economics of a consulting practice and in particular, the basis for budgeting and setting up management controls for the practice.

Chapters **2** and **3** look at client relationship management from the time of marketing a professional service, through starting to discuss a prospective project and carrying it out, to disengagement.

Chapters **4** and **5** cover two of the core skills of a management consultant – creating change and data collection.

Chapters **6**, **7** and **8** deal with written and oral communications and Chapter **9** develops one aspect of the latter, namely rational persuasion.

Finally, Chapter **10** provides some career advice to people contemplating or engaged in a job as a consultant.

In my experience, these topics are the ones which create most difficulties for consultants and in which they need most support. This book should be of particular use to those new to the profession, but I hope it will prove interesting for experienced consultants to revisit the basics. The contents should also prove helpful to consultants other than management consultants, but whose work calls on similar professional skills.

Since the publication of the first edition, it has become clear that the rapidly changing environment in which organisations exist requires managers to be increasingly able in dealing with change. Consultancy skills can prove particularly helpful in this context.

I hope also that this book will appeal to purchasers of consultancy – our clients. Consultancy projects are cooperative efforts involving a partnership between consultant and client. It is essential that consultants understand their clients but successful consulting projects need good clients too. This book should help clients to improve their understanding of the nature of consulting thereby enabling them to use their consultants better.

1 The business of consultancy

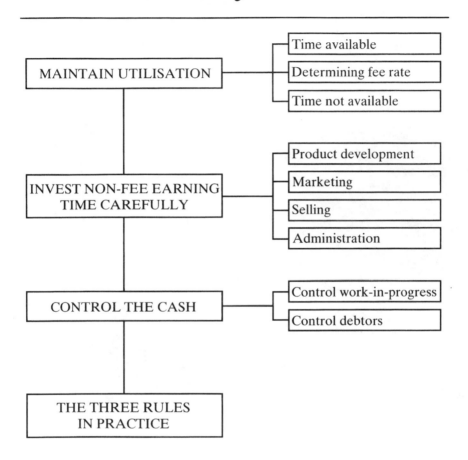

1 The business of consultancy

Annual income twenty pounds, annual expenditure nineteen nineteen six, result happiness. Annual income twenty pounds, annual expenditure twenty pounds ought and six, result misery.

Mr Micawber in *David Copperfield* (Dickens).

Some years ago I was involved with a specialist consultancy – not a management consultancy – staffed in the main by individuals with a formal professional qualification – largely barristers and accountants, and the occasional chartered secretary. Each was an expert in their field and the firm provided first class advice to its clients.

The chief executive had a problem, however. 'Our profits are falling', he confided one evening after work. 'What is more, our cash flow is poor and the amount of work-in-progress we have is far too high.'

When I looked into the problem, I found that although the professional staff were immensely capable within their own fields of expertise, they were far less effective at creating new engagements or invoicing their clients. It was not a problem of ability but one of willingness. The professionals would put these tasks at the bottom of their lists of priorities; other tasks would almost always supervene.

I have seen this frequently replicated in professional firms – not only in firms of lawyers and accountants, but also in medical practices, research laboratories, stockbrokers, chartered surveyors and management consultants – and it is, I believe, a universal truth:

Professional people do not like administration. They will give it low priority and avoid it whenever possible.

Why is this? It is probably because professionals have been schooled for a long time in their specialisation. The emphases are on quality of advice and breadth of experience in the area of their expertise. The professional's reputation grows because of specialist ability, not because they do administration well! But if a professional firm is to survive and prosper, it is vital that its business is managed to an adequate standard.

This, then, is the reason for starting a book on practical consulting with a chapter on the business of consultancy. The purpose of this chapter is to illustrate some of the important commercial aspects of running a consultancy business: for example, in the way that you organise your work.

You need to keep a record of how you spend your time, and this can be a chore. The need to achieve results within tight deadlines can also be difficult, particularly if the consultant is fascinated by the technical ramifications of the problem. The commercial imperatives of running a consultancy business can therefore conflict with the inclination of the consultant to avoid administration and become preoccupied with the projects they are undertaking.

If the new consultant understands this, they should be able to appreciate – though not necessarily enjoy – some of the pressures to which they are subject. If, alternatively, you are planning to set up a consulting business, it is vital that you understand how it works. A capacity to provide professional advice is rarely sufficient by itself to ensure commercial success!

The economics of a consultancy firm

There are three key rules (at least!) in running a consultancy business; they are:

1 Maintain the proportion of time earning fees (the utilisation).
2 Carefully invest the time not earning fees.
3 Control the cash.

Tom, Dick and Harriet work together in a consulting practice and Tom has prepared a budget for the forthcoming year. Figure 1.1, opposite, shows the breakdown of the costs expected.

The firm (TDH Ltd) consists of Tom, Dick, Harriet and a secretary. They are based in a small office they rent outside London. They try to keep their commitment to expenditure to a minimum, so use outside services to supplement their own where required. The secretary acts as a message-taker, types reports and letters, etc. Temporary staff are used when she is sick and on holiday.

Tom has budgeted basic salaries of £40,000 p.a. for himself, Dick and Harriet, which will be supplemented by a share of the profits at the year end. Each also has a company car, which the firm has supplied and pays running costs.

As far as possible, expenses incurred in carrying out their work are recharged to their clients. But there are other expenses in carrying out their business which they cannot recover – for example, in connection with attempting to sell to prospective clients who do not buy – and these are also shown.

Figure 1.1   *TDH Ltd: Fixed costs*

	£ p.a.
Consultants' salaries (3 × £40,000)	120,000
Pensions, National Insurance (25% of above)	30,000
Company cars and non-recoverable expenses	20,000
Office expenses	12,000
Telephone	3,000
Secretary/receptionist (inc. pension and National Insurance)	20,000
Other office costs	10,000
	£215,000

The budgeted expenses of the business therefore amount to £215,000 and at least this amount of revenue needs to be generated to break even. In fact, Tom, Dick and Harriet would be disappointed if the revenue was as little as this, because they would like incomes more than £40,000 p.a.

Rule 1: Maintain utilisation

Tom, Dick and Harriet get their revenue by selling their time – they do not provide product-related services. So they do not sell the results of research as reports, organise conferences or sell proprietary software for computers, which are some of the other ways in which a consultancy firm can generate revenue. Rather, when making a sale, TDH Ltd estimates how many days work it will need and multiply it by a daily fee rate to estimate the price.

So their revenue is determined by:

how many days they work on fees x the daily fee rate.

Tom has estimated how many days could be available for earning fees and Figure 1.2 shows his calculations.

Out of a total of 260 days, only 212 are left after allowances for holidays, illness and training.

This time cannot be spent entirely earning fees – it has to be allocated to selling, marketing, administration and other activities throughout the year. Small consultancy firms which do not reserve time for these can alternate between feast and famine. A consultant engaged full time on a project for several months has no time for developing further business and at the end of the project, therefore, has nothing to do. A consultant then has a period of no revenue whilst they sell the next engagement, which then occupies

---

Figure 1.2   *TDH Ltd: Working days available per consultant*

	Days
Total days available: 52 weeks x 5 days	260
Statutory holidays:	8
Annual holidays (5 weeks)	25
Illness: (minor ailments only – each of the consultants has an insurance policy in case of disability or long-term sickness)	5
Training: attendance at courses and conferences is necessary to keep up to date, so TDH Ltd budgets two weeks per year per person for this.	10
Total time unavailable	48
Net time available	212

---

them full time. This effect diminishes with increasing numbers, and independent professionals sometimes associate formally or informally to smooth it out.

A good rule of thumb for a management consulting practice is to aim for an average of about 60% of total time earning fees. This is 156 days per year per person (60% x 260 days = 156 days). More than this means more revenue, but you have to take care that the remaining time is sufficient for the non-fee-earning activities.

With a large consulting practice, of course, the work is not uniformly distributed; more senior people may spend time in selling and marketing than their junior colleagues, who will spend most of their time earning fees. Thus, in a large firm, senior people may spend only a few days per month earning fees, whilst junior consultants might be full time engaged on doing this.

By contrast, sole practitioners (who are truly **sole** practitioners – i.e., getting no work as a subcontractor to other consultants) typically find they work 100–140 days per year on fees.

The percentage of total time spent earning fees is called the utilisation on fees (hereafter referred to as utilisation).

Determining fee rate

Tom has also to decide what fee rate to charge; he knows that competitors charge from £500 per day to more than £1000 per day.

Tom therefore has to analyse how total revenue might vary according to different fee rates, assuming that Tom, Dick and Harriet each earn fees for 156 days in the year.

The result is shown in the graph in Figure 1.3, which shows how annual revenue varies with different fee rates. Also shown is the estimate of total cost from Figure 1.1 – £215,000. The breakeven point – where revenue equals cost – is at a daily fee rate of £460. So the fee rate must be more than this.

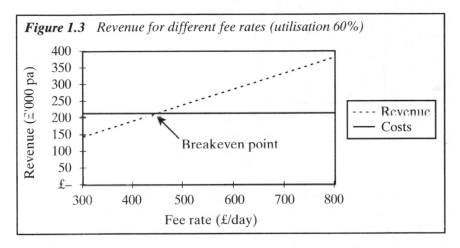

Figure 1.3 *Revenue for different fee rates (utilisation 60%)*

Tom should know from experience what fee rate is acceptable to most of his firm's current or prospective clients, but in practice some may be willing to pay more, others less. (Generally, clients are less price sensitive than consultants.) So he budgets for an *average* fee rate, and this is assumed to be £600 per day.

Having established this, he then needs a further analysis which shows the effect of varying utilisation – and this is shown in Figure 1.4. What Tom notes from this is that if budgeted utilisation is achieved, profit should be £65,800.

	£
Revenue: 156 days x £600/day x 3 people	280,800
Costs (from Figure 1.1)	215,000
Profit	65,800

If utilisation is only 50% instead of 60%, however, profits are reduced considerably:

	£
Revenue: 130 days x £600/day x 3 people	234,000
Costs (from Figure 1.1)	215,000
Profit	19,000

Thus a 10% fall in utilisation (from 60% to 50%) reduces profits to less than a third of what they were.

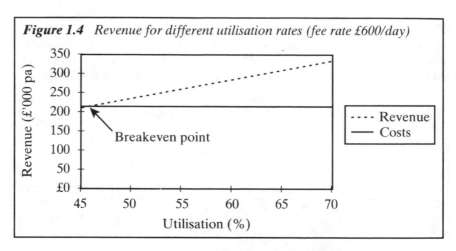

Figure 1.4 *Revenue for different utilisation rates (fee rate £600/day)*

Utilisation, therefore, is a key factor to control in any consulting firm. Income depends on utilisation and fee rates. Whereas fee rates are set on an infrequent basis – maybe annually, or at the start of a project – utilisation has to be controlled on a daily basis. Once a day that could have been spent fee earning has passed in less profitable activity, it can never be recovered.

- I have a friend – an architect – who works from home. He does not have a large income, although he claims he cannot take on more work. In fact, he is a great potterer; he will find odd tasks to do round the house, articles to read, games to play on his home computer; he works probably no more than two or, at most, three hours each day. He could easily double his income by increasing the number of hours he works each day. But there is the man, there is his lifestyle, and it is not something he would wish or needs to change.

In commercial consulting practices such freedom is rarely possible. There is – or there should be – pressure on the consultant to maintain utilisation at what may seem high levels if a practice is to prosper.

Time not available

But what of the time *not* earning fees? At this point, let us review the assumptions made in Figure 1.2 about time available.

We have assumed a five-day week and five weeks' annual holiday. Statutory holidays are also taken off from work.

Also assumed is that consultants are at work for the average working day on the principle that it is wrong to budget on the basis that individuals are to put in excessive effort. There is a certain machismo attached to long hours, working weekends, not taking holiday and so on. This is totally wrong. There is no intrinsic merit in spending excessive time at work – indeed, it can be counter-productive.

- A friend, who works for a prestigious firm of management consultants, appeared one Sunday at lunch, having spent the morning working at his office. I asked if this was a frequent occurrence, and did he get 'brownie points' for doing it? His comment was that it depended on your existing reputation. If it was good, you would be credited with having worked the extra hours; if it was poor, the comment would be 'he has to come in on Sundays to keep up with the rest of the team'.

Inevitably there will be occasions when it is necessary to work extra hours, but they should be the exception rather than the rule, and be in response to a peak of workload.

Holidays away from work are of benefit to the business as well as the individual. After a break, the consultant comes back refreshed and recharged. It is tempting to postpone or forgo holiday; avoid temptation if you can. Often the benefit of a break can be seen only in retrospect.

Illness

Ideally – from the point of view of both the business and the individual – there should be no time lost through illness. In the example an allowance has been made based on the average of past years. If it is less, that is good fortune; if more, bad luck.

Training

It can be very easy, given the pressures of day-to-day work, to allow other activities to take priority over training. And time away from work has an easily measurable opportunity cost for consultants, so training is very expensive. Consultancy, however, is a knowledge-based profession, and it behoves consultants to maintain their knowledge assets. This can be achieved partly through their work experience, but time needs to be allocated to attend refresher and updating courses, and appropriate conferences.

Time might also be spent on sharing experience internally. One of the critical activities for any knowledge-based organisation is to capture individual experience and make it corporately available.

Moreover, professional institutes (such as the Institute of Management Consultants) insist on at least a minimum amount of time spent each year on Continuing Professional Development (CPD) and the time allocated to training in Figure 1.2 should cover this.

In the example in Figure 1.2, holidays, illness and training are budgeted at 48 days per person per year, leaving 212 days, of which 156 are budgeted for fee earning. How should the remaining 56 days be allocated?

Rule 2: Invest non-fee-earning time carefully

Time spent not on fees has to be allocated to:

- marketing;
- selling;
- developing new services;
- administration.

The way these fit together in the consulting process is illustrated in Figure 1.5 opposite.

Product development

Consultants of all kinds have to be able to describe what they do for their clients, and product development consists of refining the details of these descriptions. Descriptions may be concrete (e.g., 'we are a firm of recruitment consultants; we generate a shortlist of candidates willing and able to fill a vacancy') through to the abstract (e.g., 'as a process consultant, I engage with your people to help them carry out their work more effectively').

The 'product' is the method by which individual consultants' capabilities are delivered to a client. A sole practitioner may have a narrow range of simple products, whilst a large practice may combine the capabilities of many consultants to conduct long term, complex projects. The choice of product will also influence the size of a sale; a small practice may sell a few consultant-weeks each sale, whilst a large one might seel many work-years in a single sale.

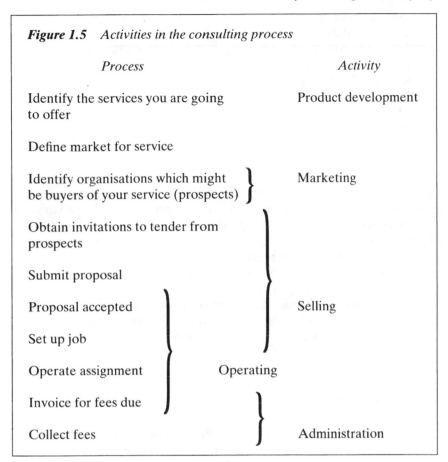

Figure 1.5 *Activities in the consulting process*

Process	Activity
Identify the services you are going to offer	Product development
Define market for service	
Identify organisations which might be buyers of your service (prospects) }	Marketing
Obtain invitations to tender from prospects	
Submit proposal	
Proposal accepted	Selling
Set up job	
Operate assignment	Operating
Invoice for fees due	
Collect fees	Administration

Equally important is defining what you are **not** going to do.

- Recently a new client approached me. 'We have been given your name by XYZ, who have been doing some excellent work for us in team building. They no longer wish to do it, and have suggested you could help.' XYZ is a major practice, which is following a focused strategy. This means defining clearly what they will and will not do. The piece of work they were doing for this client was excellent, and seen to be so, but it now fell outside their chosen area of business, so they turned it down. I admire them; in implementing strategy, the difficult task is declining promising opportunities outside the area of business chosen.

Product development can be carried out as a specific activity, but often combines theoretical development with operating experience.

So, in practice, time spent on product development is spent packaging consultants' capabilities and experience, and directing these to address client needs. It might consist of developing software for computers, a training course on a specific topic, or – as a lawyer or accountant – exploiting a change in legislation to the benefit of clients.

Consultancy services do become outmoded and need refreshing and – as with all aspects of the business – require an investment of time. The investment needs to be focussed carefully – perhaps it is in this area that time can be most easily wasted.

One of the most effective ways of developing new products in manufacturing has been the sponsorship of a 'product champion'. A product champion is an individual who believes in a product concept and is enthusiastic and energetic enough to develop an idea into a marketable reality. Similarly, in a consultancy an enthusiastic product champion is much better than a half-hearted individual who sees the task as a chore.

The rules for allocating time to product development are similar to those for marketing – the plan should fit the resources, and the resources the plan. In a commercial consulting firm, the amount of time usually given to product development will be among the least of the non-fee-earning activities

Marketing

There are as many definitions of marketing as there are people prepared to define it, and it is easy to start an argument on what the difference is between marketing and selling.

I differentiate them as follows: selling is directed at specific prospective clients, whereas marketing is aimed at raising awareness of the firm and its services more generally. Marketing therefore covers promotional activities such as:

- advertising and publicity material – e.g., brochures;
- publicity about the firm and its work;
- speaking at conferences;
- running seminars;
- publishing articles in journals and newspapers;
- other publications – e.g., books, manuals, software, periodicals.

Marketing will include other activities which can be generally categorised as 'networking'. These are occasions when you can come into contact with prospective clients informally; attendance at a conference may lead to this, but there will be other occasions – for example, through membership of a club – which will bring prospective clients into contact.

An important group of people to include in a network are 'connectors'. These are third parties who can introduce business to your own firm. For example, an accountant may be asked to recommend a consultant who can advise on the selection of computer systems, or a banker asked to recommend a consultant who can give sales training. The object of marketing, therefore, is to raise awareness of your services amongst not only clients but also connectors, so that they will contact you when they know of an organisation needing the service you offer.

Marketing your firm's services is just as much a project as any of those carried out on behalf of clients. It therefore needs good project management – a set of objectives, plans for their attainment, resources allocated, and controls for monitoring progress. The time budgeted for marketing will depend on the marketing plan.

In the case of TDH Ltd – and possibly larger firms too – this is worked out by a process of compromise and opportunism!

In practice, selling work and earning fees are likely to take priority over marketing, since they are 'closer' to cash revenue (see Figure 1.5). Marketing is fitted in between times, but there must be a minimum level of activity to secure the future.

In preparing his budget, therefore, Tom should see how much time ought to be spent on selling before allocating time to marketing.

Selling

Selling takes time, but it does not always result in sales. Time spent on selling therefore has to be jealously husbanded.

- Some years ago, during a recession in consultancy, I remember a team of consultancy salespeople who seemed to be spending a lot of time around the office rather than out with clients. One of the salespeople explained to me, 'It's easy to be a busy fool. It would be easy to rush around the country – with the resultant costs – meeting people with whom there is no prospect of doing business. We are concentrating our efforts on identifying and selling only to good prospects and spending the rest of our time on longer-term marketing'.

The best opportunities for selling are amongst existing clients, either by extending projects or spotting opportunities in other areas.

An extension to a project might come about by repeating the work for another part of the company. For example, a firm may call on a consultant to help in designing and introducing cost control procedures in one factory. Having succeeded there, they may be asked to repeat the process in other factories. Extension work might also occur within a project, evolving from help in planning it to help in implementing it.

Because large firms of consultants offer a wider range of services, there is usually more opportunity for them to be able to offer help in areas outside the scope of existing projects. In this respect, therefore, a small firm, engaged with a client, and spotting a sales opportunity it cannot help with itself, might act as a connector for a different firm (hoping perhaps for a *quid pro quo* in the long term). These have to be dealt with carefully, however.

- At the start of my consulting career, I saw scope at a client's to start a new project. A senior colleague stopped me. 'I realise they can do this, and it is needed,' he said, 'but it is not amongst their present top priorities as a business. We would lose face as a consultancy practice if we were to advise them to undertake a project of low priority'.

The amount of time to win a request for a proposal (RFP) or an invitation to tender (ITT) depends on the effectiveness of marketing and, as illustrated in Figure 1.5, there is an overlap with selling. It is difficult to conclusively align success with a specific marketing initiative, but it is sensible to analyse sales performance. The analysis may show a pattern amongst successful sales and suggest ways in which the sales level could be increased.

For the purpose of budgeting time, it is useful to have some idea of the 'score rate' of successful versus total proposals. Experience may show, for example:

- 90 per cent of proposals to existing clients are accepted;
- 50 per cent of proposals to new clients are accepted.

These figures could be applied to the firm in the example, TDH Ltd. Tom's budget is shown in Figure 1.6. It shows that 97 days should be allocated to selling.

This is of course only for budgeting purposes; sales may be of different sizes and success rates vary. During a recession, more effort will be needed to secure sales – the market may diminish and there will be more competition for fewer opportunities.

Figure 1.6 *TDH Ltd: Sales budget*

Average size of sale: 4 weeks' work
Value of average size of sale: £12,000
  (£600/day)

Assume that 90% of new sales lead to an extension sale. A new sale would then be worth, with its extension sale:

Value of new sale = £12,000 + (90% × £12,000)
      = £22,800

The number of new sales required would be

$$= \frac{\text{Revenue required}}{\text{Value of new sale}}$$

$$= \frac{£280,800}{£22,800}$$

$$= 13 \text{ (rounded up)}$$

Assuming that proposals for new sales are only 50% effective, the budget shows 26 proposals for new sales and 13 extension proposals would be needed.

Time therefore needs to be allowed for 39 proposals. Assume–say–$2\frac{1}{2}$-days' selling time is required on average to secure the RFP, create and present the proposal, the total time for selling in the budget

  $= 2\frac{1}{2}$ x 39 $= 97\frac{1}{2}$ days.

Administration

Finally, some time should be allowed for the administration of the business. (This does not include administrative work associated with specific projects, such as billing, writing letters or proofreading reports; these should be charged to the appropriate project.)

The business will need time spent to plan and review its development; for example, if they are successful, TDH Ltd may want to add further consultants to the team, and time has to be allowed for recruitment.

An allocation of half a day per month per person for administration has been made by Tom in his budget.

For Tom, Dick and Harriet, then, in their consulting practice, their annual budget could be as follows:

	Days per person per year
Net days available	212
Operating	156
Selling	32
Marketing	10
Product development	8
Administration	6
	212

Rule 3: Control the cash

Consultancy firms have two principal features which militate against good cash control.

Firstly, expenses are mainly fixed, and because the largest portion relates to salaries, it is difficult to finance working capital by deferring payment of creditors. (There are ways of coping with this. One firm increased its working capital by moving its salary payment date back a week. Another firm pays salary well in arrears, unlike most organisations which pay salaries in the current month.) TDH Ltd have made their expenses more variable by guaranteeing only a proportion of Tom, Dick and Harriet's remuneration; the balance is payable as a profit share at the end of the financial year. None the less, there is a continual flow of cash out of the firm irrespective of the level of business.

Secondly, there is usually a considerable interval between making the sale and collecting payment for it, whilst the assignment is being carried out. The result is that high levels of work-in-progress can build up – i.e., work done for clients for which they have not yet been charged – unless there are special measures introduced to avoid this.

The monthly income and expenditure budget for TDH Ltd is shown in Figure 1.7.

Note that item 2 in Figure 1.7 shows the flow of work into feeable work-in-progress – not cash in. Cash will not arrive until after the client has been invoiced for the work. In some cases, a client may not be invoiced until the project has been completed – the worst case for cashflow. It could also leave an unhealthy balance of initiative with the client. For example, if TDH Ltd have £50,000 of fees outstanding to a single client, they would be vulnerable in any dispute with that client. Indeed, in consultant mythology there have been several companies which purposely created disputes with their consultants so as to reduce the size of the outstanding bills.

Figure 1. 7 *Monthly income and expenditure budget for TDH Ltd*

1. Monthly cash flow out of the firm (based on cost budget shown in Figure 1.1).

		£
Salaries and associated expenses		12,500
Company car expenses and other non-recoverable expenses (excluding depreciation)		750
Office expenses		3,750
	Total	17,000

2. Assuming budget utilisation and fee rates, the feeable work transferred to work in progress each month is as follows:

Days on fees per month = 3 × (156 ÷ 12)

= 39 days

Value of work done = 39 × £600

= £23,400

Where possible, therefore, it is sensible to bill clients at regular stages during a project – say on a monthly basis. Even so, the working capital required is usually about three months' work-in-progress. Work done in month 1 will be invoiced in month 2 and paid (all being well) in month 3. TDH would therefore need about £50,000 working capital.

This would increase *pro rata* if they were to expand by taking on another consultant. Cashflow out would go up by more than £4,000 per month, and a further £12,000 worth of working capital would be required. (Note that this is a substantial proportion of their budgeted profits.) This is typical of an expanding consultancy: previous years' surpluses can quickly be absorbed in financing increasing work-in-progress.

Some firms require stage payments at more frequent intervals than a month, but this of course represents an increase in administrative workload and is not suitable for projects which are thinly spread. An alternative is to bill at pre-determined work-in-progress limits – e.g., at £10,000 intervals for TDH Ltd.

A further possibility is payment partly in advance; this is ideal from the point of view of your cashflow, but the reverse for the client's, and therefore less usual. Where there is some doubt about the client's ability or willing-ness to pay, however, the consultant may insist on payment in advance. No provision has been made for bad debts in Tom's budget, and he is relying on the quality of his credit control to see that they do not occur.

What do the three rules mean in practice?

Experienced consultants will be familiar with the consequences of the three rules; those new to consultancy, particularly those who have not worked in a professional practice before, will become aware of them because of the administrative disciplines placed on them. Summarised below, therefore, are some of the peculiar features of consulting practice which result from the rules.

Rule 1: Maintain utilisation results in pressure on consultants to:

- keep a record of how they spend their time;
- maintain the proportion of time spent on feeable work;
- complete projects within the working time allocated;
- control their diaries ahead so that utilisation can be maintained.

Rule 2: Invest non-fee-earning time carefully: time has to be spent on activities other than earning fees but to be done well, it requires that:

- the time invested is controlled as strictly, and the same disciplines applied, as in fee earning work;
- it is given the correct priority with respect to other work. Fee earning work can always take higher priority than non-fee-earning work in the short term, but may be detrimental in the long term.

Rule 3: Control the cash: cash control is a chore to consultants and it is better to have systems for invoicing and cash collection from clients which need little, if any, effort from consultants. Failing that, however, the consequences of this rule are:

- agree payment terms with the client at the start of a project. If it is of any size or duration, insist on stage payments;
- ensure that this agreement is adhered to on your part – do not overlook invoicing in the flurry of other activities;
- monitor the value of work-in-progress on each project to ensure it does not become too large.

The major difficulties specialist professionals have in making the transition to commercial consulting arise from the commercial context of the business. The rules set out must be observed if the consulting firm is to survive and prosper and professionals be enabled to practise their specialisms.

2 Marketing, selling and setting up consultancy projects

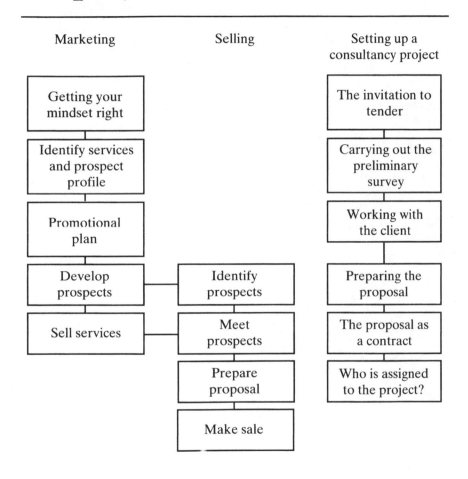

Marketing	Selling	Setting up a consultancy project
Getting your mindset right		The invitation to tender
Identify services and prospect profile		Carrying out the preliminary survey
Promotional plan		Working with the client
Develop prospects	Identify prospects	Preparing the proposal
Sell services	Meet prospects	The proposal as a contract
	Prepare proposal	Who is assigned to the project?
	Make sale	

2 Marketing, selling and setting up consultancy projects

Whenever you're sitting across from some important person, always picture him in a suit of long red underwear. That's the way I always operated in business.

Joseph P. Kennedy

Consultancy projects rarely appear out of the blue. Before any assignment can be carried out, it must first be sold. Increasingly, organisations are augmenting their own resources with consultants and becoming experienced in using them. Similarly, consultants will have spent time and effort in creating an identity for themselves (in terms of general or specific capability) by marketing activities.

Figure 1.5 in Chapter **1** shows the activities involved in a consulting practice; in this chapter we consider the pre-sales activities of marketing, selling and setting up consultancy projects.

Getting your mindset right

Many professionals feel uncomfortable about selling, and we know – for example, from the lessons of sports psychology – that if you feel uncomfortable about a task, you are less likely to perform it well. So it is essential that you approach marketing and selling consultancy with the right mindset.

There are two reasons why professionals feel uncomfortable about selling:

1 They believe that they have to change their personality to that of a stereotypical 'high pressure salesperson'.
2 Fear of failure: rarely in operating consultancy do you get such black and white outcomes as in winning or losing a sale.

As we shall see in this chapter, the first point is simply wrong. On the domestic front, each of us makes hundreds of purchases each year, and each one of those purchases was sold to us. Now, if you look back over your personal purchasing experience, particularly over items of major expenditure, how often did you experience a high pressure sales technique, and to what extent was it successful? And, if it was successful, would you happily deal with that salesperson again?

I have asked these questions of hundreds of consultants, and the constant reply is that the salespeople who succeed are:

- those who listen to what you want; and
- those who take an active interest in helping you to find the right product to meet your needs.

These are good rules for a consultant salesperson, and should help to raise the confidence of any professional specialist called on to sell – i.e.:

1 Listen carefully to what the client says, and try to identify clearly what they want.
2 Show an active interest in their problems, and work out what you can do to help.

And it also follows that if you cannot help, you should say so.

The second point – fear of failure – depends entirely on how you define failure.

- The senior partner of a large firm of consultants told of a major sale they had recently lost. 'We had put tremendous effort into this bid and were obviously very disappointed that the project had been awarded to a competitor. I and my two partners who had led the bidding team sought a meeting with the client to review what had happened. The client was apprehensive about the meeting, and visibly relieved when we conducted an objective review of why we had not been chosen. The way we conducted this review encouraged this client to do more business with us thereafter.'

The point of this story is that, although the transaction was lost, the relationship was strengthened. The relationship between consultant and client is like a bridge, whilst separate sales are like the traffic passing over it. If there is no bridge, you cannot have any traffic; conversely, there is little point in having a bridge with no traffic either! So winning a sale should never be at the expense of the relationship. If you lose a sale, do two things:

1 Find a way of using this to strengthen the relationship with the client.
2 Use it to learn: what will you do different or better next time?

Marketing and selling consultancy

The process by which marketing leads to selling is illustrated in Figure 2.1.

The *services* a consultancy might offer depend on the skills and experience of its consultants. It is as well to define the services that are on offer; if you cannot explain your services, it is unlikely that clients will understand them. For this reason, it is particularly helpful for a newly-formed consultancy to produce a brochure. I am not convinced that a brochure functions as anything more than a substantial calling card; the value of preparing one lies, however, in the discipline of having to define your services, the needs they address, and so on.

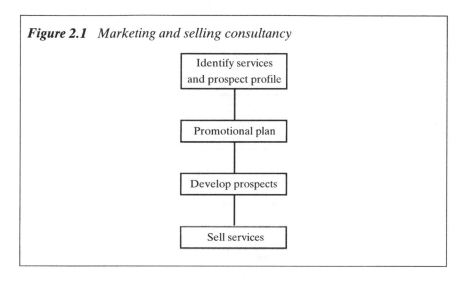

Figure 2.1   Marketing and selling consultancy

Some organisations may be excluded as clients once the service has been defined. For example, a company with no international business is unlikely to be interested in international marketing, nor is a services organisation likely to be interested in manufacturing control systems. You need therefore, to identify a *prospect profile* that defines the characteristics of the sort of organisation that might be a client for the services on offer.

These prospects need to be made aware of the service, which the consultancy can do by carrying out a *promotional plan* to publicise it. Brochures, seminars and conferences, publicity and articles in the press and so on will all help the consultancy's service to become known.

Some organisations may express an interest in the service, thereby becoming *prospects*. In my view, marketing finishes and selling begins in consultancy once a specific prospect is identified. The consultancy will therefore seek to sell its services to the prospects it has identified.

Figure 2.2 shows the stages involved in selling. Each leads to the next.

The purpose of *identifying prospects* is to choose which organisations you wish to pursue as potential clients. As it is unlikely to be a good investment of time, or even possible, to meet every prospect, there needs to be some basis for selecting which you follow up. Indeed, the whole process of selling consists of whittling down intelligently at each stage.

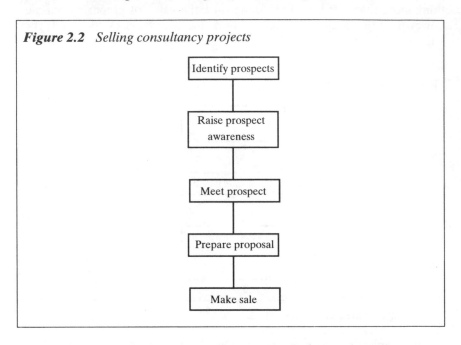

Figure 2.2   *Selling consultancy projects*

The next stage is to *raise the prospect's awareness* of your consultancy and the services you have on offer. This might be done by writing to them, perhaps by sending them some promotional material. It is unlikely that any sales will result directly from this activity; the purpose is to create a selling opportunity, which is usually at a meeting with or presentation to the prospect.

The purpose of the *meeting* is to secure authorisation to put in a proposal for carrying out a consultancy assignment. (Of course, there is no point in submitting a proposal if there is no chance that the client will buy it.) At the meeting, the salesperson has to listen very carefully to find out what the client wants. A rule of consulting is, 'Sell them what they need in terms of what they want'. There may well need to be more than one meeting before the authorisation to put in a proposal is given. This can take some considerable time; for example, I have a client with whom I had meetings intermittently over three years before being asked to submit a proposal.

The purpose of the *proposal* is to secure the sale. A proposal is the written specification of the work that is to be undertaken by the consultancy and the terms on which it is to be carried out. It may also contain the arguments for conducting the project and the benefits that might accrue by so doing. If the meeting has been conducted well, the proposal may simply be the written confirmation of what has already been agreed. In other cases, there may be quite a bit of work involved after the proposal has been submitted. For example, there may be questions to be answered; the proposal may need to be modified or refined to reflect more closely what the client wants. Some clients may want an oral presentation following submission of the proposal. Some may have elaborate procedures for deciding whether or not to accept a proposal.

Finally – you hope – the *sale* will be made. But the process is, in reality, much like a leaky pipe: not all the prospects who enter at one end emerge at the other as clients.

At each stage there is a loss. The proportion of prospects which finally become sales is usually very small – a few per cent at most. So you have to approach quite a lot of prospects before you get a sale. But this leads to two messages of hope for those who are new to selling consultancy:

(i) Don't be depressed by prospects who don't get to the meeting stage, or meetings which fail to lead to proposals, etc. This is all part of the normal process.
(ii) Provided you have identified the right prospects (and your sales technique is not disastrous!) eventually some sales will emerge from the pipeline.

It also indicates the priorities for salespeople in using their time: sales effort is best put in at the point closest to making the sale.

Of course, the consultancy sales process has to be matched by the client's buying process, and both are illustrated in Figure 2.3 over.

The figure shows that a consulting assignment is the culmination of separate and joint activities in the client and consultant.

The figure also shows that a consultancy project is in reality a joint venture between consultancy and client, and the selling/buying activity is directed to sorting out the details of the joint venture. This concept is often of help to those new to selling consultancy, many of whom think that selling involves persuading people to buy things they don't want. This is certainly not the case in selling consultancy; if you sell a client a project they don't need, you run the risk of:

• engaging in a project doomed to disappoint the client;
• ruining the client relationship.

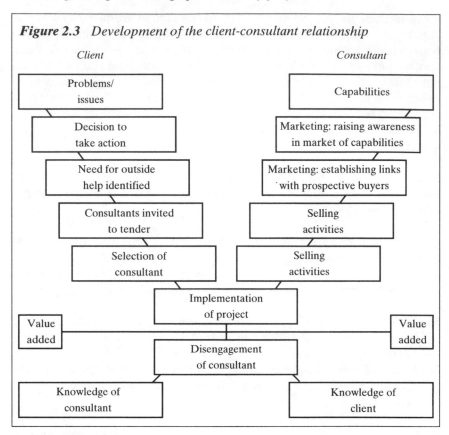

Figure 2.3 *Development of the client-consultant relationship*

So, selling consultancy involves identifying an overlap of interest between consultancy and client to your mutual benefit.

Consultants have capabilities which their clients do not have, or have in insufficient measure. Conversely, the client has a whole bundle of issues or problems which consultants could help to resolve, but which have to meet several criteria before outside help is sought:

(i) The problem must be recognised as such, and the client must have decided that they want to do something about it. Problems may be evident (for example, when relocating an office or factory). But consultants themselves can create needs through marketing activities. Over the last few years, for example, activity-based costing and process re-engineering have been used as a basis for deciding how to deploy resources to best effect.

(ii) The resolution of the problem must be a matter of priority – something the client has to do something about, now.

(iii) The client must believe the problem can be solved. Marketing by consultants can help in both meeting this and the previous criterion: the possibility that a problem previously thought to be insoluble can now be solved can make it become a matter of priority. For example, a certain level of absenteeism is accepted in all organisations; if it became known that it was easily possible to halve it, many organisations previously content would seek to do this.

(iv) The client recognises the need for outside help – whether it is expertise, or experience, or the objectivity of a professionally qualified outsider.

Part of the process of selling a consultancy service consists of getting the agreement of purchasers that these criteria are met. In the selling situation you are trying to get the prospective client to acknowledge:

- this issue is relevant to my business and needs to be addressed;
- it merits attention now;
- the issue can be resolved . . . with outside help (provided by you!).

Note that the client's perspective is from the issues that concern him. A task of the salesperson is to establish a link between these issues and the services the practice has to offer.

Once the client has decided to launch a project and seek outside help a consultant will need to be selected from those the client knows or who have a reputation in the required specialism. If you have helped the client to identify the issue and launch the project in the first place, you will be well placed to secure the assignment. If not, whether your firm is picked will depend on whether the client knows of you and your reputation – and this in turn will depend on the effectiveness of your marketing.

For these reasons, the attractiveness of any prospect can be ranked in the following order (the least attractive first):

(i) *Cold calls*: here the consultant has taken the initiative. Consultant and client will be personally unknown to each other. Although cold calling is unattractive by comparison with the other sources of prospects set out below, it can still be worth doing.

(ii) *Introductions* to new clients. Existing clients can provide introductions; there are also 'connectors' (other professional firms, banks, etc.) who can provide introductions.

(iii) *Leads*: the difference between a lead and an introduction is that with a lead a probable need for consultancy services has been identified. Leads can again arise from clients, contacts, connectors, and so on.

(iv) *Extensions*: this is the further work you might conduct with existing clients. Note that one of the outcomes of doing a consultancy project is a different – closer – relationship between consultant and client. This means that you have an inside track when bidding to do work with existing clients.

Domestic experience confirms the validity of this. If a house painter calls at your door, the chances of your needing some painting doing, and wanting him to do it now are small; likewise, so too is the probability of success from a specific cold call. Friends might be using a painter to decorate their house, and recommend him – this is an introduction. The lead would be if you wanted some painting doing, and you asked friends who recently had had their house redecorated to recommend a painter. Finally, an extension occurs when you ask the decorator – with whom you are well satisfied – to quote for doing a couple more rooms.

Sales statistics in consultancy practices reflect the relative ease of each of these. Business with current or past clients can account for two-thirds or more of sales. Indeed, global practices may have a defined target client list that means that – say, in the UK – of necessity 90 per cent or more of their sales must be to existing clients.

Referrals (leads and introductions) will account for most of the balance of sales in all cases; only a small percentage of sales will come from cold calling. And, as cold calling is the least fruitful – and hence most time consuming – of sales activities, it follows that you have to put a disproportionate amount of time into selling if you are launching a new consultancy practice.

The important point to emerge from this is that an important asset for any consultancy is its network of relationships – the contacts it has with past and present clients, connectors, and so on. A job for every consultant is to create and maintain a network.

Setting up a consultancy project

A consultancy project is thus only one part of an ongoing relationship between a client and consultant. It represents a particularly intense period of the relationship and can influence it significantly – well or adversely. And after the project has finished, the relationship will continue to need managing if the consultant is to obtain follow-on work or new projects.

Having good client relations is vital in maintaining a network for a professional practice and the foundation of this is how the relationship starts. When consultant and client come together, there will be expectations and obligations on both sides. The basis of a successful consultancy project (and hence a good ongoing relationship) is therefore a clear understanding between consultant and client about:

- the scope of the assignment;
- how it is to be conducted;
- how much it will cost;
- what deliverables the client will receive.

This means that clear terms of reference need to be established at the start; indeed, many difficulties on a consulting project arise because of a mismatch of expectations at the very start of an assignment.

In some larger firms of consultants the job of the 'salesperson' has traditionally been separated from that of the operator. Nowadays, because of the degree of specialisation often involved and the insistence of clients, operating consultants are usually involved in the selling process at least in the final stages. Consultancy salespeople may take responsibility for managing the client relationship; they will be the first point of contact for a client, but will then involve an appropriate specialist who will carry out the assignment. All consultants therefore need to be familiar with the commercial aspects of setting up a consultancy project.

TDH Ltd (introduced in Chapter **1**) will be used to illustrate the selling process. For simplicity we will assume that they are consultants on basic matters of organisation and methods, and the first contact they have with the prospective client is a telephone enquiry.

The invitation to tender

The first contact might be by letter or telephone. A government department or agency may issue a general invitation to tender containing carefully thought out terms of reference and a background briefing but this is rare elsewhere. Suppose then that Dick, of TDH Ltd, receives a telephone enquiry from a director of ABC Ltd. After introducing himself, the director might continue:

Director
'I'm told that you might be able to help us on a problem we have on our stock control system. We're thinking of installing a new computer-based system and want some external consultants to work with us. I gather you can help'.

Dick might query how the director knows about TDH Ltd, e.g., was it from general marketing or a reference from another client? This information could help in planning future marketing.

Dick
'We've done a number of projects of varying scales for a wide variety of clients in this area. Perhaps you could give me some background on your firm and the stock control system.'

Dick establishes in principle that TDH is able to help. He may never have heard of ABC Ltd, so he needs some background information.

So, they discuss the nature and context of the problem and the selling process has started. For example, the client will be forming an opinion of TDH Ltd by how well Dick demonstrates his understanding of the problem and the quality of his questions.

At this stage, it is not necessary for Dick to suggest possible solutions – quite the reverse; even if the problem is technically easy to solve there may be serious barriers to getting acceptance within the organisation.

The conversation could conclude:

Dick
'I think the next stage is for us to meet. Shall we fix a date now?'

Dick is fixing the next step in the selling process.

Director
'Can I come back to you on that – I'll call you in the next day or so.'

Not a particularly well-organised director but the point is to illustrate Dick's response . . .

Dick
'Fine; can I contact you next week if I've heard nothing in the meantime?'

Which allows Dick to take the initiative in contacting the director again should it be necessary.

They will need to arrange a venue for this meeting; a visit to a client's office or factory can tell you a lot about the business, so I try to arrange that at least one of the early meetings takes place on the client's premises.

Carrying out the preliminary survey

Prior to contracting to work on a particular project a consultant will carry out a preliminary investigation or survey to assess its nature and scope. It is a mini-project in itself to:

- collect data about the problem as defined;
- analyse it to identify the key issues;
- decide the type of approach which will lead to resolving the issues;
- plan how the project is to proceed;
- determine the consultant and other resources required.

In some projects this may already have been done by the client – for example, if the consultant is required to make a defined contribution as a specialist to a complex project already being undertaken. In other cases, a preliminary investigation might be the first stage of a multiphase project. In some cases a consultant might provide considerable help to the client simply through diagnosising the problem, and might therefore charge fees for this preliminary survey. In this example, however, we will assume that the consultant is involved in defining all the stages above before the assignment starts.

So Dick arranges to carry out his survey. Prior to visiting the prospective client he might do some more research on ABC Ltd. If he can get hold of a company report and accounts for ABC Ltd plus publicity material on its products, he will be able to learn something of ABC in advance and to focus his enquiries during his visit rather better. (He could even ask the director to provide him beforehand with information that might be available and helpful.)

Dick will have a mental, if not a written, checklist of points he will want to cover during his first visit. He may want to tour the (relevant) factory/offices/stores and be introduced to key people. (But remember that this is not always appropriate; it is an intervention into the organisation, and therefore has to be considered in the context of the project's goals. See Chapter 5 on data collection.)

Where matters of opinion (rather than hard data) are concerned, he may wish to talk to more than one person to distinguish between commonly held and individual views.

It is vital during a preliminary survey to try to identify what the real problem is rather than the symptoms. Consultants have a touching faith in their own abilities and some cynicism about their clients' skills in separating symptoms from causes. That this endures is because it is often borne out by fact. Thus Dick will find the presentation of the stock control problem is:

- we want a new computer-based stock control system;
- the current system, installed two years ago, has been outgrown, and indeed has never worked satisfactorily.

On further probing, he will probably find that:

- production and sales do not talk to each other and . . .
- . . . the only thing they agree on is that they hate the computer department . . .
- . . . who hate them equally, because they do not provide the data required, or it is inaccurate or late . . .
- . . . and the computer system *is* inadequate.

Now, whether or not he expresses it to his client, Dick is not going to get very far with the project unless he gets everybody working together. There are people issues involved as well as technical ones, and the approach Dick adopts has to allow for both dimensions of the problem.

Working with this client

Dick will also need to assess at the survey stage what sort of client he is dealing with and the nature of the working relationship they will have.

He will need to rate how good a client the organisation is; is it accustomed to using management consultants and able to manage consulting projects? If not, Dick will need to provide more project management support than otherwise and guide the client in using a consultant effectively.

There will be assumptions on both sides about the nature of the client–consultant relationship, and Dick should consider the following points in particular.

(i)   What is the relationship of the member of client staff commissioning the assignment (whom I call the 'sponsor') to the overall project? Is it his brainchild or has he been deputed to look after it? If the latter, who is the real client? How committed is he to its success and what personal objectives might it be meeting? Are there any 'unwritten expectations'? Beware of taking on projects to which the sponsor is uncommitted; more junior staff will sense this with the result that the project will be low in their priorities and the consultant will have a tough job carrying out the project. Again, beware the sponsor who is initiating a project as a personal crusade in the organisation. Others may be interested in seeing the project fail and if it does, the sponsor may find it politically expedient to blame the consultant.

(ii) What will the sponsor's involvement be after the assignment starts? If he is not going to be the principal point of contact, who is? What will your reporting relationship be to the organisation? As a strategic ploy, you should keep the reporting relationship as high as you can. In practice, this means that even if the sponsor delegates day-to-day contact to one of his subordinates, you should make sure you continue to deal with the sponsor as your client. The reason for this is that your power to get things done will depend in part on the level of your connections in the client organisation. (For more on this see Chapter **4** on creating change.)

(iii) What client staff will be available to work with you? At the very least it is helpful to have a 'Mr Fixit' who can act as your guide to the organisation, arrange meetings and make internal information available to you. Beyond this, you may need advice about the nature of the business and the industry; after all, clients should be expert about their own business! In short, therefore, consultants need support from client staff to help them work effectively. It is important that the client understands this, and provides the necessary help.

(iv) How should the assignment be publicised within the client organisation? Who needs to be told, and in what detail? This will depend on the nature of the project but it is better to take the initiative in informing staff rather than having to react to rumours and gossip.

These points need to be resolved before starting the assignment and should – at least in outline – be taken into account in preparing the proposal.

Preparing the proposal

Having carried out this survey, Dick should have collected enough data to prepare a proposal, which is the document embodying the terms of reference for the project.

On the first occasion of working with a client the proposal will probably need to be written out in some detail, but once a good consulting relationship has been achieved, a client may be happy with a short confirmatory letter covering the key points which have been orally agreed.

In *all* cases, however, the key points below must be considered in detail by the consultant and agreed – at least in principle – by the client, whether or not they are written down, so that the expectations of both the consultant and the client are the same.

(i) Your *appreciation* of the problem: at the very least this is simply feeding back to the client the data that has been given you. Much better, however, is to interpret the data with insight, so that the problem is seen by the client in a different, more helpful perspective than before. If you have a standard approach to a problem, this allows you to differentiate your proposal. For example, a client was seeking to appoint recruitment consultants and briefed two firms of consultants, both of whom impressed the client at the initial meeting. The choice therefore had to be made on the basis of the proposals they put forward. One consultancy provided a standard proposal; it reflected nothing of this briefing and could have applied to any client. The other provided an appraisal of the business issues relating to the appointment, developed from the briefing they had received. The latter firm was appointed.

Thus Dick's appreciation of the problem at ABC Ltd might emphasise the technical problems as manifestations of the need for better teamwork (a point he will need to express sensitively).

(ii) The *scope and objectives* of the assignment. These set the boundaries for the project and what is to be achieved within them. If ABC Ltd is a multi-site company, Dick may limit the scope of the project to one site – or even one product group – as appropriate.

The objective may be to have a new stock control system working well but Dick may suggest more precise measures of this, such as the requirements of the new computer system and when it should be installed and running.

(iii) The *method of approach*: there may be a totally standard, off-the-shelf approach to carrying out the assignment. There is nothing wrong with this. (Indeed, taking an example from another profession, whilst under the surgeon's knife on an operating table, we much prefer he uses a standard, well-proven approach.) On the other hand, consultants should not fall into the trap of fitting clients' problems to their solutions. Innovation, therefore, is not a *sine qua non* – it must be introduced wisely.

So Dick might use a standard approach to stock control in ABC Ltd, but be innovative in introducing it so as to achieve better team working.

(iv) The *programme of work* entailed. This is getting much closer to planning, and at this stage the principal tasks should be described at least in outline. An assignment might fall into a number of discrete phases of work and in the case of ABC Ltd, consist of:

- specification of the new system;
- delivery and introduction of the new equipment;
- parallel running with new and old systems;
- complete transfer to new system.

In this section you should explain what the client will be getting for their money – i.e., the deliverables – and when they should expect them, for example, when a new system will have been designed, when a report will have been delivered and the points it will cover, and so on.

(v) A summary of the prospective *benefits* arising from the project. This is particularly relevant in written proposals, which may be used for selling the project concept as well as your firm's services, to your sponsor's colleagues. Thus in this proposal Dick may quantify the reduction of working capital, and the consequent savings in interest payable resulting from the expected reductions in stock levels.

(vi) The *resources required*. This will cover the time required from the consultant and the consequent fees. With a multi-stage project, the size of
later stages may be contingent on the first; even so, it is helpful for budgeting purposes to give a client an indication of what future costs might
be. As almost all consulting projects involve input from client's staff,
there should also be some indication of the resources required from
the client.

An outline plan may also be included, but for the purpose of this example
we will assume that detailed planning is done after the survey stage, when
the programme of work will be elaborated and set against a timescale.

You will probably also need to state why you believe you are qualified to
carry out the assignment. This may relate to academic qualifications, but in
most cases will consist of a history of relevant assignment experience. In
Dick's example, he will cite similar assignments on which he has worked
involving stock control issues. A large firm of consultants may quote a
summary of the jobs it has carried out and add brief CVs of the consultants
expected to work on this particular assignment. CVs should be tailored to
projects in hand rather than standardised, to show why each consultant is
qualified to work on this project.

The need for previous experience of a similar assignment or knowledge of
the business sector will depend on the nature of the work being undertaken
by the consultant. In all cases, however, clients should ask sufficient questions to reassure themselves that the firm and/or consultant has appropriate experience and professionalism. Reputable individuals or firms of
consultants will be equally anxious to do a good job – if they fail they will
lose their reputation. One bad job can cost 100 good ones.

References from other clients may be useful in validating the reliability of
consultants new to a client. High-risk projects should, of course, not be
entrusted to any consultant whatsoever unless the client has complete confidence in them.

The proposal as a contract

The proposal is also the basis of the contract between client and consultant,
and in this sense the points it should particularly contain are:

- the work to be done by the consultant and the deliverables (and the work
  specifically excluded);
- resources which the client must provide;
- the timing and duration of the project;
- the basis on which fees will be charged.

Sometimes these may change during the course of a project. If this happens, it is as well to document the changes, e.g., in a letter to the client confirming them.

You will also need to indicate the basis of your terms of business, including:

- how long the offer remains firm: you may want to review the fee estimate if the client does not decide for six months, or if the consultants originally assigned are no longer available;
- what is covered: does it include expenses and VAT, or are they separate? Are secretarial and other services to be provided by the client or by the consultant? If the latter, is a separate charge to be made for them?
- whether fee rates are to be subject to revision during the course of the assignment;
- the terms on which the fees will be paid;
- the conditions under which the assignment may be terminated by either side.

In these litigious times, it is as well to put in a clause which disclaims responsibility for achieving particular results or for any consequential losses. (Whether it will provide total protection is arguable, but at least it will help in removing any ambiguity on this point.) Some professionals – such as architects – are not able to disclaim this, but management consultants are, and probably rightly so, as much of their work does depend on the effective cooperation of the client's staff. It is rare for a consultant to be able to guarantee the benefits arising from a project and written proposals should reflect this, e.g., by using 'should' instead of 'will' in refering to future events.

Clients may also want some guarantees of confidentiality. Other clauses might cover matters such as rights to copyright, patents, royalties and other intellectual property and any restrictions applying to consultants – such as taking up employment with the client, or doing similar work on sensitive matters for other clients within the same sector. (It would be clearly unethical for an individual consultant to prepare a marketing strategy for a company with a particular product range, having just done the same for the major competitor.)

Who is assigned to the project?

If the consultant who has worked on selling the assignment is to be involved in its execution, there is no problem of transition. In some circumstances, particularly in a large firm, however, there may need to be a handover from a salesexecutive to the operator.

One of the 'deadly sins' mentioned most often by clients of consultants is the gap between the expertise of the impressive senior consultant who wins the contract and that of the consultant who does the work. Anthony Jay commented in a *Harvard Business Review* article on 'Rate yourself as a client' (Jay, 1977):

'There was a famous London management consultant in the 1950s whose craggy face, bushy eyebrows, deep perception and penetrating analysis were almost hypnotically irresistible to the boards of large corporations But once the corporation was hooked, he was never seen again. For the next 18 months the offices were overrun with hordes of fresh-faced business graduates completing their management education at the corporation's expense.'

If there is to be a transition, part of the handover process should be a thorough briefing about the client and the assignment. Some years ago I had to start an assignment with totally inadequate briefing; in particular, I did not know exactly what expertise the client's chief executive was expecting from me. We had the following exchange during our first meeting:

Me: (fishing for a clue), 'I'd be interested in your view of how you expect me to contribute to the project'.

Chief Executive: (not helping in the slightest), 'I'd like you to use your own particular expertise to help us'.

Fortunately things were sorted out eventually, with no ill effects – but a good briefing would have avoided that dangerous corner.

Typically, the problems of handover are not only lack of briefing, but also:

- being committed to an approach which the sales consultant knows and likes, but with which the operating consultant has little sympathy;
- after a rather more extensive investigation finding the situation is fundamentally different from that assumed when the project was conceived.

The message is simple: the consultant who sold the assignment must remain in close contact with its execution.

3 Conducting consultancy projects

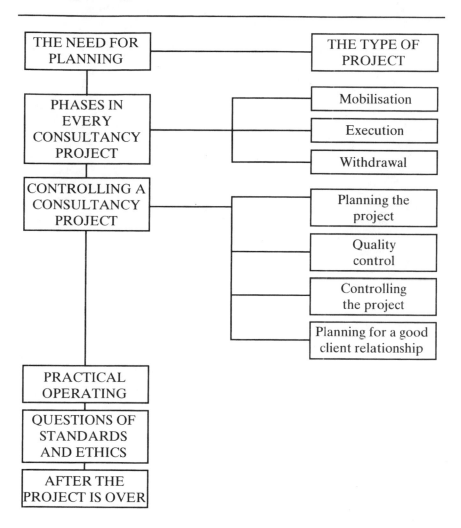

THE NEED FOR PLANNING — THE TYPE OF PROJECT

PHASES IN EVERY CONSULTANCY PROJECT
- Mobilisation
- Execution
- Withdrawal

CONTROLLING A CONSULTANCY PROJECT
- Planning the project
- Quality control
- Controlling the project
- Planning for a good client relationship

PRACTICAL OPERATING

QUESTIONS OF STANDARDS AND ETHICS

AFTER THE PROJECT IS OVER

3 Conducting consultancy projects

They said that the job could never be done,
But I with a will set to it;
And I tackled that job that couldn't be done –
And found that I couldn't do it!

Anon

The work of a consultant is usually project-based, and we have covered some of the significant consequences of this in Chapter **1**, such as the need to record and monitor time spent on each project. There is further need to plan and control the allocation of resources and the timing of activities, which is the subject of this chapter.

As well as achieving the proposal promises, a consultant responsible for operating a project has other priorities, notably:

- to keep the client happy – delighted would be better – so that repeat business is placed with the practice;
- to complete the project within the time and cost limits established at the outset.

These objectives can be met by careful planning, monitoring performance against plan, and conducting the project competently.

Not all professionals plan their projects; for example, a solicitor working on a particular matter may simply respond to outside initiatives and charge for the consequent time spent. Such an approach will be risky for consultants who are engaged with projects all of which are different and which have to meet the project objectives against a fixed fee budget. In 99 per cent of cases, therefore, consultants need to plan their projects.

A plan for a consultancy project should show:

- what is going to happen;
- when it is going to happen;
- the resources required.

These elements lead to the benefits of planning:

- it enables you to monitor progress;

- it helps to provide a standard of performance to pace your work – it is easy otherwise to let one project fall behind because of pressures of other commitments;
- planning enables you to schedule consultant resources – you know whether you have space in your diary for more work;
- it provides a basis for estimating fees;
- it can be used to communicate expectations to the client.

Good planning is required for the simple commercial reason that consultants are selling time. It is consultancy stock control.

Planning is important in managing the client's expectations, because the client will need to schedule their resources and, at a more prosaic level, need to know if you are going to be around two days a week or full time.

The type of project

Consultancy projects fall into different categories according to the ease with which they can be planned. There are two categories in which the time required is fairly predictable:

(i) *The standard service*: this is a highly 'product-orientated' approach. The client is buying a standard service which will vary very little in the amount of time required (or, if it is likely to vary, the swings and roundabouts cancel each other out). Examples might be:

- a house conveyance by a solicitor;
- personality profiling using psychometrics.

In each case, the service will be much the same on each occasion and its design requires little or no new planning. Very little management consultancy falls into this category:

(ii) *Royal roads* are standard approaches, adapted to the circumstances of a client. Examples might be:

- introducing a work-study-based incentive scheme into a factory:
- computerising a stock control system.

The work content of royal road type projects can be predicted with some certainty – not only because the work content is fairly well known, but also because of previous experience. The amount of time required to conduct a 'royal road' approach will depend on the nature of the application. The details of the work involved may also vary.

But much of management consultancy consists of a journey of exploration rather than a walk along a well-worn track. These projects must also be planned, which presents more of a challenge than the 'standard service' or 'royal road' approaches.

Phases in every consultancy project

A project plan needs to be based on a model of the steps involved in a consultancy project. Figure 3.1 summarises the major steps involved in a consultancy project.

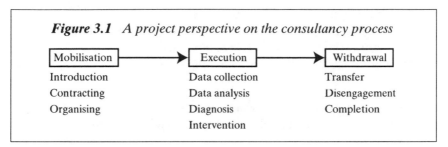

Figure 3.1 *A project perspective on the consultancy process*

Mobilisation	Execution	Withdrawal
Introduction	Data collection	Transfer
Contracting	Data analysis	Disengagement
Organising	Diagnosis	Completion
	Intervention	

There are three major stages to a consultancy project:

- *mobilisation* is all the preparatory work required at the start;
- *execution* is carrying out the project;
- *withdrawal* is finishing the project.

The steps in each one of these major phases are described below.

Mobilisation

Introduction
A consultant's first contact with a client may be either in selling an assignment or starting a project which has already been sold. In either case, careful preparation is required and you should aim to make a favourable impact.

Preparation should ensure that you know:

- background client information;
- key aspects of their business, recent performance and so on;
- the history of any previous relationship between your consultancy and the client, and particularly any previous discussions that might have a bearing on the project;
- what the objectives of the introductory meeting are;
- what expectations the client has of the first meeting; (often you can set these yourself by a preliminary letter or telephone call – see Chapter **2**, p. 33).

Conducting consultancy projects

The client will be seeking to form an impression of you throughout your early contacts. This will be from the first contacts by letter or telephone, but the first meeting is when the client will be particularly able to do so. There is no second chance to form a first impression and so you should aim to make as favourable an impact as you can.

Early in a project it is important to allow time for familiarisation. This will be necessary not only for practical matters (such as who's who, office layout, etc.) but also for understanding the informal rules and climate of the organisation. The latter includes such items as:

- specialised language used in the business;
- ways in which people work together (e.g., can you walk in to people's offices, or do you have to schedule a meeting first?);
- current affairs or hot topics for the organisation.

Contracting
As soon as contact is made there will be expectations and obligations created on both sides besides the formal agreement set out in the terms of reference.

(i) *Expectations*: a major cause of client dissatisfaction is when a consultant fails to meet the client's expectations. These expectations relate not only to meeting commitments in the terms of reference, but also in how consultant carries out the project, e.g.:

- the consultant's conduct
- what the consultant wears;
- when the consultant arrives and leaves client premises;
- the apparent priority the consultant attaches to the work done for the client.

Likewise the consultant will also have expectations of the client; these will be reflected largely in the commitment the client shows towards the project.

(ii) *Commitment*: the sponsor – the member of the client's staff commissioning the project – will, presumably, be committed to it, but you will have to consider the commitment of others. Will the project require the cooperation of more senior or more junior staff and, if so, are they committed to its success? Beware of sponsors who do not appear to be committed to the project or who are carrying it out as a personal crusade.

Organising
Organising covers the logistics of a project:

- Where will you be working and with what facilities?

- What is the project plan (if this has not been included in the terms of reference)?
- What support will you be receiving from the client and what form will this take?
- Whom will you be dealing with amongst client staff?
- What have client staff been told about the project (i.e., what are their expectations)?

Execution

Data collection and analysis
Paradoxically, you need to consider analysis before deciding what data you need to gather: you have to know what you are going to do with it when you have got it. Data gathering is time-consuming and you need to make sure you confine yourself to gathering only that which is necessary and sufficient for your purposes.

The consultant will start the project with a view of what the detailed nature of the problem is and how it might be solved. Data gathering will be initially to verify these hypotheses, and subsequent data gathering will be used to form new hypotheses or add more detail to the original ones. Data analysis will lead to possible solutions. Almost certainly you will have to be selective in your choice of data. You will also have to choose an appropriate data-collection technique. (See Chapter 5 for more on data collection.)

Diagnosis
Diagnosis will lead to a more detailed understanding of the issues and the ways in which they might be addressed, both substantiated by the data collected. Diagnoses might be represented by a series of conclusions, and provides the bridge between the data collected and the formulation of suitable interventions.

Intervention
By 'intervention' is meant the culmination of the project when the consultant engages with the client on the topic of the issues to be addressed. Most often, the intervention wil consist of recommendations.

In making your proposals they have not only to be technically 'right' but also acceptable to those responsible for authorising their implementation. During the project you should develop an idea of what is or is not acceptable, and devote effort to 'pre-selling' your preferred solution.

Your proposals should also be feasible, that is, the client must be able to implement them. No points for making technically excellent recommendations, which the client embraces enthusiastically, and then finds cannot be implemented because the resources or competancy to do so are not available.

Proposals should therefore also include recommendations for how they might be implemented in practice.

Withdrawal

Transfer
Transfer means leaving the client with the ongoing capability to maintain the changes and systems you have introduced as a result of your work. Transfer therefore includes:

- training client staff;
- setting standards and procedures;
- establishing systems and records;
- providing manuals.

Remember these are a major chunk of your legacy to your client on this project and therefore should be provided to a high standard.

It may be appropriate to provide ongoing help after the project is complete, for example through servicing visits. As well as the obvious benefit to the client, this allows the consultant further 'rights of entry' to the client that might reveal opportunities for extension sales.

Extension or disengagement
Withdrawal may mean the end of this particular relationship, but there may be extension work – other projects you can carry out to the benefit of the client.

How you treat this final stage depends on how you see the relationship between you and your client. Ideally, you are one of your client's specialist advisers to whom they will turn whenever there is a problem you can help with. But whilst working with this client you have the chance to find other areas where your practice can help develop the client's business. Hopefully, you can turn these opportunities into extension sales.

If you cannot extend, you disengage. This is not the end of the relationship; you and your client will have better knowledge of each other, and you should keep in touch. Remember that past clients are the best sales prospects for the future.

Completion
The ending of a consultancy project is as significant as its launch; quite apart from the commercial aspects of completion, the consultancy practice needs

to make sure that other aspects of value are also drawn from the experience of conducting this project.

Remember that some of the value of an assignment consists of the corporate experience gained by conducting it; it might also provide a reference for future work. It is important, therefore, even when no formal evaluation is conducted, to assess the value of an assignment and what the consultancy has learned, which will benefit it for the future.

You may also wish to conduct a formal evaluation of the project. This consists of comparing what actually happened with the original terms of reference (and as they were subsequently amended, if appropriate).

You should keep the terms of reference to hand throughout a project and refer to them frequently to ensure that the work you are doing remains relevant (it is easy to go on interesting, but time-consuming, digressions).

Ideally, all clients will be satisfied at the end of an assignment, but when they are not, it is frequently because you had different expectations at the outset rather than through any failure of operating. It is thus essential to make sure that the terms of reference are clear throughout.

Controlling a consultancy project

Planning a consultancy project

Although an outline plan may have been set out in the proposal, for any project other than the most simple, the consultant will need to prepare a detailed operating plan. The principles of planning a consultancy assignment are the same as those for planning any other project, but it is worthwhile briefly recapping on them.

Figure 3.2 *Outline programme*

Phase 1: Specification of the new system

1.1 Familiarisation.
1.2 Appraisal of present production and stock control procedures.
1.3 Formation of project panel.
1.4 Identification of priorities and requirements for new system.
1.5 Specification for new system drafted for discussion and approval.

(i)   Break the job into discrete tasks, and break these tasks themselves, if they are large, into separate elements. Figure 3.2 shows the breakdown for the first phase of Dick's assignment at ABC Ltd.

Again, each one of these steps themselves consist of smaller steps, as shown in Figure 3.3.

Where there is a distinct order to the tasks (as in Figures 3.2 and 3.3) then it may be helpful to show the tasks on a logic chart reflecting these relationships.

(ii) Assess the time required for each step, in terms of both consultant input and calendar time. Calendar time is usually more than consultant time, to allow for delays whilst client staff are carrying out part of the project, or are unavailable. Remember to allow time for yourself for thinking about the project, or discussing it with professional colleagues.

For complex projects, more sophisticated tools, such as network analysis might be useful. For short or simple projects, however, I have found the Gantt chart quite adequate for my needs, and an example of this, for a quite different assignment this time, is shown in Figure 3.4 on page 54. The practical test of any plan is: does this plan tell me – or can I infer from it – what I am meant to be doing on this project today? If it does not, it is probably inadequate.

(iii) If there are several consultants on a project they will need to be allocated specific tasks. The job of project management is made more simple if these tasks are 'mini-projects' – i.e., the consultant has to achieve defined goals or deliverables, within a certain fee budget and calendar time.

Figure 3.3   *Detailed programme*

Phase 1.3: Formation of Project Panel

1.3.1 Determine who are the most influential people in sales and production.
1.3.2 Draft shortlist of possible panel members and consider solicitation method.
1.3.3 Discuss shortlist and method at progress meeting on 7 April. Get confirmation/alterations.
1.3.4 Carry out solicitation programme.
1.3.5 Convene first meeting of panel for 21 April.

Here are some practical tips to consider when planning consultancy projects:

(i) Allow some time for familiarisation with new clients at the start of a project. Familiarisation can include:

- visiting the various sites of factories and offices;
- knowing 'who's who';
- understanding the key processes in the organisation (for example, in a profit-making organisation, the principal methods of adding value);
- understanding the jargon used in the business – every organisation has words or phrases that it uses in a specialised way.

After this initial immersion into the client culture, the consultant should have sufficient knowledge to speak the language of the client. I remember some years ago a banking client commenting that the consultant team spoke his language so well he forgot that they were not employees of the bank. (Of course, 'protective coloration' can be taken too far. Consultants who spend too long working with a particular client can lose their objectivity and start to look at things as members of the client's staff. This is a process known as 'going native'.)

(ii) Accept that planning cannot be comprehensive at the start of a project and allow for this. It may not be possible to define what later phases of a project may contain in detail, until the initial diagnosis is carried out. It is after this that detailed planning can then be done. All you can do in making your estimate at the outset is to use your best guess.

Quality control

In this context, I mean the quality of *output* of the consultancy project.

Management consultancy projects often break new ground by the novel application of existing techniques and thus the consultant is undertaking work that in some respects is unique. This creates difficulties in controlling quality because there are no basic standards to compare with. If, by contrast, you are manufacturing a standard product, you can decide what the key quality characteristics should be, establish measurable criteria of acceptability and check whether each item falls within the criteria. It is less easy to do this in a service industry, and particularly difficult to do it within a consultancy project. It is important, however, to define what standard is adequate. Given more resources, any job can be improved (and consultants are by nature relentless improvers), so where do you stop? The starting point is to establish the standards by which an a project is to be judged, and these should be embodied in the terms of reference. (Indeed, it is a good test of terms of reference to see whether they indeed do provide a basis for this judgement.)

Figure 3.4 *Introduction of performance appraisal system: pilot trial plan*

Activity	6 OCT	13 OCT	20 OCT	27 OCT	3 NOV	10 NOV	17 NOV	24 NOV	1 DEC	8 DEC	15 DEC
1. *Completion of systems design*											
1.1 Preparation of draft documentation	X										
1.2 Review of draft documentation		X									
1.3 Final documentation and procedures agreed			X								
2. *Pilot trial*											
2.1 Announce the pilot trial to staff				X							
2.2 Training assessors					X						
2.3 Preparation of performance appraisals											
2.4 Performance appraisal 'clinic'						X					
2.5 Review of performance assessments							X				
2.6 Appraisal meetings held											
2.7 Review of system with assessors and those assessed									X		
2.8 Evaluation of pilot trial										X	

There are some fairly obvious other criteria to be met, such as having a satisfied client, and carrying out the job in an appropriate manner. But there is something more required, which is professional integrity. A major trap for the new consultant is to assume that a satisfied client means that they have done a good job. This may not necessarily be the case; for example:

(i) Given a choice of alternative courses of action, the client may be relying on the consultant to recommend the best. Initially, the client will not be able to judge the choice, but will be satisfied because a choice has been recommended.
(ii) The client may not want to hear or do what is best, but to speak the unspeakable could be the most helpful thing a consultant does – this is the advantage of being an outsider.

Most assignments should result in satisfied clients, but professional judgement is the responsibility of the consultant.

How in practice should quality be controlled?

Two heads are certainly better than one for quality control in consultancy, and it is well worthwhile involving a colleague in an assignment for other reasons too.

- Often the discussion of a project is a helpful way of identifying the key issues, solving problems and creating new ideas.
- You can be blind to flaws in your thinking that may be obvious to someone else – better that the 'someone else' is not the client!
- You may have rationalised away the need to deal with certain important issues; working with a colleague should spur you to confront them.
- It is as well to review key items of documentation, particularly reports with a colleague who can check them for clarity, as well as proofread them.
- It may also be useful to refer to a colleague's expertise, not just in technical matters, but also to tap into their expertise on consultancy matters.

Larger firms often embody this role into a supervisory system; a more experienced consultant is appointed to supervise less experienced ones on projects perhaps with written procedures to be followed. The supervisor might have other responsibilities too, such as training the consultant. If you are a sole practitioner, however, this approach becomes more difficult; none the less, sole practitioners can and do seek the help of fellow professionals to ensure high-quality work.

Individuals new to consulting firms can be daunted by the quality control procedures. In their previous jobs they may not have been subjected to such high standards and; some find it difficult to adjust to having their professional judgement questioned.

Controlling the project

Whereas quality control was about controlling the output of an assignment, controlling a project also involves controlling the input – the consultant's time.

Once the plan is made, it is necessary as with any project to monitor progress. As there are plenty of excellent texts about project management, we will here consider only those features that are peculiar to control in a consultancy project.

The consultancy time spent must be carefully controlled. It is useless waiting until the end of a project of any size to see what time was spent on it. It needs to be monitored at suitable milestones, and an agenda item at each progress review.

The availability of client resources to work on a project is a constraint on its pace; there are others too.

- The availability of hardware; if a project requires new hardware, there may be a lead time associated with acquiring it.
- The availability of client staff to contribute to the project – this means being available for meetings, and carrying out other work entailed by the project. (A consultancy project usually entails an increase in the workload on a client.)
- The pace at which change can be absorbed within the client organisation.

These factors should have been considered at the time the consultant and client agreed to carry out the project. The agreement will have probably estimated:

- the number of consultant days required;
- the calendar time for its completion.

The control of time on a project interfaces with the internal accounting system for the consulting company (see Figure 3.5).

As emphasised in Chapter **1**, it is essential that consultants ensure they are spending their time gainfully employed. This means careful diary control. There are therefore two essential controls required for internal accounting for time spent, namely:

- how time was spent during the last period;
- how time is to be spent in the future.

Figure 3.5 *Controlling time*

Internal accounts

- Time spent on various projects
- Forward loading

Project data

- Time spent on this project
- Time required for project

The same breakdown can be used for both and Figure 3.6 over, shows the type of form that might be used.

Professionals often charge by the hour – or, indeed, a fraction of it if their work does not usually occur in large enough units to merit a whole hour's effort. On the other hand, an audit clerk may be assigned to a client for days or weeks. So the nature of the work does help to determine what is the most appropriate method of monitoring a consultant's time. I believe that accounting for consultant's time on fees by the day or half-day is most appropriate for fee-earning work. Other aspects, however, such as selling, marketing or administration, do not necessarily occur in such convenient periods, so you may wish to account for these in smaller units.

Data on time spent can be collected weekly or less frequently, depending on the nature of assignments and the invoicing cycle. For example, if invoicing is done weekly (to keep accounts receivable to a minimum), then time needs to be booked weekly. If the projects are long term – say a full time engagement, typically for a month at a time, then a monthly interval may be more appropriate

Forward loading typically is difficult to do in any detail more than a few weeks ahead, but even so, it is worthwhile looking beyond that. There needs to be some distinction on the plan between certain commitments to fee-earning jobs and those which are only tentative. A method of showing this is also given in Figure 3.6, within the category 'allocated'.

Data from the internal system then can be used to monitor how much time has been spent on the project. Figure 3.7 on page 59 shows a simple control sheet which Dick might use on the ABC Ltd assignment, assuming that Tom and Harriet also have an input to make.

Figure 3.6 *Loading chart*

Name

Week commencing	3/4	10/4	17/4	24/4	1/5	8/5	15/5	22/5	29/5	5/6	12/6	19/6
CHARGEABLE												
Alpha Ltd	2	1	1		$^1/_2$		1	3				
Delta Ltd		2		2		2						
Gamma Ltd	$^1/_2$	1	2	1								
ALLOCATED												
Zeta Ltd					1	1	1	1	2	2		
TOTAL	$2^1/_2$	4	3	4	$1^1/_2$	3	2	4	2	2		
SELLING												
Bloggs	$^1/_4$	1	$^1/_4$									
Cloggs				$^1/_4$	$^1/_4$							
Floggs			1			$^1/_4$	$^1/_4$					
TOTAL SELLING	$^1/_4$	1	$1^1/_4$	$^1/_4$	$^1/_4$	$^1/_4$	$^1/_4$					
Projects	1											
Course/Conference					1							
Office Admin.												
Holiday	1				1				1		4	
Total other	2				2				1		4	
Total allocation	$4^3/_4$	5	$4^1/_4$	$4^1/_4$	$3^3/_4$	$3^1/_4$	$2^1/_4$	4	3	2	4	–
Free days	$^1/_4$	–	$^3/_4$	$1^3/_4$	$1^1/_4$	$1^3/_4$	$2^3/_4$	1	2	3	1	5

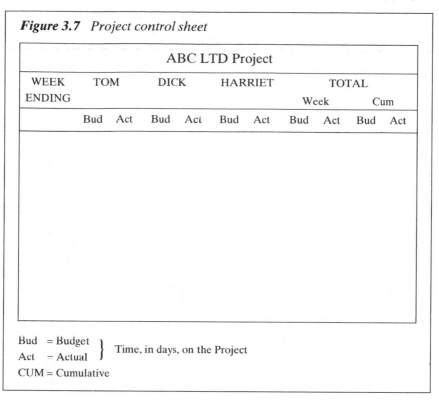

Figure 3.7   *Project control sheet*

ABC LTD Project										
WEEK ENDING	TOM		DICK		HARRIET		TOTAL Week		Cum	
	Bud	Act	Bud	Act	Bud	Act	Bud	Act	Bud	Act

Bud = Budget
Act = Actual   } Time, in days, on the Project
CUM = Cumulative

One of the great dangers for a consultant is overcommitment. They need to control future commitments so that they have sufficient flexibility to respond to any additional operating requirements on existing jobs.

Planning for a good client relationship

As well as achieving the results promised in his proposal, Dick will have the aims of keeping his client happy throughout the work and establishing a good relationship so that TDH Ltd will be considered when the next requirement for outside help arises.

To this end your planning should enable you to do the following:

(i)   Keep the client informed about progress: the plan should schedule regular progress meetings with the client to report on progress, problems and successes, and future plans. Make sure you do not leave long gaps between reports, particularly at the start of the assignment, and above all avoid unpleasant surprises to your client.

Whatever the rank of your client, not only do they have to be assured of the continuing success of your project, but they also have to be able to assure their boss, colleagues and subordinates too, some of whom may not be as enthusiastic. A well-informed client is able to refute rumour – and of course, will be more convinced that the assignment is being professionally run.

(ii) Allow yourself a safety margin in both consultant and calendar time for completing a project. It is embarrassing (and makes for poor client relations) if you have to increase the fees, or fail to meet deadlines.

Remember, too, that operating several assignments part-time is less efficient than a single full-time assignment (as encapsulated in the equation: $2\frac{1}{2}$ days/week + $2\frac{1}{2}$ days/week = $5\frac{1}{2}$ days/week).

Part-time operating has to be more carefully planned and organised than full-time; it wastes time, and it can be frustrating to visit a client and find the people you need to see are away.

(iii) Within a short time of the project starting you should demonstrate some 'quick successes'. A quick success consists of delivering a benefit to the client before completing the project. In Dick's case, he might find a way of reducing inventories of finished goods in a few areas. If this can be done very soon after starting, he will have shown his worth.

(iv) Aim to do a little more than was promised. This can vary from doing more on the project to providing help in other areas of the business.This has to be kept in check, however – no points for providing so much extra in other areas that the original project falls behind.

(v) Schedule your invoicing so that the client has a bill to pay when they have a sense of having received value from you, e.g., after delivering a report rather than before it.

Practical operating

This chapter concludes with a few practical tips on operating management consulting assignments.

Keep the initiative

The consultant should provide a sense of direction and set the pace on a project – the client should strive to keep up with you rather than the other way around. Initiative applies not only to project management, however, but also to thinking. The consultant should be presenting the ideas and recommendations on a project rather than the client. Bear in mind what Robert Townsend said about consultants (see the quotation heading Chapter 5).

Keep client staff informed

This is not simply those in contact with the project, but also other senior staff, whose impression of the project may be formed solely from casual conversations with you. You should be careful what you say on these occasions as an unguarded remark can have unfortunate repercussions. Years ago, a colleague advised me how to cope with this. 'Always have a "news item" up your sleeve' he said. 'A "news item" is some simple, quotable recent piece of information about your project which puts it in good light. It will be passed along by word of mouth and generally result in the project getting a good name'. Examples are:

- 'savings should be more than we originally expected';
- 'we have completed this phase of the work faster than we expected';
- 'old Harry (who had been against the project) is now putting a lot of support into the project'.

(If you are a junior consultant working in a large firm of consultants, this technique might also be used to impress senior colleagues.)

Keeping a project diary

Some consultants habitually maintain a diary – a log of events, meetings, agreements, etc. – on all projects. Others rely on progress reports. A project diary is more appropriate, however, if the project is long or complex, or is likely to be contentious – e.g., if there is a large industrial relations or commercial content.

Keep documentation secure

Many projects involve sensitive information which should not be freely available to client's staff, so when committed to paper, it needs to be kept secure. This means keeping it under lock and key if it is left at the client's premises.

My observation of security in many organisations is that it is very slack, and that anyone with sufficient determination could get access to any paperwork they wanted. The filing systems in most organisations, however, are so dreadful that it is difficult enough for staff, let alone the industrial spy, to find specific documents!

Documentation, of course, is often computer-based, and so you should ensure that your computer files are appropriately secure. Nowadays, a lap top computer seems to be a standard tool in the consultant's kit; obviously, this too should be kept secure when used on client premises.

First-name terms

There comes a time when you have to decide whether to get on first-name terms with client staff. If in doubt, err on the side of formality.

Look like a consultant

Knowing that you are well-dressed and presentable adds to your self confidence – and you have to look worth whatever exorbitant fee rate you are charging. You should also *behave like a consultant*. From the point of view of the client this means:

- you should be seen to act in their interest;
- you should be working for them whilst charging them fees (i.e., not be always on the phone to your office or other clients);
- you should be seen to be operating at a high work rate (one firm advised its consultants always to walk quickly on client's premises, and always to carry a piece of paper or a file to give an impression of great industry);
- if you are working at the client's offices, you should keep their office hours and preferably those of the client's executives, which will be longer;
- you should bring a standard of excellence to other activities you undertake – for example, in chairing or contributing to meetings, in responding to queries promptly and so on.

Remember that, if you work for a firm of consultants, you are the embodiment of that firm to your client. A record of first-class operating is enormously valuable to individuals consultants and a tremendous sales aid to their firms.

Do not undervalue the assignment project

It can be undervalued in two ways – by you or by the client. Because it is competing with other pressures for your time, it should none the less receive the necessary attention from you. If the client feels you are not giving sufficient priority or attention to the project, they will rapidly become discontented.

Similarly, the happiest outcome for some client staff might be that the project stops and you go away. They may therefore belittle the project, and hope that you will do the same. Don't.

On being thrown out

Sooner or later it happens that a consultant gets thrown off a job. This can happen to inexperienced and experienced consultants alike; it may be obvious and dramatic or become clear only in restrospect and can be no fault of the consultant. The fastest I have come across this was years ago when a consultant, who went to start a project in the morning, was back in his office just after lunch because 'his face didn't fit'. Another example was the consultant who worked with a client on a project for 18 months who was then asked to withdraw because of a change in political balance – he was identified with the old regime.

Happily, this does not happen very often, but when it does it can devastate a consultant's self-confidence. The only consolation is that it has happened to a lot of good consultants, who are still highly regarded by their other clients.

When things go wrong, in your role as account manager, consider what you can do to build the relationship. Bear in mind that the test of a service organisation is how well it handles breakdowns in service. And bear in mind this is a problem for the client as well as you; joint problem solving can be a powerful way of building a relationship, and dealing expeditiously with an operating problem as a way of so doing.

Questions of standards and ethics

Questions of standards and ethics arise for the consultant in two areas:

1 What are the standards of professional behaviour and personal conduct that I should adopt in my work?
2 How should I resolve dilemmas arising from the applications of these standards?

The Institute of Management Consultants (IMC) has published a helpful *Code of Professional Conduct* which gives direction on the professional standards to be adopted by management consultants which is given in full in Appendix **5**. The code interprets three explicit principles:

1 *Meeting the client's requirements*: A member [of the IMC] shall regard the client's requirements and interests as paramount at all times.
2 *Integrity, independence, objectivity*: A member shall avoid any action or situation consistent with the member's professional obligations or which in any way might be seen to impair the member's integrity. In formulating advice and recommendations the member will be guided solely by the member's objective view of the client's best interests.

3 *Responsibility to the Profession and to the Institute*: A member's conduct shall at all times endeavour to enhance the standing and public recognition of the profession and the Institute.

These are sound principles; I have a simple test that I also apply to any question of standards:

'If this action were reported fully and fairly in the press, or to my clients, would this enhance or detract from my professional reputation?'

It is not, however, questions of professional standards themselves that give most difficulty, but their interpretation in different situations can be tricky, when there can be a conflict in doing what is right for more than one party. Examples of dilemmas arise in:

1 Engaging in work for a client whose culture and ethics are different from ours. For example, the attitude towards bribes, or the treatment of women, is quite different in some countries outside the UK. How should consultants respond? Do they refuse to change from the standards in use in the UK, or should they adapt to the local practice?
2 Situations arising in a client where serving their wishes and interests may be in conflict with our own standards. For example, the marketing director of the client confides to you that he is about to change jobs, but does not plan to announce it until the annual bonus (which will be substantial in his case) is paid. The CEO – your client – at a subsequent meeting asks you if there are any foreseeable defections. Do you tell him about the marketing director?
3 Conflicts between the demands of our own practice and that of a client. For example, a consultant was assigned to a project where – unbeknown to him – his qualifications had been exaggerated to the client by the colleague who made the sale. It would be embarrassing (and commercially difficult) to withdraw – besides which, the colleague comments, 'the job is 90 per cent common sense – if you need some specialist help outside your expertise, just ask for it'. What should the consultant do?

As you can see, each of these dilemmas ends with a question. In many cases, any given answer to the question is going to upset somebody – there is not necessarily a perfect answer which will satisfy all.

It is often difficult to take an objective view of an ethical dilemma that involves you. For this reason, managing ethics does not consist of prescribing the answers to sets of dilemmas; it involves communicating principles (such as those to do with transparency and vulnerability contained in the IMC code) and acting in accordance with them within an organisation so as to encourage good practice.

If you are in a large consultancy practice, therefore, this is what should be done. Smaller firms and sole practitioners may not have the resources to set up an internal system; a qualified outsider in all cases, though, may be helpful to resolve ethical dilemmas. The IMC recognised this when, in 1996, it set up a 'helpline' for those faced with ethical dilemmas; notes on their ethical guidelines are reproduced in Appendix **5**.

After the project is over

At the completion of a project there should be a standard procedure to ensure that maximum value has been obtained from the work, for the consultancy. A project might have value in that it provides operating credibility in a particular business sector, or provides useful experience in the development or application of particular techniques. The larger the practice, the more important it is that there is a formal system for ensuring that project experience is recorded so that it can be used with effect throughout the practice.

The completion of the project need not mark the end of the consultant-client relationship. On a practical point, there may be the need for follow up servicing visits to ensure that new systems continue to work well or to carry out further training of client's staff.

A consultancy project offers commercial opportunities beyond this, firstly by extending the work with the client. There may be scope for greater involvement in the current project, for example, by:

- taking on work which would otherwise be less well done by client's staff;
- becoming involved in later stages of the project, e.g., its implementation, or replication at other sites.

The consultant may also be able to see opportunities for additional work outside the present project with the client, either for themself or for other members of the firm. (See also p. 18 in Chapter **1**.)

The client will have their own network of contacts locally and in the industry. If you have done a good job, they will probably spread the word. If you ask they may be prepared to introduce you to other organisations which could be interested in your services. Less directly, the project may be a useful reference, both in terms of the work carried out and the experience of working in a particular business sector. This can help in bidding in future for similar projects or work in the same industry.

Finally, when you have finished working with a client, keep in contact. There are all sorts of vehicles for doing this, e.g., lunches, seminars, circulation of newsletters, new brochures and so on. This has to be managed sensitively – you do not want the client to feel you are too importunate. A good rule of thumb is that you should limit prospection meetings to about twice a year (unless the client indicates otherwise), but you can circulate documents more frequently. How often you do this depends on the breadth of your product range; I know one practice with a relatively small number of target clients which makes sure that they get something once a month. This is probably more frequent than most practices, which might aim for circulars three or four times a year.

The pressure of present projects can crowd out this important work, however, and it is best to have a systematic approach to follow up. Do not neglect your former clients – they can be your best market.

4　Creating change

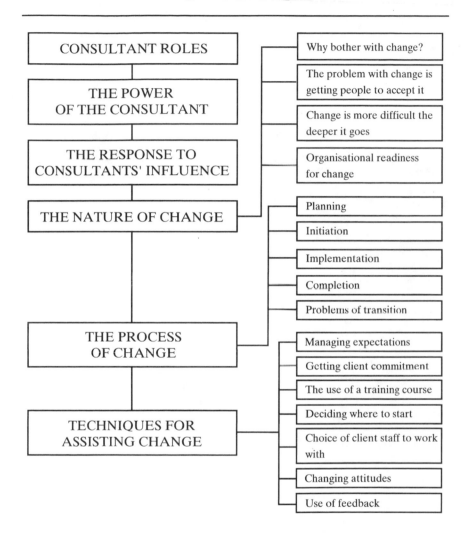

CONSULTANT ROLES	Why bother with change?
	The problem with change is getting people to accept it
THE POWER OF THE CONSULTANT	Change is more difficult the deeper it goes
THE RESPONSE TO CONSULTANTS' INFLUENCE	Organisational readiness for change
THE NATURE OF CHANGE	Planning
	Initiation
	Implementation
	Completion
	Problems of transition
THE PROCESS OF CHANGE	Managing expectations
	Getting client commitment
	The use of a training course
	Deciding where to start
TECHNIQUES FOR ASSISTING CHANGE	Choice of client staff to work with
	Changing attitudes
	Use of feedback

4   Creating change

We trained hard, but it seemed every time we were beginning to form a team we would be reorganised . . . we tend to meet every situation by reorganising, and a wonderful method it can be for creating the illusion of progress while producing confusion, inefficiency and demoralisation.

Satyricon, Petronius Arbiter

- The client was a manufacturing company in the Midlands; the project was to improve business performance, which had been falling drastically. On the first day of their assignment the two consultants drove up to the head office and parked their car in the spot directly outside the front door, marked 'Reserved for the Chairman'. They marched in to announce their arrival. 'Tell the managing director', they said to the receptionist, 'that the consultants have arrived!'

I have always liked this story, which a former colleague swears to be the truth. It portrays the consultant as Superman, and it is delightful to be regarded as such. Sadly, however, in reality a consultant is more like Donald Duck; sailing forward serenely on the surface but paddling furiously under the water.

Much of the paddling is to do with creating change. Change is at the core of consulting assignments and the management consultant has a key role in helping it happen. Organisations of people are amongst the most complex entities on this planet and there has been – and, undoubtedly, will continue to be – a considerable volume of research into their behaviour. This research has thrown up a host of theories and models, all of which give insights into the behaviour of organisations in different circumstances. To date, however, there is no universally applicable theory which the consultant can use to determine what has to be done to create particular changes. The best approach, in my experience, is to select those theories and models which help you and provide you with some insight.

But I do not believe that you need a tremendous body of theoretical knowledge to create change. Change is normal and we encounter it throughout every aspect of our lives. Everybody has their own theories, based on experience, of how and why organisations and people change, and will apply them to consultancy projects. Furthermore, a consultant is rarely concerned with change *per se*, but changing *something* as a means to an end.

In this chapter, therefore, we consider change in the context of a consultancy project. In the first part we cover the factors which need to be taken into account. Consultants have a variety of roles and types of power available to them and these will affect how they work with their clients and how they are able to exert influence for change. The relevant characteristics of change are:

- how important its acceptance is among staff for its successful implementation;
- how profoundly the change affects the organisation;
- how ready the organisation is for it.

The last part of this section assesses the possible responses to the consultants' attempts to influence the client.

Later sections of the chapter consider the process of change and some techniques for its successful implementation. Appendix 2 gives some techniques for analysing change.

Consultant roles

One way of looking at the client-consultant relationship is as doctor and patient; the patient has an ailment of some kind and goes to the doctor to diagnose and cure it. But there are other ways in which a consultant can provide help.

In certain circumstances a consultant might be appointed to hold an executive position temporarily. For example, a company may appoint a consultant as general manager for a short while to mastermind a turn-around. Once complete, the consultant can leave and an individual with different qualities be appointed to rebuild the company.

In a less dramatic way, an organisation may find it needs a data processing manager to bridge the loss of one and the arrival of a replacement, and call on a consultant to help.

These are highly interventionist roles – ones in which consultants are taking decisions as if they were executive employees of the organisation. At the other extreme is the role of consultant as facilitator, working totally through the client's staff; in this situation the work of the consultant enables the client organisation to initiate and manage change for itself. For example, the management team of a UK company, which had been acquired by a US conglomerate, had to reorganise its structure and systems to meet the requirements of its new parent. This was a new task for the management team, and one which required them to work together in a way they had never done before. The job of the consultant who worked with the team was not to plan the reorganisation required, but to help the group to do it for themselves.

The roles of executive and facilitator are widely divergent. Schmidt and Johnson (1970) analysed consultant roles in more detail and suggested a continuum of behaviours which is shown in Figure 4.1. The continuum is from client-centred to consultant-centred. Client-centred behaviours use the client's experience and knowledge: the role of the consultant is to help the client use this experience and knowledge effectively. At the other end of the spectrum are consultant-centred behaviours which focus more on the consultant's direct knowledge and experience.

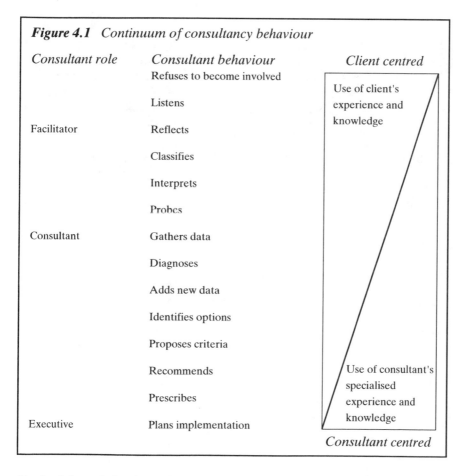

Figure 4.1 *Continuum of consultancy behaviour*

Consultant role	Consultant behaviour	Client centred
	Refuses to become involved	Use of client's experience and knowledge
	Listens	
Facilitator	Reflects	
	Classifies	
	Interprets	
	Probes	
Consultant	Gathers data	
	Diagnoses	
	Adds new data	
	Identifies options	
	Proposes criteria	
	Recommends	Use of consultant's specialised experience and knowledge
	Prescribes	
Executive	Plans implementation	
		Consultant centred

Each of these behaviours is defined in Appendix 1.

Schmidt and Johnson also considered the circumstances favouring behaviours towards either end of the spectrum and classified them according to:

- factors unique to the client;
- factors unique to the consultant;

Creating change

- factors in the client-consultant relationship;
- factors in the situation.

These have been simplified and presented in Figure 4.2 below.

Figure 4.2   *Factors influencing the consultant role*

	Favouring client centred	*Favouring consultant centered*
Factors unique to the client	Client wants: • Independence • To understand and learn about the problem • To take the decisions	Client has: • Little experience • High need for help • No great ownership of status quo • No vested interest
Factors unique to the consultant	Consultant wants: • Client to grow and develop • To prevent dependency	Consultant has: • Considerable relevant experience and expertise • Established reputation • High understanding of client
Factors in the client–consultant relationship	• Little empathy • Consultant not totally acceptable	• High mutual trust • Previous experience of working together • Congruent goals • Open communication
Factors in the situation	• Penalty for wrong solution is high • Affects complex systems • Problem is dynamic or has long time perspective	Problem is: • Clearly defined • Urgent • Of low complexity • Of little consequence on culture

---

This analysis brings home the point that consultancy projects are joint efforts between consultant and client and the consultant should vary his role according to the circumstances to get the best results. So, whether you are an experienced consultant or a novice, it is worth reviewing on assignments:

- Where on the continuum am I functioning and is this appropriate?
- Do I tend to operate at one position on the continuum, and not take the other roles when they might be more suitable?

The power of the consultant

Whatever role consultants are performing, they need influence to be able to create change. Influence is the exercise of power and is underwritten by it. It is important for consultants to understand whence they draw their power, and also to recognise where power lies in the client organisation and of what sort it is.

A helpful analysis of different types of power has been provided by Hersey, Blanchard and Natemeyer (1979) in connection with their studies of leadership, under the seven headings, reproduced in Figure 4.3 over.

The availability and usefulness of different sorts of power will vary according to circumstances. It is rare to have only one kind of power or to exercise influence through only one kind.

There are some points of particular interest to consultants arising from this analysis.

(i) Although on internal consultant usually has some defined position within the organisation and thus has some legitimate power this is usually of little use in influencing change. By definition the external consultant rarely has any legitimate power. This is in distinct contrast to a line manager or executive, accustomed to using legitimate power to get things done. Managers or executives who transfer to a staff role, or that of external consultant, need to adjust their approaches to influencing to take account of this change in their power base.

(ii) The foundation of consultants' power is their expertise. If working for a firm of consultants, it is probably this which they have hired and almost certainly it will be what the client buys. Even so, the consultant has other power bases available, and connection power is particularly useful in influencing change. Most consultancy projects are commissioned by senior management, and the consultant thus has influence over more junior staff because of the connection with senior management. This can present a problem to the consultants having been hired by middle management but who have to influence senior management – they have no connection power.

- This was illustrated on a project after the go-ahead had been given by the personnel manager commissioning it. It involved working in factories at different locations, all under the control of the operations director. He felt he had not been adequately consulted by the personnel manager about the project and stopped it shortly after it started. It could not be restarted until the operations director had satisfied himself on the details.

Figure 4.3 *Types of power*

Coercive power is based on fear. A leader high in coercive power is seen as inducing compliance because failure to comply will lead to punishment such as undesirable work assignments, reprimands, or dismissal.

Connection power is based on the leader's 'connections' with influential or important persons inside or outside the organisation. A leader high in connection power induces compliance from others because they aim at gaining the favour or avoiding the disfavour of the powerful connection.

Expert power is based on the leader's possession of expertise, skill, and knowledge, which, through respect, influences others. A leader high in expert power is seen as possessing the expertise to facilitate the work behaviour of others.

Information power is based on the leader's possession of or access to information that is perceived as valuable to others. This power base influences others because they need this information or want to be 'in on things'.

Legitimate power is based on the position held by the leader. Normally, the higher the position, the higher the legitimate power tends to be. A leader high in legitimate power induces compliance or influences others because they feel that this person has the right, by virtue of position in the organisation, to expect that suggestions will be followed.

Referent power is based on the leader's personal traits. A leader high in referent power is generally liked and admired by others because of personality. This liking for, admiration for, and identification with the leader influences others.

Reward power is based on the leader's ability to provide rewards for other people. They believe that their compliance will lead to gaining positive incentives such as pay, promotion, or recognition.

(iii) One of the features of expert power is that it is situational; thus the plumber has expert power over the lawyer when the central heating has broken down. Expert power does, however, diminish in the presence of a greater expert. For example, new consultants could find that their expert power diminishes in client meetings at which they are accompanied by more senior people from their own firm.

(iv) Legitimate power must be underwritten with other types of power if it is to be meaningful. For example, line managers may need access to all the power bases in some measure to do their jobs. From the consultant's point of view, it is interesting to consider the power bases of senior individuals in an organisation to find out who really has influence, particularly 'ministers without portfolio' – are they has-beens with high-sounding titles or are they the power behind the throne?

One kind of power has not been listed in Figure 4.3 and that is negative power – the power to say 'No'. Given that the job of a consultant is to promote change rather than prevent it, they are unlikely to use it often. More significant is the fact that negative power is widely distributed in an organisation; the factory hand and secretary both have considerable negative power – both can make life difficult for a manager or executive. If negative power is the only source of influence available over organisational matters, it will be used. Consultants should remember this in introducing change and to provide consultative procedures which avoid the need for staff to exercise negative power.

Consultants need an acute sense of the nature and distribution of power – both their own and that within their clients – if they are to be successful. Although their power lies in their expertise, at more junior levels in the client organisation it is their connection power which enables consultants to get things done. It is therefore important for the consultant to maintain links as high up the organisation as possible. To a lesser extent, referent and information power are also available to the consultant to influence change.

The response to consultants' influence

Before moving on to analyse change, it is worth considering the possible responses to the consultant's attempts to influence a client. Leaving aside rejection, Charles Handy (1981) has suggested that responses to influence fall into the following categories:

- compliance – 'I'm doing this because I have to';
- identification – 'I'm doing this because it is you who has asked me';
- internalisation – 'I'm doing this because it is my choice'.

All these responses imply that the change has been accepted; all are therefore effective, but each has pros and cons.

Compliance requires that there is sufficient power behind the change to ensure a positive response. Thus the change must be backed by – for example – the legitimate power of a line manager within the organisation. For instance, the introduction of a new accounting procedure may only require the chief accountant to authorise it, following which the accounting staff will use it. The consultant, too, may have sufficient connection power to ensure a compliant response.

The drawback of compliance is that as soon as the pressure for change has disappeared, things may revert as they were before. A similar difficulty applies to the *identification* response – once the consultant withdraws, the changes introduced may be undone. Referent power is required by the consultant to effect the identification response.

The *internalised* response is generally regarded as the most enduring and is required for any change of a fundamental nature (i.e., in the goals or culture of the organisation). It does not require a particular power base, but it does require time and skill on the part of the consultant, to introduce changes using processes which are most likely to lead to an internalised response. These processes will be participative and the consultant's role will be towards the client centred end of the spectrum in Figure 4.1.

From a commercial point of view, the identification response is more gratifying and rewarding than internalisation. Internalisation implies 'We changed because we wanted to', and very possibly the consultant may be seen as irrelevant to the change. This is not the way a consultant can demonstrably earn their keep and so there is a strong temptation to prefer identification!

The nature of change

Why bother with change?

One of my associates comments, 'If you always do what you've always done, you always get what you always got.'

Another colleague notes, 'Organisations are perfectly designed for the results they achieve.'

The corollary of both these comments is that if you want to achieve something different, you have to do something different. Interestingly, the behavioural requirements of change to a superficial observer are small; people will often see little change in:

- their place of work;
- when they have to be at work;
- the activities they engage in (e.g., meetings, making telephone calls, operating a machine).

The significance of change is the human dimension – the change of status; the loss of authority, and so on. The human dimension is all important.

The problem with change is getting people to accept it

The problems in making changes are not only concerned with the technical adequacy of the change, but more often with getting those affected to accept it. Perhaps people can be ordered to comply with the change but the result will always be less satisfactory than if their commitment had been won.

Resistance impedes commitment and it would be tempting to see winning commitment as simply overcoming resistance. This is an inadequate view. What is required is to mobilise the energies of those involved so that they carry through the change successfully. That is commitment. Where energies are directed to opposing the change, that is resistance.

One writer has suggested that resistance should be honoured. This view emphasises that there is usually (in the mind of the other person) a sound foundation for that resistance. Recognising, understanding and accommodating resistance may lead to better ideas, improved methods of implementation and greater acceptance of change.

Many people enter consultancy from a technical background which emphasises finding solutions that are 'right'. The people dimension can easily be overlooked. Much of the remainder of this chapter is therefore about people and change.

Change is more difficult the deeper it goes

Figure 4.4 suggests an empirical hierarchy of change.*

Projects for the purposes of this definition are accomplished within the existing systems, structures and procedures of the organisation. Examples may be the test marketing of a new product, the repainting of a factory, or the installation of new equipment. Projects may be part of a more fundamental change – for instance, new computer equipment will probably entail changes in systems and possibly some changes in organisation structure.

*I am indebted to Alan Elliott of the City University Business School who has conducted research into the validity of this model. As a result of this he has suggested the interpolation of 'strategies' into the hierarchy.

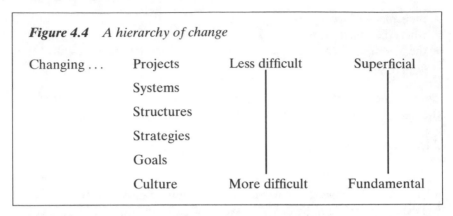

Systems are the processes regulating activities within the organisation. As well as the management information system – for reporting and control – there will be many other systems manifest as procedures, for example, for regulating when people arrive at and leave their work, for determining the allocation and use of resources, the flow of work and so on.

By *structures* I mean the organisation of tasks within the enterprise. One way of looking at an enterprise is to see it as having to accomplish a host of tasks relating to internal and external transactions. These tasks are collected into convenient groups and called jobs. Structure is all about these task groupings and how the jobs relate to one another.

Changing *strategies* involves redirecting the business of the organisation, which occurs when entering a new market or business. Strategies are the routes by which the goals of the organisation are achieved.

Goals are about the purpose of the organisation – goals in this context do not mean transient targets or budgets (e.g., £1m profit this year). What is meant are the mission(s) of the organisation, for example:

- 'To provide health care to all residents in the UK'.
- 'To be the largest supplier of automobiles in the world'.
- 'To make a living repairing TV sets'.

A redefinition of goals can have dramatic repercussions for a business. Thus, a bank might change its mission from 'To provide credit, banking and money transmission facilities' to 'To provide financial services to the general public', which might involve entering new lines of business such as insurance and pensions, and withdrawing from corporate finance.

All this is grist to the mill of the corporate strategist. More fundamental though, is organisation *culture* – the underlying values and norms of the organisation. This will be manifest in an enormous variety of aspects: what dress is *de rigueur*, the manner of addressing one another and all the traditions and habits of the organisation. It is the corporate personality.

Only in a few situations will it be necessary for a consultant to intervene at the corporate culture level. Indeed, many of the superficial interventions will themselves effect a change, albeit slight, in corporate culture. Thus, a change in organisation structure or in the systems in use will have an effect on the organisation's culture (in the same way that experience can affect the personality of an individual).

Modifications of a corporate culture ought to be approached with some moral caution, as it is in effect altering the corporate 'personality'. The consultant has to be able to justify the changes to be made and this cannot simply be the superimposition of their own value system on that of the client. There must be sound business reasons for cultural change. Occasions when a change in culture might be required are the following:

(i) The retirement of an autocratic and long-standing chief executive (possibly the founder of the company) who has no obvious successor. In this case the organisation would need to change from being centred on a particular individual to, perhaps, one where the organisation structure was more significant. (Roger Harrison has developed an organisation typology in which this change would be typified as from 'power-centred' to 'role-centred' – see Harrison 1972.)

(ii) A decline in traditional markets requiring a firm to become innovative and entrepreneurial. In a mature market, the usual practice would be to maintain the status quo – standard production processes, routine selling and distribution patterns and so on. Innovation and entrepreneurialism run counter to the status quo. (Large organisations may form separate business divisions or subsidiaries to accommodate those different styles to avoid conflict between the two cultures.)

Organisational readiness for change

The ease with which change can be accomplished also depends on how ready the organisation is for it. Research shows that change in organisations occurs discontinuously – periods of upheaval are separated by interludes of relative stability. Change often coincides with the arrival of a new leader or in response to circumstances which threaten the organisation.

Gleicher, quoted in Beckhard and Harris (1977), has developed a formula which gives an insight to this: it looks at the 'cost' of change:

Creating change

$$C = (ABD) > X$$

where:

C = change
A = level of dissatisfaction with the status quo
B = clear desired state
D = practical first steps towards the desired state
X = cost of the change – not simply the financial cost, also disadvantages to those involved.

The formula shows that, if change is to take place, the elements A, B and D must be present. Moreover, they should together weigh more than the 'cost' of undertaking the change – the upheaval, the time, the discomfort and so on. Organisational readiness for change will be insufficient if A, B or D are too small. Deficiencies in each of these can be characterised as follows:

> A: 'We're happy with the way things are'.
> B: 'Although we're not very happy with the way things are, we've no clear idea about how they could be better'.
> D: 'We know how we'd like things to be, but we don't know how to start'.

Analysing readiness can help the consultant decide where effort might most profitably be invested to achieve the required change, for example, by:

- confronting the client with the facts to show how unsatisfactory the situation is (A). (Sometimes, the act of carrying out this data can by itself increase the level of dissatisfaction);
- helping the client to define the 'ideal state' of affairs, or investigate the potential for improvement (e.g. by market research) (B);
- using experience from elsewhere to show how the improved state can be achieved (D).

And do not overlook X, the 'cost' of change; even though the elements A, B and D may be significant, they may be less than the perceived cost. As an alternative to increasing A, B or D it may be possible to reduce X. Remember it is the perceived cost – so reducing X can be achieved by changing people's perceptions of the cost, as well as the cost itself. For example, part of the perceived cost could arise from fear of the unknown. Good communications and explanations from the consultant could reduce this fear, and hence the perceived cost.

The process of change

Consultants need an understanding of the change process as it evolves in a consultancy project. In this section it is unbundled into four stages, and we consider the key elements that apply to each stage. The stages are:

(i) *planning*, in which the change is dealt with only in concept;
(ii) *initiation*, in which the change is started;
(iii) *implementation*, in which the change is carried out;
(iv) *completion*, in which the change is 'cemented' into the organisation.

These are not watertight compartments; often the understanding of the nature of the change may develop during implementation. Planning has to be flexible to accommodate this.

In each stage of change, the consultant needs to be able to answer the questions:

• What is going on?
• What ought I to be doing about it?

Figure 4.5 illustrates the answers to these questions for each stage.

Figure 4.5 *Building commitment*	What is going on?	The critical items to manage to deal with this
Planning	Vision – defining where we are heading	Mobilise influential opinion
Initiation	Reaction: • welcome • questioning • uncertainty • resistance	Energy-raising Expectation Communication Processes
Implementation	Response: • acceptance • fall in performance • alienation	Participation Confidence-building
Completion	Making change permanent: • internalisation • revisionism	Reward Review

Planning

The starting point of a change is a *vision* held by the client of how things will be after the change has been accomplished. Sometimes it may be the task of the consultant to help the client to articulate this vision.

It is worth noting that the vision may alter or develop as the change proceeds. Initially it may be only broadly understood; with time its detailed nature will become more apparent. Next, there has to be a *climate of opinion* among the client's colleagues, superiors and necessary opinion-formers that supports the vision. Obviously, the more powerful a manager, the less reliant they are on others' support; usually, however, the manager needs to drum up support as part of the planning stage. The consultant can help in forming an assessment of the degree of support; the technique of Force Field Analysis, described later in this chapter, is helpful in doing this.

Initiation

Whenever a change is announced there will be a *reaction* amongst those affected. Some may *welcome* it; others may *resist*. All will *question* what it means and, for many, it will occasion *uncertainty*. That there is a reaction is inevitable; the task of the consultant is to try to get a reaction most conducive to the change being introduced.

People will base their judgement of a change in terms of its personal impact on themselves. If they feel they are going to be adversely affected, then they will resist; if they think they will be better off, they will support it. This will depend on their perceptions of the change – not necessarily objective reality!

Before a change can take place in a group, they have to be ready. Gleicher's formula, described earlier in this chapter, is useful in analysing this. To recap, three conditions have to be satisfied:

(i)   there is dissatisfaction with the status quo;
(ii)   there is a vision of how things might be after the change has been implemented;
(iii) there is some idea of at least the first few steps in getting the change started.

These criteria have to be satisfied for all those who are involved in the change. In particular, there has to be an incentive to change; if everybody is fat and happy, then there is no reason to change. Consultants can use data feedback to show the disadvantages of maintaining the status quo. Remember, however, that the announcement of an impending change may itself create a climate in which change is more likely to be accepted.

- For example, one organisation was often undergoing change. The technique the general manager used was to let it be known informally through his immediate subordinates that a reorganisation was impending. He then waited for an interval, by which time everybody was so tired of the ambiguity that they welcomed any change that resolved the situation.

This method is described to show the effects of uncertainty rather than as a prescribed method. Indeed, the effect was devastating on the morale of this organisation, and it has since gone out of business.

Having created an awareness of the need for change, the consultant has helped the client to 'sell' the vision of how things might be after the change to those who are likely to be affected by it.

These activities serve to *raise energy levels* of all concerned and direct them towards the change. This is also known as 'unfreezing', and it is aimed to make people more receptive to the idea of change. Unfreezing involves:

- clear signal(s) that things are going to be different;
- encouraging behaviours that are different.

Symbolic behaviours by the leaders in an organisation can raise the awareness of change.

- For example, a new chief executive who wanted to transform the organisation quite deliberately always ran, rather than walked, up the stairs whenever visiting any of the outlying offices. This demonstration of energy was symbolic of the new energy to be released in the business.

It is easy to underestimate the importance of symbolic behaviours in change unless you recognise the impact of past experience. All organisations have stories (myths, legends), 'case law' and so on, into which a newcomer will informally be indoctrinated. These have a powerful effect in that they illustrate what are meant to be the right ways of behaving or taking decisions. When you introduce change, you have quickly to change the appropriate aspects of organisational folklore by promulgating examples which underscore the new behaviours or ways of taking decisions.

Again, change programmes are sometimes launched by seminars, conferences or other meetings. As well as performing their role in facilitating communication, these can act as 'rites of passage', which encourage people to behave differently after attending them. (An example of a 'rite of passage' in everyday life is a wedding ceremony. Although it lasts a very short time, it has a profound impact in the way in which a couple think about themselves and on how society regards them.)

Expectations are a key component in change; what people expect of the change and how it might affect them is going to condition their response.

Managing expectations is vital. One result of uncertainty is that if people do not know what to expect, they will draw their own conclusions – which may be totally wrong. So good *communications* are essential.

Good communications at times of change may require special efforts; the routine methods may be inadequate to deal with the communication requirements of a major change. Organisations deal with this by having special briefing sessions, newsletters, meetings, etc. Often these communication channels are one-way (such as a newsletter), but communication must be two-way; not only should managers tell their people about the change, but should also listen carefully to their response. The consultant must ensure that the right communication channels are in place, so that people know what the change is, why it is necessary and how it will affect them.

In the same way that change may require new methods of communication, it may also require new *processes* of problem-solving and decision making. Different problems require different approaches; one method alone is insufficient for all managerial problems and decisions. The consultant should make the client aware of this and introduce new (often more participative) methods of problem solving as required.

Implementation

Implementation is the body of change and can take a considerable time – months, if not years.

Some people will *accept* the change quite happily. They represent an asset for the consultant, as they can help to persuade those who are as yet unconvinced. It is easy to become preoccupied only with those who are being resistant, but those who have accepted the change can help to build the confidence of those who have not.

Sometimes the confidence of managers can be eroded *when performance falls after the introduction of a change*. The fact is that change usually involves people doing things differently, and doing things differently requires people to learn to do them. While they are learning, people cannot be expected to attain optimal performance immediately.

Change, therefore, often entails a decline in performance in the short term. A client who is unprepared for this may be tempted to abandon the change.

Performance will suffer particularly if people become *alienated* by the change. Alienation results when people:

- have no idea of what the change means, what it requires of them or where they now fit in;

- feel powerless: they have no influence over the change or how it affects them.

The result of alienation is, at the least, resistance to the change. In extreme cases it can create considerable stress and lead to people 'psychologically resigning' from the organisation – i.e., losing all interest in their work and caring little about their performance.

A key area of consideration for consultants in counselling clients in avoiding alienation amongst employees is that of *participation*; to what extent should people share in:

- information: knowing what is going on and what is planned for the future;
- decisions, concerning the implementation of the change.

A consequence of excluding people from participation of any kind is that they will become alienated from the change. Far from being committed to it, it will create a climate of uncertainty and stress.

The importance of two-way communication has already been mentioned; this leads on to the influence which the rank and file have over decisions – how much attention is going to be paid to the information that is fed back?

If people feel that whatever they say they are powerless to influence the change, they will become alienated; change will be something that is 'done' to them. If they can influence it, they will become more committed. This 'empowerment' of people is a major factor in implementing change.

In practice this means delegating decision-making. The decisions over which people most want influence are those which affect them personally. Delegating these decisions has the advantage too that they are being taken by experts – those who are actually doing the job. So a consultant should encourage managers to delegate decisions – within the necessary constraints – as far as possible.

Confidence-building is the other important dimension during implementation. Where a change is spread across different areas, the confidence of those involved may not be all the same. In such cases, you can only work within the level of commitment of whichever group you are dealing with. Some groups may be able to progress well; others more slowly. Attempting to change a group more quickly than it can cope with will be frustrating for all concerned. Confidence-building can be achieved often by allowing those who are less confident to observe the success of those who are more advanced in implementing the change.

'War stories' of success elsewhere can help in building confidence in a group. Likewise, early success can also help in building the confidence of a group.

One further feature of change is saying goodbye to the past. Change is like a journey; to go elsewhere, you have to leave where you are now. Sometimes it can be very hard to leave the old ways behind, particularly if the change implies that the past was wrong. A consultant can sometimes help by getting clients to 'honour the past', by some form of exhibition, for example, or a souvenir edition of the company newspaper.

As a consultant, it is often difficult to understand resistance to change; from our position, it may seem rational, for the benefit of the majority, and so on. But to implement change, you have to start from where people are at – not assume that they are with you.

A helpful analogy is that of giving someone a lift in your car; if you are to arrive at your destination together, you have first to rendezvous at the beginning of your journey. If you are the one with the car, you are the one responsible for getting together with your passenger to start off with. Likewise, consultants have fully to appreciate the starting points of those undertaking change.

Completion

The desired state after implementation of a change is that people have taken it into their usual way of working – it is no longer seen as a change, but as the norm. This process is called *internalisation*. But there may be those who want to go back to the old ways – the *revisionists*. They are like those who, when everybody else is undertaking a journey, do not want to leave home. If they cannot be persuaded to leave home, they must ultimately be left behind. If a person finds it very difficult to accept a change, sometimes the only way forward is to put them in a position where they do not need to accept it. Sometimes it may mean a job transfer; sometimes it may mean the individual looks for a more congenial job elsewhere. It is often painful for managers to deal with this type of problem, so the consultant should help them confront the issues and deal with them.

People respond to where they see their *rewards* lying. In this context reward does not mean only what they are paid – its how they obtain career advance, the approbation of their superiors, recognition from their colleagues and so on. The basis on which people are rewarded needs to underwrite the change. A change will founder if the basis on which people are rewarded is not also changed to fit the new circumstances.

As well as money, a key motivator of people at work is: 'How do I please my boss?' If the boss is not committed to the new order of things, then it will be difficult for their subordinates to make the change. Commitment to a change has therefore to percolate through all the layers of an organisation if it is to be successful.

Finally, there is the process of *review* – what can the client learn from the way in which this change was carried out? The learning from one change may help the organisation to be better equipped to carry out the next. The consultant can see that a review is carried out as part of the closing stages of a change programme.

Problems of transition

Before moving on to techniques for assisting change, it is worth mentioning one final point about the process of change. It is this: in any change, an effort must be made to distinguish between the problems of acceptance of the new scheme of things *after* change, and the problems of getting there. Sometimes the difficulties of making a change do not lie in getting a client's agreement to the promised land that lies at the end of the change – rather, the difficulties lie in plotting out the route which will take him from here to there and getting agreement to it. Resistance to change goals may therefore arise because the client cannot see how they might be achieved. Very often there will therefore need to be a number of modest transitions en route to achieving the desired changes in the longer term (see also 'Managing expectations', below).

The problems of transition (as compared with those of goals) are the problems of 'how?' rather than 'why?'.

Confronting the client with transition problems and working with him to address them can help the changes required take root. A small-scale instance is the following:

• A client was setting up a new business and the new management team came together for a two-day meeting to discuss procedures.

  There was rapid agreement about the objectives of the new operation, and the session seemed complete after the first half-day. The consultant then suggested the group should draw up action plans (who was going to do what, and when) to achieve the objectives they had set out.

  What then emerged was that the general language of objectives masked a considerable divergence of views about details and confusion about how the group should work together.

By working on the problems of transition for the rest of the meeting, the group was not only able to develop plans (which were subsequently successfully implemented) but also to build up its strength as a team.

Techniques for assisting change

This section covers a number of techniques which can be used on consultancy projects. But beware the trap of making change seem more complicated than it really is. If the change required is only superficial, and all that is required is for those subject to it to agree to comply with management instructions, then special techniques are unlikely to be needed. On the other hand, I have found all the following techniques useful at some time or another.

Managing expectations

Even before you set foot on a client's premises, there will be expectations about you and the project you are going to undertake, if held only by senior management. When working with a wider constituency of client staff, they too will have expectations. Sometimes these can be counter productive; for example, if there is little trust between the top and the bottom of the organisation, then there may be great suspicion about you as an emissary of top management.

Expectations are managed by managing communications. With a few notable exceptions, communications within organisations are not particularly good and so it does not take much effort on the part of the consultant to improve on the regular channels. If solid information is not available, rumour – probably ill-informed – will take its place. So it is important that within all projects the consultant actively controls the information which is disseminated. (This point is expanded on in Chapter 3 – see p. 61.)

But managing expectations goes beyond this; consultants also need to ensure that they do not themselves create unwarranted expectations. This is particularly easy to do at the data collection stage of a project. You can imagine the reactions of client staff who are asked questions such as:

- 'Are you happy with your remuneration?'
- 'Would you relocate if the office were to move to Wales?'
- 'Where is there scope to cut staff numbers?'

The obvious inferences from these questions are respectively, 'Pay is going to be improved'; 'The office is to be moved to Wales'; and 'There are going to be redundancies'. The consultant has to decide whether rumours along these lines are helpful and, if not, avoid creating them.

Expectations are also an important factor in motivation, as shown in the equation:

motivation (to do something) = desire (for the reward promised if I do it) x expectation (that if I do it, I will get the reward)

For example, suppose you were stopped in the street by a man who offered you £100 to borrow your watch for an hour, payable on returning the watch to you. Most of us would consider £100 for an hour's hire of a watch a very generous payback. Equally, however, we would be concerned that once we parted with the watch we would not see it or the man again, let alone the £100. Notwithstanding our desire for the reward, our expectations would lead us to turn down the man's offer – irrespective of whether it was genuinely made.

A similar process can occur during a consultancy assignment; everybody may subscribe to the goals the consultant is trying to achieve, but still not be motivated to cooperate. Often this occurs because of lack of trust or cynicism about the intentions of senior management. 'We tried this before, but management went back to their old ways after three months', or 'They say there'll be no redundancies, but they said the same five years ago, and 50 people had to go within the year.' (These are all part of the organisational 'folklore' described above on p. 83.)

Irrespective of the truth of these, if they are what people believe, they constitute a problem for the consultant trying to create change. Those involved with the change have to be convinced to put in the effort required to make it happen – otherwise the consultant will be faced with a self-fulfilling prophecy of failure.

Sometimes reassurances from top management can be adequate; beyond this, a demonstration of support – such as senior executives chairing project meetings or speaking at training sessions – can serve to convince doubters of management's *bona fides*. A pilot trial is also useful for showing the workability of a project (see p. 92).

Getting client commitment

There will always be client staff whose attitude is, 'If you're so clever, go on and prove it!' But unless he is acting in an executive role, a consultant will be creating change via other people, who will therefore have their part to play and should be clear about and accept their responsibilities.

Clients should identify with the success or failure of consultancy projects for which they have engaged the help of consultants; it is far easier to create change in an organisation which accepts joint responsibility for success or failure than one in which the project is totally identified with the consultant. The consultant from Smith Associates should therefore avoid the project being labelled as the 'Smith Associates Project'. The consultant should position himself as assisting in the client's project, so that the client accepts responsibility.

• Quality circles are problem-solving groups set up and led by supervisors from among their own teams. A feature of quality circle programmes is that they are voluntary. In the programmes I have been involved with, first-line supervisors are invited to attend a training course as a circle leader, at the end of which we would call for volunteers to start their own circles. If no one volunteers, then there can be no circles.

Obviously we make as sure as we reasonably can that those who attended the training programme are likely to volunteer, but the end of the course, when volunteers are requested, is always a nail-biting point for the consultant.

Needless to say, on one occasion, through an unfortunate combination of circumstances, I got no volunteers.

The group was then confronted with the consequences of its decision in respect of the programme and the effect on the company. We had agreed earlier in the course on the value of the goals the programme set out to achieve, and these would be lost if the programme folded.

Because of this, one supervisor changed his mind and said that he would have a go, and others followed suit. But no such result would have been achieved if they had not accepted their personal responsibility for ensuring the success of the programme.

Commitment to a project and acceptance of its outcomes is best achieved amongst client staff by giving them opportunities to participate in it. Consultancy projects are joint endeavours between consultant and client, and there is a better chance of achieving acceptance if client staff have been able to contribute to determining the changes required. A participative approach is essential if there is to be an internalised response from client staff.

The level of commitment must reach a 'critical mass' if change is to endure. Many initiatives wither and die because commitment has not been built up to this critical level. Not only are numbers important but also who is committed. In every organisation there will be easy 'converts', but they (unfortunately) are not always the opinion leaders. Every change project should include a plan for identifying the key client staff who might make up the critical mass (and that could be as few as one person) and obtaining their support.

The use of a training course

Training obviously can be used to increase performance by increasing capability. But a training course can also be used to legitimise new behaviour, and as such is similar to an anthropological rite of passage. (See above under Initiation, p. 82.)

Hence, a training course can be used in a change programme to encourage a change of attitudes and behaviour. To be effective, the course should:

- be away from the workplace (and preferably residential);
- last at least a whole day and preferably longer;
- be intensive (and the intensity can apply to the informal sessions around the bar as well as classroom).

These arrangements are distinctively different from what goes on at work. They must be a punctuation mark in the working lives of participants and thus the event must have impact. The overall effect should be to unfreeze the attitudes of participants, to make them receptive to new ideas and willing and able to undertake the changes required. The content of the training given on the course should complement these processes.

- By way of an example, a major company wanted to improve managerial performance significantly. The programme adopted had two components:

  (i) a performance improvement element with an incentive; if a work-group could show an improvement in performance of 10 per cent, staff within the group would get a 10 per cent pay rise;
  (ii) a training element, aimed at helping managers in the programme to carry out the process involved as well as performing the new tasks required of them.

  A very large number of managers went through the training programme which developed a reputation conducive to its success:

- participants were expected to behave differently on their return;
- they enthused about the training they had received;
- people competed to attend the training programme.

  Those who had attended were able to display a certificate which showed they had been through the training programme.

The reason for giving the example is that it illustrates how a training programme can be successfully used as a rite of passage – and in the example, it achieved its objective: the improvements in managerial performance were achieved.

Deciding where to start

If you are introducing a change into an organisation, it may be something which is all or nothing (e.g., the amalgamation of two divisions), but very frequently there may be scope for more gradual introduction. In these circumstances you need to decide where to start.

One way of doing this is to select a part of the client organisation that is going to be easiest to change, introduce the change there and use this to demonstrate its effectiveness to other departments who might be less receptive.

You thus start with a 'pilot trial' prior to general implementation. Advantages of this approach are:

(i)   it reduces change to more manageable proportions – for example, there will be fewer people involved and therefore less time involved in briefing, training, meetings and so on;
(ii) it allows you to 'debug' the new system prior to its general implementation – almost inevitably there will be unanticipated difficulties in any new way of working, necessitating changes in design and so on;
(iii) it provides demonstrable proof of the viability and usefulness of the change. Furthermore, there will be a caucus of client staff involved who can speak with authority on what is entailed and the pros and cons.

The difficulty lies in selecting the starting point. Some parts of the organisation may be ruled out for administrative or other reasons, such as a peak of workload, so the choice may be limited anyhow. The most sympathetic part of the organisation may not be the best place to start, either, if success does not carry much weight elsewhere. Only once, however, have I come across an organisation who wanted the consultants to start a project off in a difficult area; their reason was, 'If we wanted to work in an easy area, we'd do it ourselves'.

A related question is, should you start change at the top of the organisation and work down, or at the bottom and work up?

In almost all circumstances it is best to start at the top. Senior management has greater power to get things done – or to stop them happening. The circumstances in which you might start at the bottom of the organisation are:

- if the change affects only this level;
- if it is essential that people at this level cooperate for the project to work – i.e., the balance of power is shifted because they have considerable negative power.

Choice of client staff to work with

It is rare for a change project not to involve client staff in some role or other in the project team. For example, if engaged on a data-processing project, they may be seconded from the client's own data-processing department. There may be no choice of who works with you – it may be simply by virtue of the job incumbent. But on other occasions, it may be possible to set up project teams over whose membership you have some choice. Referring back to the start of this chapter, it is worth choosing a team which has the right type and amount of power and influence.

- A good example of this was a project within a local education authority. It involved devising a work pack for use by teachers in schools within the county to encourage children to save energy. Experience had shown that the work pack would be most likely to be accepted if it was devised by a team of teachers who worked in the authority. In the past teachers in the county had not been receptive to work packs designed by non-teachers, and were even inhibited about using those designed by teachers from another authority. So the project team was comprised mainly of teachers drawn from the county, and the work pack was well received.

Such an approach could have emerged by using a combination of force field analysis (FFA, described in Appendix **2**) and the power analysis mentioned earlier in the chapter. FFA would have shown that a key factor was to get the support of class teachers, and an analysis of influence would have shown that they were most strongly influenced by the recommendations of their colleagues.

Changing attitudes

Organisations and people often behave like a large block of rubber in respect of change; they change under pressure, but when the pressure disappears, they revert to their old habits. With many of the changes introduced by consultants, the option of changing back will not exist: for example, the old computer system has been replaced, so the new system must be used. But with more fundamental changes (as defined in Figure 4.4), the opportunity of changing back is more likely to exist, and so a real change of attitudes is required.

Many eminent psychologists have investigated the process of attitude change and it would be tempting, but not particularly helpful, to quote some of the theories here, but, as this book is about *practice*, there seem to me to be three general points to be made:

(i) We are not too concerned about what goes on inside a person's head. The consultant has to be concerned about what people do – the decisions they make or actions they take.

(ii) People are not inherently opposed to change *per se*. Resistance to change occurs more often as a failure in communication, its insensitive introduction or that the change is simply wrong. (I leave aside here those changes which adversely affect the individual. Few will welcome a change against their self-interest – for example, being put out of a job.)

(iii) Attitudes can frequently be changed by changing the way people look at things, and this in turn can be achieved by providing them with activities and experience which change their perspective.

Taking the last point, for example, resistance to change often comes from fear of the unknown, and so special effort needs to be put into explaining the change, the reasons for it and what the consequences are likely to be (see also 'Managing expectations' on p. 88). Even then there will still be those who feel threatened and with whom the consultant must use confidence-building measures. An example of a confidence-building measure would be, prior to making a change, allowing those subject to it to discuss it with others who have made it already, thereby allaying their fears. For example, the introduction of a new piece of equipment could be facilitated by seeing it operating in another location where it has already been successfully introduced. It becomes more difficult to demonstrate new managerial systems, unless there has been a successful pilot trial carried out already – hence the value of a pilot trial to demonstrate what really happens.

Further confidence-building measures need to be taken at the implementation of a change. However careful the preparation, however good the communications and training prior to its introduction, at its early introduction a change needs a high level of support – what some consultants call nursing. This means being on hand to answer queries, overcome difficulties and put right those things which inevitably go wrong.

What can you do when, despite your confidence building efforts, participants lack the confidence to go on? First, of course, you need to reassure yourself that their lack of confidence is not well founded: is there some factor that you may have overlooked that gives substance to their doubts? You could also work with them on a cause and effect diagram, to assess all the possible causes of failure and see that they have been addressed.

These, of course, address rational concerns, but fear can be irrational. Ultimately, you may have to give them a push – like an able swimmer lacking the confidence to go out of his depth. Once they have made the change successfully, they should have the confidence to continue.

Use of feedback

Finally, there is the use of feedback to encourage change. At its simplest level, numerous tests have shown that people seem to perform better if they know how well they are doing. Combined with target-setting, this can be a powerful motivator.

- A colliery displayed the cumulative weight of coal mined, year to date, on a big sign at its entrance. One year, it became clear that the workforce might achieve a million tons for the first time. By unprecedented effort and teamwork they achieved this – but it would not have happened without feedback on a regular basis on how they were doing.

In the context of change, feedback between different levels and groups can be effective, as well as that among individuals. Examples illustrating this are:

- A group of managers who had similar concerns about certain aspects of their performance, but who had never discussed them. The consultant discovered this, and was able to raise the subject at one of their group meetings. Therefore the discussion of a subject which previously they had felt uncomfortable raising was legitimised.
- Managements often see employee communication only as a downward process. But it should also be upward. The consultant can encourage the feedback of views from junior levels to senior levels, and this can frequently be instrumental in changing top management attitudes. For example, a management which considered it did a good job of keeping employees informed would need to reconsider its views if they found out that staff felt poorly informed.

One of the key jobs, therefore, for a consultant concerned with change, is to keep client staff informed about how things are going. Beyond this, remember that recognition is a most powerful motivator; in the UK we have the whole honours system to prove it! So make sure that top management recognise and congratulate those involved in a change for their achievement.

Some final words of consolation

Organisations are the most complex systems with which a consultant has to deal. No surprise, then, that no one has devised a comprehensive way of ensuring that change is guaranteed. (And if they had, by definition, we would not know of it.) All you can do is improve the odds for change being successful and this chapter should provide a basis for doing so. Even so – if it is any comfort – like all consultants, you will have your failures.

There is a danger as well that 'change' becomes overplayed, that it is made to appear overly hard. But change, not stasis, is a natural state of affairs. Everybody from the moment they are born undergoes continuous change and as a species we are fairly well adapted to it. So, notwithstanding all the advice in this chapter, the best way of achieving a change may simply be to ask people to get on with it.

A final exhortation, however. Everybody has their own theory of how individuals or groups or organisations respond to change. It will be based largely on past experience and may include precepts and rules which are empirically deduced. It is well worthwhile bringing your own particular theory out from the back of your mind to examine it carefully. Do the beliefs and assumptions you have made about change make sense in the context of the projects you are now handling? Maybe you should change *your* views about change.

5 Data collection and analysis

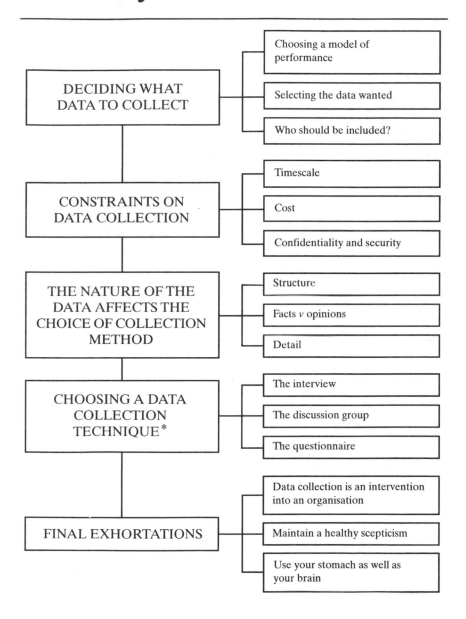

DECIDING WHAT DATA TO COLLECT
- Choosing a model of performance
- Selecting the data wanted
- Who should be included?

CONSTRAINTS ON DATA COLLECTION
- Timescale
- Cost
- Confidentiality and security

THE NATURE OF THE DATA AFFECTS THE CHOICE OF COLLECTION METHOD
- Structure
- Facts *v* opinions
- Detail

CHOOSING A DATA COLLECTION TECHNIQUE*
- The interview
- The discussion group
- The questionnaire

FINAL EXHORTATIONS
- Data collection is an intervention into an organisation
- Maintain a healthy scepticism
- Use your stomach as well as your brain

*See also Appendix **3**

5   Data collection and analysis

- A hot-air balloonist had lost his bearings when he landed in a field and saw a man approaching on foot. The balloonist asked the man where he was. 'You are in the basket of a hot-air balloon, in the middle of a field' came the reply. Factually correct but totally unhelpful.

In management consultancy – as with all problem solving – you need to identify the data you require very carefully. From childhood, our life is taken up with collecting and sorting data and trying to make sense of the world. Similarly, management consultants collect and sort data to make sense of the organisation and issues they are working with.

A difficulty facing the consultant, however, is not the shortage of information but its abundance, and it can be problematical choosing what information is relevant.

Perversely, of course, despite the availability of data, it is rare to have all the information you ideally would like. This applies particularly to predictions about the future, especially people's behaviour. Cost is also an element; the more accurate or extensive the data required, the more costly it is to collect. Moreover, I suspect it obeys the 'law of diminishing returns': the effort involved in getting data to 1 per cent accuracy is an order of magnitude greater than getting it to 10 per cent accuracy.

Management consultancy has its roots in work study, which itself is based on the careful observation, measurement and analysis of work and involves large amounts of data collection and analysis.

Similarly, in the other areas into which management consultancy has developed, projects almost always involve some initial research; it is rare for data to be readily available in the form required to address a particular issue. The data the consultant collects will be facts and statistics – i.e., hard data – but soft data, such as opinions, signals, assumptions, speculations and other clues can be just as relevant to the successful implementation of a project.

In this chapter, you will see that no distinction has been made between data collection and data analysis because there is little point in collecting data unless you have some idea of what you are to do with it. Data collection can be very time-consuming (indeed, it can be the single most time-consuming element in a consultancy project), and a lot of time – and thus money – can be wasted if it is not done properly. The specific and detailed techniques associated with any discipline can be seductive: it can be easy to embark on a highly structured programme of data collection without reflecting what the data is to be used for. Once started, the danger is that the means become the end – the process of collecting, analysing and presenting data over-shadows the original purpose of the project. There are a mass of consultants' reports languishing on managers' shelves around the world which, although masterpieces of data collection, have failed to address the important issues. Alternatively, the important issues have been recognised, but too late; the data collected does not match that required to address the issues, and the conclusions are inadequately supported.

Starting a new consultancy project is a bit like being the balloonist referred to at the start of the chapter: you are put down in the middle of a field and have to find your way around. There is some comfort in taking action – any action – and rushing around collecting data may give you the comfort of action and your client the impression of progress. The purpose of this chapter is to avoid doing unnecessary work. At the start of an assignment, therefore, don't just do something – sit there and think!

Deciding what data to collect

One of the popular methods of teaching business analysis has been the use of case studies. I have a book of them in front of me and they vary in length from two to more than 20 pages of closely typeset information. Even so, 'real life' is vastly more complex; a case study – however long – offers a small volume of data compared with the real world in which the significance of data may not be appreciated, or it is unavailable, or there are other priorities competing for attention. Deciding what data to collect is trying to sort the signal from the noise. It is an important task, and can be a hard one. A helpful first step is to choose an appropriate model of performance.

Choosing a model of performance

The relevance of data is a function of the model being used to understand the nature of the problem; for example, market research data may be highly relevant to a sales problem but not to an engineering one. Thus there are at least two levels of data collection required:

(i) to determine the nature of the problem and the model to be used to understand it;
(ii) to build a more detailed picture according to the model chosen.

Turning again to the balloonist analogy, the former is like deciding which of many maps to refer to and the latter, having chosen the map, to find out where you are on it.

Chapter **3** mentioned the need for a 'wallow' at the start of a project – the process of familiarisation. This stage helps the consultant to select and build a mental model of the issue to sort out. Often this model will not be articulated; it may be intuitive, but it will be there. Consultants with different specialisations look at situations from their own specialist point of view. The marketeer will see problems from the marketing standpoint, the informations systems specialist will see the data-processing problems and so on. Inevitably consultants bring their own specialist biases to a project but this should be no disadvantage – after all, consultants are chosen on the basis of their expertise being expected to be of use.

The process of familiarisation helps in gaining an insight to the nature of a problem.

Referring back to the stock control problem in ABC Ltd, mentioned in Chapter **2**. The problem initially cited by the director is that of wishing to introduce a new computerised stock control system. Although recognising that the problem is not necessarily about logistics, Dick's experience might indicate that the process of familiarisation could be best accomplished by drawing up a material flow diagram. His first step will be to collect data at level (i) above to understand what the material flows are. The results are depicted in Figure 5.1 on page 103.

He would build up this picture by discussions with a few key people in the company, at the same time illuminating the problem he has to address. Dick may wish therefore to check what models are in use in ABC Ltd in relation to stock control. Two questions that Dick might ask at this stage are therefore:

(i) What measures are used to determine the performance of the stock control system wholly and in part?

(Various measures might be:

- to deliver goods within a given time of receiving the order;
- to keep inventories of stocks low;
- to keep rejects below a given percentage.

These objectives will be in conflict, and the stock control system will have to lead to the right trade-offs.)

(ii) Who takes decisions which affect the performance of each part of the system? (If different managers are responsible for pursuing each of the objectives above, then the system could itself cause conflicts between the managers.)

Selecting the data wanted

Very often consultancy assignments are a process of hypothesis testing: the consultant is able at an early point in the assignment to have a pretty good guess at what the likely recommendations might be and thus orientate data collection to test whether these are right.

For example, Dick's initial hypothesis concerning the stock control problems at ABC Ltd following the formalisation stage could be that managers are working towards conflicting performance goals. The data he will choose to collect initially will therefore be about performance measures and managerial responsibilities.

Consultants are great *post hoc* rationalisers (they are not alone in this) and when reporting retrospectively on a project, will show that the process of data collection is in the following sequence:

- define the objectives of the project;
- determine the data required;
- develop and implement a plan for collecting the data;
- analyse the data;
- draw conclusions and make recommendations.

In practice, unless the project follows a 'royal road' (see Chapter **3**), the process is more messy and, for example, Dick's project would probably follow a series of iterations:

- definition of the project objectives beforehand;
- initial wallow;
- new slants to the issues identified. Possibly project objectives are slightly shifted, and initial hypotheses formed;
- crude data collection;
- items worth exploring identified in more detail;
- revise/substantiate hypotheses;
  and so on.

Despite this process of reaching hypothetical conclusions early on in the assignment, the consultant must keep an open mind.

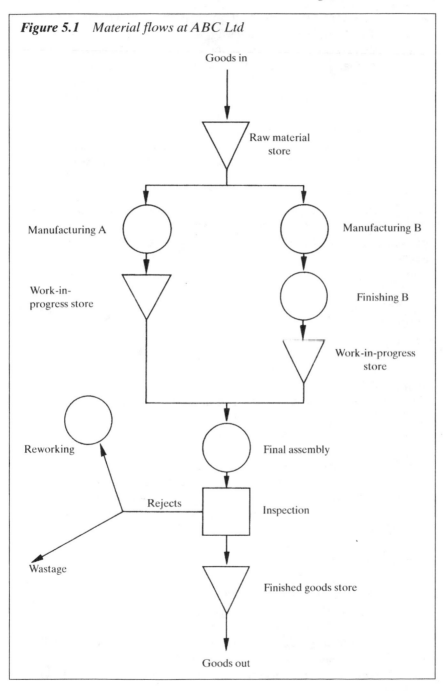

Figure 5.1   *Material flows at ABC Ltd*

Goods in

Raw material
store

Manufacturing A

Manufacturing B

Work-in-
progress store

Finishing B

Work-in-progress
store

Reworking

Final assembly

Rejects

Inspection

Wastage

Finished goods store

Goods out

- On one assignment the consultant quickly identified what he considered should be the outcome of the investigation. A number of data collection meetings with senior executives in the company had been set up but the consultant made the mistake of pre-selling the proposed solution at the meetings. In the event, most of the executives agreed with his conclusion, except the chairman of the company, who was the last to be seen. He totally disagreed with the consultant's solution. The consultant lost face with the chairman, for having reached what appeared to be a firm conclusion without sounding the chairman out, and also lost face with the executives because he could not deliver the proposals to which he had got their agreement.

A development of this method of choosing what data to collect comes from giving some thought to the content and structure of the final report early on in the assignment. If Dick, for instance, reckons that ABC Ltd ought to have a new stock control system, he might decide that his case will be best made by presenting data on:

- benchmarking of stock levels in ABC Ltd with those expected in high performance organisations elsewhere;
- quality of delivery;
- timeliness and accuracy of information produced by the system.

Having decided what evidence he will want to present in his final report, Dick could then go one step further to lay out how it might be presented. This would consist of drawing up the tables, diagrams, graphs and charts, etc., to assess what data would be needed to complete them.

A further refinement is to fill in the charts and tables with dummy data (before starting data collection) to make sure that there are no gaps, nor is data to be collected which is unlikely to be of much use. You need an active imagination to do this effectively, and it is more difficult with qualitative than with quantitative data.

Who should be included?

In the story of Sleeping Beauty, a curse was placed on the princess by a fairy who was not invited to her christening. Beware the same process happening on your assignments! If you are to carry out a survey, it is important to cover not only those who have data but also those powerful individuals who will feel that they should have been consulted. It is better to see too many people than run the risk of needlessly creating a powerful antagonist.

Data collection also provides an opportunity to meet a wider cross-section of the top people in the organisation than the consultant otherwise would.

It gives a chance to assess what they are like whilst at the same time being able to make your number with them. There is a military maxim that 'time spent in reconnaissance is rarely wasted'. The same is true of data collection; you may well have a complete compendium of hard data to collect, but equally you need to have information about the key people in the organisation and their views relevant to your project. And, as is obviously the case, you can learn a lot from meeting them.

For example, sometimes consultants will receive a certain amount of disinformation – information that purports to be accurate, but which at best is only partially so. This is often provided by those wishing to score political points or follow their own agenda, particularly at senior levels.

Happily consultants can often spot this happening, and so have acquired a useful piece of data in itself – the peculiar objectives being followed by the provider of disinformation.

Constraints on data collection

Dick will have to make sure that he does his assignment within the consultant time allocated, and this might restrict the information he can collect. For example, it could be very useful to have information on how satisfied ABC's customers are with delivery times, but visits to customers could be difficult to arrange and time-consuming. Moreover, there is the danger that asking questions about the adequacy of delivery dates may create questions in the customers' minds which were not there before.
Summarised below are the major constraints on data collection, which will limit both the range of data collected and the methods of its collection.

Timescale

The first constraint is the calendar time available for the project. (The amount of effort and the consequent limitations in terms of cost, are discussed in the next section.)

The effect of a limited timescale may itself constrain the amount of effort which can be put in by a project team. For example, if a new product is to be launched to catch the retail Christmas market, there may be severely limited time for test marketing if it is started too late.

- On the other hand, do not let a limited timescale deter you from collecting vital information. This happened to a consultant pressed for time on a number of projects, who had to take on another which had to be completed within a short timescale. Most of the factual information required was collected, but because of the time constraints the deeply political environment in the organisation the consultant was required to advise had not been recognised. The consequence was that a major presentation to the board of directors went very badly and jeopardised the project the consultant was engaged with.

The moral is, if there is insufficient time to collect vital data, either extend the timescale, or limit the terms of reference of the project – at least initially – to that which can be accomplished within the available timescale. If clients expect work to be completed within an unreasonably short timescale, a firm stand by the consultant is necessary to persuade them otherwise. If this is not possible, you have to question whether you should be involved with the project at all.

Cost

The expense of data collection arises mainly from:

- the consultant's time and the expenses incurred;
- the method of data collection and analysis;
- the time and effort of client staff.

For example, if attitudes are to be assessed throughout an organisation using a questionnaire, costs will arise from design and printing, the time spent completing it, and the collation and analysis of completed questionnaires.

Travel expenses can also add considerably to the costs of the project, as they did in a project run from the UK in an African country, part of which was to advise on the suitability of particular computer software. The software was available and in use only in the USA, and so the consultants had to make several intercontinental trips, which added significantly to the project cost.

Sometimes a consultancy may subcontract research work and this can be another form of expense. Published editions of market or economic research reports focusing on highly specialised topics can cost thousands of dollars. Similarly, there are research organisations which, for example, will carry out consumer-based market research on a bespoke basis.

Expenses can also arise from using specialist survey techniques involving proprietary questionnaires and the computer software required to analyse them.

If the expense of data collection is likely to be significant, it should be included in the preliminary cost estimate. Remember also that clients are often as concerned about the 'expense' of the time of their own people becoming involved in meetings and so on. The consultant needs to be prepared for, and sensitive, to this point.

Confidentiality and security

Consultants are sometimes used to carry out external research where the client wishes their identity, or the fact that they are engaged in a particular project, to be kept confidential. Executive search (headhunting) is an example of this: the client may not want it to be generally known that they are seeking to fill a particular position (perhaps because of personnel or commercial repercussions), or wishes to sound out a prospective candidate's interest through an intermediary.

It is sometimes difficult, however, to collect data if the identity of the client is to be kept secret from those providing the data – for instance, if you require competitors to pool data. The way around this is to offer respondents a suitably edited version of the research carried out in exchange for their taking part. Product managers will be more ready to give their views on the changing market for widgets if they know that they are going to receive a distillation of the views of similar managers amongst competitors, than if they are to receive nothing in return.

Sources of information sometimes have to be kept confidential from your clients. Thus, a consultant commissioned to carry out a salary survey may have got data on the basis that specific providers would not be identified; to do otherwise would therefore be a breach of confidentiality.

Perhaps the most difficult problem of confidentiality is that of keeping the nature of an enquiry from staff. For example, a consultant advising on the feasibility of a company moving its head office from one location to another may need to know how many staff would consequently resign, preferring not to move. One way of finding out is to ask them – and indeed, that may well be done later on in the project – but at the stage of a feasibility study, the resultant speculation would not be in the client's best interest. So an alternative method of data collection would have to be used, so as to keep the reason for it confidential.

One consultant faced with exactly this problem asked heads of departments – who knew about the prospective move – to guess for each employee whether they would resign. A further alternative might have been to collect the data under the guise of a survey oriented to a different end – for example, one on job satisfaction. (Although this needs care too, to make sure you do not jump out of the frying pan into the fire.)

In any case, a consultant is a new face in an organisation and, inevitably, questions will be asked about who they are and what they are doing there. If you are not going to tell the whole truth, you must ensure you have a good cover story beforehand!

The nature of the data affects the choice of collection method

The general considerations in the last section (cost, timescale, etc.) will influence the choice of data collection method. But the nature of the data you seek will also affect how you go about collecting it.

It might exist already in a form you can use. Hard data abounds in an organisation on matters to do with its business, and so there is much to be gleaned by examining documents such as:

- management accounts;
- business results and forecasts;
- business plans;
- organisation charts;
- personnel statistics;
- advertising material.

There are sources outside the company too, for example:

- published market research;
- stockbrokers' reports (for large companies or sectors);
- newspapers and periodicals.

Proprietary databases can be used to access details on companies or specific topics, based on abstracts of published information, and a lot of other information in the public domain as well as within the client may potentially be of use to the consultant.

Most assignments, however, involve the consultant having to research data. In selecting the method you have to consider the structure, nature and detail of the data required.

Structure

By structure is meant the degree of variety in the answers which can be given to the question asked. A highly structured question is, 'How many people work in this factory?' The answer will be a number. An unstructured question is, 'How effective is the stock control system in this company?'

Unstructured questions invite further qualification; in the case above, it might be, 'effective in what terms?' It invites comparison with a number of yardsticks; does the stock control system:

- Keep working capital requirements low?
- Minimise waiting time on key pieces of manufacturing machinery?
- Enable customers' orders to be delivered within the required time?
- Help production operations to be planned efficiently?

There will need to be some research into which of these – or any other – yardsticks should be used to assess the stock control system.

The nature of a consulting project is to move from relatively unstructured to more structured data collection. At the start, the consultant will try to approach an issue with an open mind. The data he collected initially helps to focus later enquiries. The danger of starting with too much structure is that you are asking questions of the kind, 'When did you stop being late for work?', which contains at least four assumptions which could be wrong!

It is much easier to analyse structured data than unstructured. Examples of structured and unstructured questions are shown in Figure 5.2.

Figure 5.2 *Unstructured and structured questions*

Unstructured   What do you think of
this Company's employment
policies?

Structured   Show your degree of agreement with the following
statements using the boxes below:

                                            Agree ⟵⟶ Disagree
                                            strongly   strongly

The company pays well ☐☐☐☐☐

The company provides
secure employment ☐☐☐☐☐

The company provides
equal opportunities to
all ☐☐☐☐☐

There will be a wide variety of responses to the unstructured question which will then have to be classified. In the structured case, the classification has already been done; it assumes, for example, that pay, security of employment and equal opportunities are the appropriate measures of the attractiveness of the company's employment policies. If, however, the major concern of those surveyed is that they feel they work in unpleasant surroundings, or they do not like the hours of work, these points will not emerge in the structured questionnaire.

In summary, then, structured data needs a lot of work doing to make sure it is structured correctly before collection, but is relatively easy to analyse afterwards. Unstructured data does not require as much preliminary work, but needs a lot of analysis subsequently.

Facts *v* opinions

Facts should be verifiable, but opinions can also provide valid data. Answers to questions such as:

- What do you think of the company's employment policies?
- Is company publicity being adequately dealt with?
- Could we do our training better?

are matters of opinion.

Opinions are subjective and with all subjective data there is the danger of distortion – that respondents will slant their response to some particular end – perhaps to please the questioner. A question such as: 'Are you an honest person?' will usually get the reply 'yes'. But the replies to: 'What do you think of the company's employment policies?' could be distorted – for example, if respondents believed a critical answer would be held against them.

If distortion is likely, better quality data can be got by face-to-face data collection than by questionnaire, and by trying to eliminate value-laden language as far as possible.

The advantage of face-to-face collection is twofold: firstly, most people lie less well face-to-face – and indeed are more reluctant to do so. Moreover, the consultant can often spot if the individual is distorting the truth. Secondly – and probably more significantly – people will speak their minds face-to-face with the consultant (who, hopefully, establishes some sort of rapport with them) far more openly than if they are required to commit their comments to paper, which may be seen by anyone.

It is sensible to avoid value-laden language in all data collection. By 'value-laden' is meant the implication that some answers would be more welcome than others. Thus, 'Is your company a *good* employer?' is a value-laden question because of the use of the word 'good'. It is probably better in this context to ask a question such as: 'What employment policies in this company do you consider wholly satisfactory, and which would you like to see changed?'

People are sometimes uncomfortable being critical so if you are seeking data which requires them to disclose honest criticism, there are two further things you can do:

- allow them to make positive as well as negative comments (as in the example above);
- convey the sense that it is safe to make negative comments (and this is far more easy to do face-to-face than via a questionnaire).

Detail

The detail required may also affect the data-collection method used, and there is a major distinction between qualitative and quantitative data. Much of consultancy (particularly at strategic levels) is about qualitative data, such as:

- How do we compare with our major competitors?
- What are the most probable technological threats to us?
- Which markets offer the best growth opportunities to us?

Detailed, statistically accurate information is not necessarily required but it is important to distinguish those cases which do. For example, some years ago a financial securities firm was planning to spend £1 million on computer hardware, for a screen-based dealing system. They had specified a response time of three seconds. After some research it was found that this response time was required for only a fraction of the applications, which could be achieved by a modification to the software costing only a few thousand pounds. Arriving at this conclusion involved collecting fairly precise numerical data; the benefits of a cheaper solution had to be balanced with the possibility that their dealers might be at a competitive disadvantage.

Generally, the need for detailed numerical data is greater in technical consultancy such as:

- introducing a new software system;
- moving the office to another location;
- deciding on a new salary system.

Strategic consultancy is concerned with policy, and requires the definition of policy options and how choices are to be made among them. This may be a matter of opinion but it is possible, none the less, to apply statistical analysis to opinions, through such methods as the Delphi technique (see Appendix **3**).

The touchstone for determining the level of detail required is, what is the data to be used for and how much accuracy is required to define and distinguish between options?

Choosing a data-collection technique

There are essentially only three ways you can collect data:

- from observation;
- by dialogue with people;
- by examining documents or other material.

In consultancy, data is generated using investigative techniques, three of which are considered below:

(i)   the interview – a meeting with a single interviewee;
(ii) the discussion group – a meeting with several people;
(iii) the questionnaire – a way of creating documentary information.

Analytical techniques allow data to be structured in forms for particular use.

The following analytical techniques are outlined in Appendix **3** together with their advantages and disadvantages and some practical hints for using them:

- paired comparisons;
- repertory grid;
- critical incident;
- Delphi technique.

To illustrate how a data-collection method might be chosen, we will continue with the example of Dick's stock control assignment at ABC Ltd. He has used the notion of 'individual performance analysis' (described on p. 223 in Appendix **2**) to arrive at his hypothesis that the conflict between departments arises because their goals are in conflict. If he is right, he will need to clarify and possibly rearrange managerial responsibilities.

The performance model Dick uses for the next stage of data collection is shown in Figure 5.3. Business performance overall depends on the performance of its component parts; there will be measures for each of these, but performance targets have to be set suboptimally; (i.e., what is best for part of the business is not necessarily best for it overall; for example, responding to an urgent customer order may result in inefficient production, but be necessary to provide competitive customer service).

Dick's model shows that the quality of performance depends on how well key decisions are made, and these in turn depend on each manager having:

* unambiguous responsibilities;
* clear performance goals, which are consistent with those of other managers;
* the right information for the decisions he needs to take.

Dick's hypothesis implies that these criteria are not met and he needs to define and collect the data necessary to verify it.

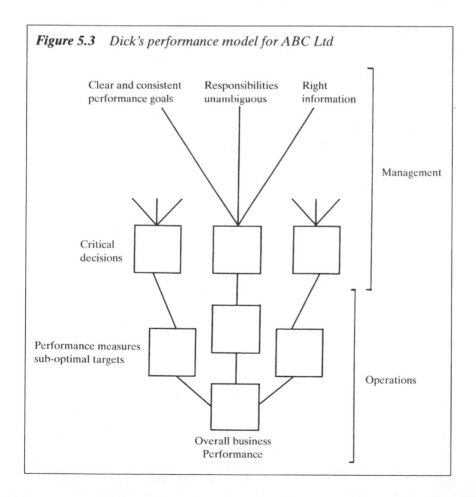

Figure 5.3   *Dick's performance model for ABC Ltd*

Clear and consistent performance goals

Responsibilities unambiguous

Right information

Management

Critical decisions

Performance measures sub-optimal targets

Operations

Overall business Performance

Suppose, then, that Dick wants to check whether managers' responsibilities are ambiguous; he needs first to define which responsibilities are relevant to the stock control system. This is highly unstructured data and his initial data collection will attempt to give it more structure. One of the features of ambiguity is that it not only arises out of fact but also because individuals' perceptions are unclear or mistaken. Dick will therefore need to use a data collection method which gathers opinion and, given that the number of respondents would be small, he should use interviewing.

The interview

The interview is a one-to-one meeting between the consultant and a member of the client's staff. (Incidentally, I rarely refer to them as interviews when discussing them with the client – I always call them meetings. Some people would object to being interviewed, but meetings are a part of their routine work.)

Advantages
(i)   It allows personal contact with client staff which may not otherwise be possible. This is particularly useful when interviewing the senior people in an organisation, which gives you the opportunity to make your mark with those who might be strongly influential in determining the success of the assignment.
(ii) It can be used in an unstructured way. It enables you to follow the interviewee's train of thought, priorities and emotions, rather than forcing them into the predetermined structures required in most other forms of data collection.
(iii) It enables client's staff to feel they have contributed to the study (and thus they are more likely to accept the conclusions).
(iv) It allows you to get a 'feel' for the organisation and people in it. If interviews are held in interviewees' offices, what is it like? Are they always being (and allowing themselves to be) interrupted? Have they got a clear or untidy desk? Are there any interesting charts or graphs on the wall. All this could be useful intelligence.
(v)   Personal contact can be used to draw out more data than otherwise might be forthcoming. (In two ways; firstly, as already remarked, the interviewee may be more confident about making disclosures face-to-face. Secondly, they may have data in their office which they can show you.)

Disadvantages
(i)   It is time consuming.
(ii) It is sometimes difficult to decide who should or should not be seen. (I usually define the criteria and let the client select. Almost always this means having to see more people than you originally budgeted for.)

(iii) As much of the data collected is unstructured, it makes subsequent analysis more difficult.

Operating hints

- Allow sufficient time for interviews. Those at the start will normally take longer because you are at the bottom of the learning curve. As you get to know more about the organisation you will need to ask fewer questions of clarification, and also the focus of your questions will become sharper.
- Ensure that you and the interviewee have a common idea of how much time is required for the interviews. It is frustrating to have only half an hour available for an hour's discussion, so if possible book the time in their diary in advance.
- Do not try to do too much. Interviewing is hard work – it requires 100 per cent attention all the time to hear and understand what is being said while at the same time directing the conversation. As a rule of thumb I operate at 50 per cent capacity: assuming I work an eight-hour day, I would schedule four one-hour interviews – perhaps at $1\frac{1}{2}$-hourly intervals. The extra half-hour can be used for extending the interviews, allowing for late arrivals and for writing up notes. I recognise that the six or seven hours thus allocated will not be totally taken up with interviews, so I usually take other work I can do to fill in the odd spaces.
- Use some form of structure which will help you to develop the discussion in a logical way and, subsequently, to analyse the response. This is particularly important if more than one consultant is carrying out the interviews. Figure 5.4 over shows the method I use of developing 'areas of enquiry'. It shows the type of question which might be used to start the discussion on the topic; the numbering system can also be applied to the responses (by noting the reference in the margin of your interview notes) so that they can be analysed more easily later. Remember, too, to introduce the interview – what it is about, what it is to be used for and how long it will take. At the end, thank the interviewee for their help and mention, if possible, what will happen next.
- It is essential to keep a good record. This can be done by writing or tape recording. I have never used the latter, but some consultants believe a complete transcript of what has been said is very useful. It does, however, require a lot of typing and of course the subsequent analysis is still needed. Other drawbacks are that interviewees may be inhibited by the presence of the microphone, and a typed transcript will not show the relative stress attached to the various points made by the interviewee.
- The advantage of taking notes is that you can keep a commentary in parentheses – remarks such as ('seems very anxious') or ('uninterested in this aspect') can help to illuminate the subsequent analysis. (I was amused once, during an interview with a headhunter, to see that he was drawing sketches of me to help his subsequent recollection.) It is also worthwhile adding a summary of your major impressions to your notes after the meeting.

Figure 5.4 *Interview agenda relating to the organisation of a finance
function in a bank*

1. Introduce selves
2. Explain purpose of interview
   - To collect information and views on
     current and future activities and
     organisation of finance department.
3. Explain meeting will be about $1^1/_2$
   hours.
4. Views are non-attributable.
5. Record name of interviewee and date.
6. Run through the agenda below. The
   questions shown are to denote areas of
   enquiry, which will need to be fleshed
   out by supplementary questions.
7. Use the numbering system in your
   interview notes to aid subsequent
   analysis.
8. At the end of the interview:
   - leave the opportunity to ask further
     points of clarification later
   - reiterate the interview is non
     attributable;
   - explain what happens next.

AGENDA
1. Current organisation of function.
   1.1 Your job and the structure
       reporting to you.
   1.2 The role of the group for which you
       are responsible.
   1.3 Responsibilities of your job and
       specialist skills/knowledge required.
   1.4 The responsibilities of those
       reporting to you and any specialist
       skills/knowledge required.

2. Operation of your function
   2.1 Imperatives and obligations:
       - imperatives: are there any statutory
         (e.g., reporting) obligations the
         function has, and what are they?
       - internal obligations – e.g., timing
         for internal accounting purposes.
   2.2 Interfaces – information flows
       and/or dicisions. Frequency
       (importance, etc.):
       - within finance function;
       - with other parts of the bank;
       - outside the bank.
   2.3 Scope (discretionary aspect?)
       - Has your group a formal remit, and
         if so, what is it and how was it set?
       - How would this remit be changed?
         In particular, how do you know if
         some things you do are no longer
         required, or if additional tasks are
         required?

2.4 Performance
   - How can you tell if your function is
     doing a good job/things are going
     wrong?
   - Priorities/vulnerability; what are the
     most important task/tasks which have
     serious repercussions if they go
     wrong?

3. Future developments
   3.1 What do you see to be the major
       influences which may change the
       nature of your function?
       - business change/organisational;
       - statutory/regulatory change;
       - information technology;
       - other.
   3.2 What are the results of these
       influences likely to be in terms of:
       - the tasks and responsibilities of your
         group;
       - the volume of work;
       - the skills required;
       - other.
   3.3 What influences are there likely to be
       on other parts of the finance function
       and what are the consequences likely
       to be:
       - influences/changes;
       - change consequences.
   3.4 Are there other changes which would
       be desirable to enable your group or
       the finance function as a whole to
       increase its performance?
   3.5 In particular, comment on:
       - the interface between central and
         local finance function with
         subsidiaries/overseas offices;
       - how the function should be organised
         to deal with:
         – different specialisations;
         – different subsidiaries/overseas
           offices;
         – different businesses.

4. Personal development
   4.1 What is your career history?
   4.2 How do you see your future?

5. Is there anything else you would like to
   add to your comments?

- I have never had anyone object to my notetaking but it is worth emphasising that remarks will be used but be non-attributable. (The information given you in an interview cannot be totally confidential – you need to reveal it to your client as part of your findings.)
- Do not forget the technique of the experienced interrogator – people will say more when they are relaxed. At the end of an interview you can put down your pad and notebook and show by your mien that it is over. At this point an interviewee will often relax and provide you with more useful data which they were uncomfortable doing during the formal part of the interview. Remember also the virtue of silence. which can sometimes prompt an interviewee to say more than intended.
- In the interests of good client relations you may wish to drop a 'thank you' note to those who have given up time to see you, either after you have seen them or at the end of the interview programme. It is not always appropriate doing this – in some circumstances it might be considered too formal – but it is worth considering.

The discussion group

The discussion group is a meeting at which more than one of the client staff are present. There is a variant called a 'focus group', which is usually more structured than an interview, and is often used in market research.

The discussion group has many similar advantages and disadvantages to those of the interview; the following points are worth noting by contrast.

Advantages
- You can meet far more people in discussion groups than in one-to-one interviews.
- A discussion group is a higher profile event than a meeting one-to-one, and can therefore be used to raise the profile of your assignment or as a building block in a change programme.
- Individuals may feel more confident about giving their views if they realise that others in the group are being open.

Disadvantages
- The more people there are, the less time there is for each to talk. You will therefore get a less comprehensive view from each individual and one or two people may dominate the discussion.
- People may be inhibited about opening up in front of colleagues.
- Meetings will probably need to be held in a meeting room – so you will not get the advantage of seeing others' offices.
- It is harder work; you have to regulate a more complex discussion as well as taking a record. For this reason it is often useful to have two consultants involved – one to lead the discussion and the other to take notes – but obviously this is more costly.

Operating hints

- Have some ground rules for determining the composition of groups. Should each consist of members from the same department or from a cross-section? Should there be a mix of levels? Take the decisions on these, bearing in mind the type of data you want to collect, and remember they can also be an instrument of change. If Dick (in our example) wants to confront departments with others' views of them in respect of the problem, he might use mixed groups.
- Unless there are strong reasons for doing so, avoid forming discussion groups with the top executives in an organisation. You will be the outsider in the group of powerful people, who will know each other well. Whatever you are trying to achieve may be overshadowed by the agendas they are working out amongst themselves.
- You have both to regulate the discussion and to keep a record, and this is more complicated in a discussion group than in an interview. You can make this task easier by:

  - *more structure*: you keep control of the topics covered more tightly than in an interview;
  - *greater focus*: you concentrate on finding out about a narrower range of more specific items;
  - *simplified notetaking*: you will not be able to collect all the data that becomes available at a discussion group meeting and the difficulty is compounded by also having to lead the discussion. The demands on your attention should be relieved particularly by the other means suggested above. Beyond this, you may wish to resort to tape recording (more difficult because of the size of the group), but an alternative with a large group is to record the key points on a flipchart. This has the additional advantage of giving participants the opportunity to make sure you have recorded and understood the key points they are making.

The questionnaire

The term 'questionnaire' is used here to include any document designed by the consultant to elicit data from respondents. Examples of their use are:

- an attitude survey, to find out the state of staff morale;
- a survey of remuneration within the computer industry;
- a study of the buying habits of car users.

Everyone will have at some time completed questionnaires and will have views on their design. Some specialist consultants may use standard questionnaires (for example, occupational psychologists use them to assess aptitudes). In what follows, we will assume that the questionnaire is non-standard and is self-administered (i.e., the respondent completes it themself rather than under the supervision of the consultant).

Advantages
- A very large number of people can be sampled if necessary, and it is cheaper than interviewing.
- Responses can be analysed fairly easily.
- It may be less time consuming for the respondent, or more easily fitted in with their work, than an interview.
- It facilitates statistical analysis.
- With large samples, optical mark or character recognition can be used to read responses into a computer.

Disadvantages
- You will get responses only to the questions you ask. You must therefore be sure these are the ones you want answered.
- You have no chance of explaining it – so it must be clear and unambiguous.
- Respondents may feel inhibited about committing themselves honestly to paper.
- Similarly, unless you provide for it in the questionnaire, you will have no idea of the relative strength of feeling attaching to a given response.
- People may ignore the questionnaire or be dilatory in completing it so a 100 per cent response is unlikely, possibly leaving you with an unbalanced sample.

Operating hints
- Whereas much of the work in interviews lies in analysing them after they have taken place, with questionnaires effort has to be put into their design before data collection takes place. In particular you must make sure that:

  - you ask questions in logical order;
  - the wording used is clear and unambiguous and does not bias the respondent toward a particular answer;
  - the questions are answerable.

- Treat the questionnaire as a document in PR terms in the same way as a report. If it has a wide circulation, it may be the only basis respondents have to form a view of you, the project you are carrying out and the organisation you represent. So make sure it is well presented and does you justice.
- It is always worthwhile having a pilot trial of the questionnaire with a small sample of prospective respondents before giving it full circulation.

This will help you to spot any poor wording or design which needs improvement.

- Use the pilot trial to test not only the questionnaire but also the subsequent processing. If you are using a computer for processing the results, is the data on the questionnaire easily loaded in? How long does it take, and will this prove a bottleneck when all the questionnaires have to be processed?
- Even after all this testing, you may wish to include a contact telephone number to be called if a respondent has difficulty in completing the questionnaire.
- Do not forget about the administration of the questionnaires. You need to ensure that you have made adequate arrangements so that:

    - the questionnaires get to the right people;
    - they know what they have to do when they have received them;
    - they know how they are to be returned;
    - the questionnaires actually get back to you.

Plan to carry out checks to make sure the administration is proceeding smoothly. It is frustrating, having received no questionnaires back from a factory two hundred miles away, to find out that they failed to arrive there in the first place.

- Do not forget to include questions about the respondents (so-called 'demographic data') covering relevant facts about them and their work. You may, for example, wish to contrast different sites, or differentiate according to age, sex or some other distinguishing feature. (I am always amused by the apocryphal personnel department which provided information on 'employees broken down by age and sex'!) Consider also whether you want to identify individual respondents, or whether you will get a better response by preserving anonymity.
- Use scales and tick boxes to record varying responses. Figure 5.5 shows an example of this.
- Beware of creating skewed scales which bias answers: for example, the scale:
    Excellent
    Good
    Above average
    Average
    Below average
is biased towards favourable remarks.

Figure 5.5 *Example of a questionnaire*

Canteen	Very Good	Good	Average	Poor	Very Poor
31. How do you rate the quality of the food?					
32. Is the variety of dishes presented...					
33. How do you rate the service?					
34. What do you think of the decor?					
35. Overall, how do you rate the canteen?					

Final exhortations

There are three comments which I believe are of great significance in data collection and analysis and which merit the attention of all consultants.

(i) Data-collection is an intervention into an organisation. Treat it as such
Since the Hawthorne experiments over 50 years ago, it has been known that an observer will have an effect on people working. Consultancy involves interacting with an organisation, and collecting data is part of that interaction. The knowledge that a consultant is involved can make people curious or feel threatened, so imagine the repercussions within an organisation resulting from the following data-collection activities of a consultant:

- they ask publicly for a printout of staff numbers;
- they ask at an interview, 'Do you think you are paid enough?';
- they ask for comments on the consequences of shutting down plant X;
- they ask why profits from product Y are not greater.

Consultants are agents of change, and any request for data, however innocent, may imply that there is to be change in the matters to which the data relates. So, in collecting data, remember there are no limits to the conclusions to which imaginative and paranoiac minds can jump.

Data collection and analysis

Data collection is also the point at which the consultant is going to become more widely known in the organisation. How well it is done will influence the organisation's view of the consultant.

- In a project involving a team of consultants, one of them circulated a questionnaire amongst client staff which was poorly designed and very difficult to understand. The only replies the consultant got were protests about the questionnaire; none was returned completed, and the episode severely dented the consultant's credibility with the client.

(ii) Maintain a healthy scepticism

One of the reasons consultants are employed is because of their objectivity. One of the ways in which this is most useful is in challenging conventional wisdom, which straitjackets thinking and stifles innovation. Comments such as, 'We tried that five years ago and it didn't work' although true carry the unspoken corollary – 'and it won't work now'. The consultant must ask 'Why?'.

Conventional wisdom – 'well-known facts' and conventional thinking – needs to be verified. Consultants must satisfy themselves that the data they are working with is sufficiently reliable.

(iii) Use your stomach as well as your brain

Not a suggestion to increase the number of business lunches attended, but encouragement to make use of gut feel.

This means trusting your instincts – those impressions or conclusions which cannot be explained wholly rationally. The brain is a powerful organ which no one fully understands and it is immensely capable. In the course of work you absorb many impressions, many of them unconsciously. Similarly there are unconscious mental processes, the output of which is gut feel.

I have always regretted the occasions I have let reason overrule gut feeling; I have always been mistaken. So, notwithstanding the apparent reliance of consultancy on data and logic, trust your instincts. You can always rationalise your conclusions afterwards.

6   Report writing

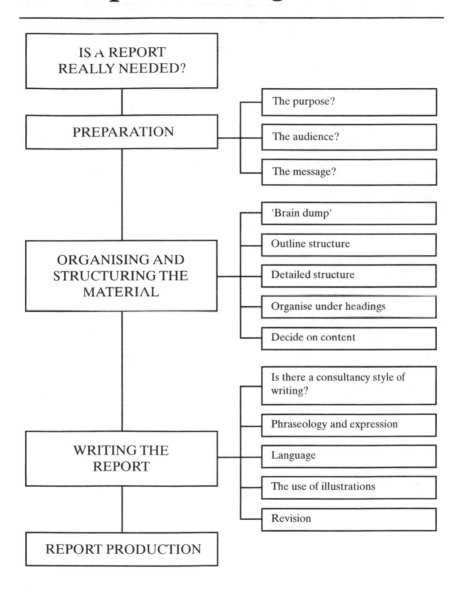

6 Report writing

What is written without effort is in general read without pleasure.

Samuel Johnson

I love being a writer. What I can't stand is the paperwork.

Peter de Vries

At a course for newly-appointed management consultants, participants were asked what they had found most difficult in making the transition to consultancy. Each gave several reasons, but the group was unanimous that report writing was a major difficulty. That is consistent with my experience in training and supervising new consultants, and writing high-quality reports can be difficult for all consultants.

Notwithstanding the increasing use of visual and electronic media, for the foreseeable future consultants will need to continue to produce written material as part of their work. The purpose of this chapter is to outline some practical guidelines for writing reports and for the production of written material generally.

Most of the difficulties occur not because of infelicities of expression or style but from lack of thought about what is to be conveyed and how. So, much of this chapter is about what to do before setting pen to paper. Initially, however, it is worth reviewing the various types of written documentation which a consultant produces. (If, on the other hand, you are sitting with a blank piece of paper in front of you and a report to write, go straight to p. 128 and start reading the section 'A work plan for writing reports'.)

Consultants' written material can be divided into:

- *Letters*: Some letters might better fit one of the categories below, but for those which do not, it is difficult to generalise. The style of a letter can be enormously varied and almost certainly will reflect the character of the sender, the nature of the relationship with the addressee and the subject matter of the letter.
- *Proposals* to undertake a particular contract or project. Sometimes these may be in the form of a relatively short letter confirming the key points of an oral agreement, but more often will be in report format.
- *Progress reports* reviewing the position of a project.
- *Position papers* intended to open or pursue a debate with the client on a particular topic.
- *Project reports* written at the conclusion of a project or the end of a phase of it, usually with recommendations for the future.

- *Manuals* relating to the operation of a system or a piece of equipment.

There are, of course, many other pieces of documentation a consultant may need to produce, such as training materials, questionnaires and other formats for data collection, as well as internal memoranda and the like if they work in a firm of consultants. These are not covered in this chapter, but the principles described can in some measure be applied to them. The remainder of this chapter is therefore concerned with:

- proposals;
- progress reports;
- position papers;
- assignment reports;

with the emphasis on the last category.

Report writing is a time-consuming activity, so the first thing you should do is ask yourself an important question.

Is a report really needed?

A client once complained: 'We did not want a report but the consultants appeared conditioned to produce a final tome'. Think carefully, then, whether a report is required to help the assignment along, or are you simply erecting a memorial for your own peace of mind? In some cases there is no discretion about whether a report is to be delivered, as when a client requires a written proposal, or the terms of reference for a project set out the timing of progress or other reports. Other circumstances in which a report should be considered are set out below.

(i) *There is something to report.* Even on projects where there is no requirement for a project report it is worthwhile considering presenting a concluding review of progress. For example, in one case a consultant who had worked with a team of managers helping them – in an environment of considerable change – to redefine their objectives and roles, concluded the project with a paper that summarised what work had been done and what had been achieved.

(ii) *Progress reports* are an excellent mechanism for maintaining good client relations. Some projects may have progress meetings or reports scheduled as an integral part of the project plan, but even if this is not the case, they are worth considering as they can be used to:

- reassure the client that the project is proceeding well, even if there is nothing otherwise to report;

- engineer a meeting with the sponsor (the individual who commissioned the project) if the consultant is usually working with the sponsor's subordinates;
- provide a record of assignment progress and a discipline for the operating consultant.

(iii) *Position papers* can provide a mechanism for thinking through a particular issue. The discipline of having to express a complex issue clearly to the client can help a project along.

- For example, in a major study lasting more than a year, a number of independent outside consultants were seconded full time to the team and there were also inputs from specialist subcontractors. The output of the study was to be a single report (which ultimately ran to more than 2,000 pages!). Coordinating the various inputs and maintaining the necessary pace throughout the project were thus of major importance.

  The project leader did this by getting the project team to submit a series of substantial position papers to the client, on subsidiary matters, throughout the course of the year. Not only was a series of milestones thereby created but also the means whereby the client could offer their own comments and contribution to the final product.

The difference between a position paper and a project report is a nice but useful one. A position paper is a means of pursuing work-in-progress and perhaps airing a subject for debate. For example, a position paper during a strategic project might discuss the pros and cons of diversification into a particular business sector. It could serve as a mechanism for verifying the issues critical to a decision on this matter as well as providing a means of eliciting the views and opinions of the key decision makers and influencers within the firm.

- You can, however, fall prey to providing too many position papers. On one particular assignment which was on a part-time basis over many months, the consultant found himself volunteering to produce position papers more and more frequently, as this was the most convenient way of dealing with the client. The consequence was that he spent an increasing amount of time working on and revising position papers and less time with the client. This was a vicious circle: the client saw less of him and his contact became weakened; his papers became less attuned to the politics of the organisation and thus needed more time on revision. Eventually, the client terminated the assignment. The moral is: writing is a means – not an end in itself.

(iv) The most common reports required of consultants, however, are *assignment reports*. These are produced at the end of an assignment, or perhaps at the end of a major stage of it. They are the documents which most new consultants (and often experienced ones) have greatest diffi- culty in writing. The emphasis on the assignment report is quite proper, however; often they are the only material manifestation of the work performed by the consultant and what the client has paid for. At the end of a project which has cost £50,000, the client needs to be presented with a document which does justice to that cost.

A note on draft reports

All written material presented to a client must be of satisfactory quality. There can be no compromise.

A pitfall for the new consultant is the so-called 'draft' report. A consultant might submit a substandard draft report to a client in the expectation that he will then subsequently have the chance to amend and upgrade it before issuing a final version. If, however, the client accepts the draft, the consul- tant will have delivered a product which is substandard. The use of the heading 'draft' on a report is to allow a client the opportunity to make an input – for example, by suggesting more persuasive ways of presenting recommendations. From the consultant's view it should be able to stand as a finished product.

A work plan for writing reports

There are four steps to writing a report (or, indeed, any written communi- cation).

(i) *Define the purpose*: what is the purpose of this report? To whom is it addressed? What are you seeking to convey?
(ii) *Organise* and structure the material.
(iii) *Write* the report.
(iv) *Produce* the report.

The sections below suggest a detailed work plan based on these steps, but before proceeding, you should consider how much time your report is going to take to write. A rule of thumb is that from start to finish you should allow one day for each 10 pages. This is obviously very approximate – some will be written far more quickly, whereas an inexperienced consultant may require much longer to produce a complex report to an acceptable standard.

The point is that reports do take a finite time to write which must be allo- cated whether it be in a project plan or in preparing a proposal. But what I have noticed is this – that the most common reason why consultants burn the midnight oil is because we have to prepare a report.

Purpose

Occasionally reports are to act as a source of reference only (e.g., the results of research, such as an opinion poll), but the majority of consultants' proposals and reports have a persuasive objective – to engage the consultant for a particular piece of work, or to accept particular recommendations as the result of a project.

This point is often overlooked by consultants – a report is meant to have some sort of effect within the client system. When considering the purpose, therefore, it is important to be clear about the nature of the effect the report is expected to make: how is the intervention of producing a report meant to advance the sales process (in the case of a proposal) or the progress of the project in which the consultants are engaged?

The report will be only part of a number of interventions in pursuit of these objectives. Indeed, in many instances, the report may be only a record of what has already been presented, discussed and agreed with the client.

In all cases, however, you must be clear about the purpose of this report: why is it being written? What are the objectives it is intended to achieve and do they merit the investments of time and cost required? Remember that a report is a form of communication and what you are seeking to convey might be better done using a different medium.

If there is a tomb to the unknown consultant, its headstone will be the contents page of a lovingly prepared and totally unread report.
At the start, therefore, it is worth reflecting on the purpose of the report. It is also worth bearing in mind that there are a host of other messages conveyed by a report – for example:

- Its appearance; does it look worthwhile?
- Its timeliness: (for example, if a proposal is delivered late, will this be a characteristic of assignment operation)?
- The quality of the content: is it well presented and argued? Does it strike the right level and balance? Does it bring out the key issues? Does it add value to the client's views or merely reflect them?

These are features of all reports and help the client to form an impression of the quality of the consultant. Similarly, the astute consultant will manage these aspects carefully to give a favourable impression, particularly with proposals, when clients may have relatively little other evidence on which to form a judgement.

It is helpful to have a picture of the reader(s) of the report in mind when you are writing it. Hopefully, you will have met at least one of the intended recipients of the report; a useful technique is to write the report with the recipient in mind as the reader. This has several advantages, in that it enables you:

- to take account of what the client knows or does not know already;
- to couch the report in language which is familiar to the client;
- to set the right level of treatment;
- to allow for particular sensibilities.

Organising and structuring the material

There are positive advantages in thinking through the structure and contents of an assignment report well before the end of an assignment. This is particularly helpful in identifying gaps in the information required and providing a focus for the work as an assignment progresses. We will assume, however, that you are starting from scratch (you are preparing a proposal, for example). What follows is a personal approach to writing a report; it works for me and I hope, perhaps with some adaptation, it may work for you.

Step 1: 'brain dump'

Firstly, I make a lot of notes of my thoughts on what might go into the report. These thoughts are based not only on reflection but are also stimulated by reviewing relevant material, which might be earlier project reports (on this or other similar earlier projects), the proposal (in the case of an assignment or progress report), progress reports, working papers and so on. The brain dump is not in any particular order – it is a series of notes without structure, of varying levels of detail and so on.

Step 2: look for the outline structure

Having made these few pages (not too many) of notes, the next step is to look for an outline structure. Figure 6.1 shows the typical structure of some different types of report. These, of course, are very general and the structure of every report has to suit the material being presented, but above all, the structure of the report must be *logical* and help the reader absorb what is being put across. A good structure will also make it easier for you to write the report. A report is a bit like a story and it is sometimes helpful to think of it as such. To this end there are some golden rules:

- Start off with what the readers know before moving on to what they do not know.
- The report should lead the reader naturally to its conclusions or recommendations. You should imagine the reader nodding their head in agreement as the argument unfolds. It is a good idea to frame the recommendations first and then structure the rest of the report to lead naturally to those recommendations.

Figure 6.1 *Typical contents of different types of report*

Proposal (*see also* Chapter **2**)

- Introduction
- Appreciation of present situation
- Scope and objectives of the project
- Method of approach
- Programme of work required
- Prospective benefits arising from the project
- Resources required (from the client as well as the consultant)
- Expected timescale and costs
- Reasons for using us as your consultants in this project (including previous relevant experience).

Terms of business might be included as an appendix.

Progress report

- Progress (against forecast programme of work)
- Significant achievements and problems
- Points on which you wish to consult the client (e.g., issues for approval or decision)
- Plans for the future.

Assignment report (*see also* Figure 6.2)

- Summary
- Introduction
- Findings
- Discussion of and commentary on the findings
- Recommendations
- Appendices.

- Put similar material together. Bearing in mind the content of most consultancy projects, reports are often about complex subjects. You can complicate understanding still further by confusing recommendations with findings and scattering them liberally throughout the report. Two tips to help the reader, then:

- Include in the introduction a few words about the structure and contents of the report.
- A summary of the report at the front (i.e., a synopsis of the principal points, trends in the argument, main conclusions and recommendations) can provide the reader with a bird's eye view of the report. I think of the summary as a map with which the reader can find his way through the report.

In reviewing your notes consider whether the material fits any of the structures suggested in Figure 6.1 or whether an alternative structure might present the material better. Figure 6.2 shows some different ways of structuring an assignment report. In all cases, however, there should be a logic underlying the structure.

Figure 6.2 *Two alternative assignment report structures*	
Basis of division	*Contents*
By business structure (e.g., factory site, business division, or functional area) or topic	Introduction Topic 1: Findings, conclusions, recommendations Topic 2: Findings, conclusions, recommendations Topic 3: Findings, conclusions, recommendations Summary of key recommendations

By recommendation	Summary of recommendations
	Recommendation 1:
	  rationale leading to this
	Recommendation 2:
	  rationale leading to this
	Recommendation 3:
	  rationale leading to this
	Summary of key steps required for implementation

Step 3: prepare a more detailed structure

Sometimes an outline structure is sufficient – I found it so for this chapter – but in dealing with a report you need to break the material down into convenient chunks. If the report is a big one, you will need to have subsections as well. Some ideas about the subsections will undoubtedly arise in preparing the outline sections; alternatively, the nature of the project may determine the structure. Figure 6.3 below shows the contents of a report on management training and development in a multi-divisional company: each of the major sections is concerned with a separate business division, but is structured in broadly the same way as the others.

Figure 6.3 *Contents*

Executive Summary

1. Introduction
   1.1 Background
   1.2 Methodology.

2. Overview of the group

3. Division one
   3.1 Nature of the business
   3.2 Development and training focus
   3.3 Selection of recruits
   3.4 Reduction of staff turnover
   3.5 Sales training
   3.6 Selection of managers
   3.7 Manager training.

4. Division two
   4.1 Nature of the business
   4.2 Development and training focus
   4.3 Professional staff utilisation
   4.4 Commercial staff performance
   4.5 Training management staff.

5. Division three
   5.1 Nature of the business
   5.2 Development and training focus
   5.3 Making the new organisation effective
   5.4 Management development system.

6. Summary of recommendations

Other ways in which a project might determine the structure of a report are:

- Operational procedures: Dick's report on stock control (using the example in earlier chapters) might follow production processes by dealing with raw materials, work-in-progress and finished goods separately.
- Project plans: for example a proposal for advice on the choice and installation of a new PABX might cover:

  - determining user requirements;
  - defining selection criteria;
  - review of suitable systems and method of choice;
  - installation;
  - commissioning.

- Conceptual framework: a report on profit sharing bonus could include sections on the key elements of how bonus is calculated, the operation of the scheme and how bonus should be distributed.

If all else has failed, think about your recommendations—how are they structured? This structure can be replicated earlier in the report. (And do *not* fall into the trap of starting to write the report before you have decided what your principal recommendations are! You may hope that by the time you get to that section, they will emerge. But the preceding part of the report will be a mystery tour for the reader and simply demonstrate the confusion of your own thought processes). So, if your report on a post-merger organisation concludes with recommendations for each function (marketing, production, etc.), then earlier parts of the report on findings and conclusions might be divided up into sections dealing with each function.

Step 4: organise your material

So you now have your notes and a detailed structure. The next step is to organise your material under the headings you have chosen.

With a large report, I allocate a half page to each subsection and rewrite the key points from my notes under each heading. With a shorter document I use the initial 'brain dump' and put a section number against each note so that I can pick up the relevant comments when I get to the appropriate section.

Of course, modern word-processing packages can render this stage quite easy if they have an 'outliner' facility, which enables you to do this on screen.

But whether you use pen and paper, or computer, this step is essential in writing a report for two reasons. The first is, that it enables you to test out the structure. If you find it difficult to allocate material to different subsections, it may mean the structure is not quite right. This is the time for fine tuning.

The second reason is if anything, more important: you are taking decisions on the content of the report – what it is to convey.

At this point, pause:

- Have you really thought through the contents of your report?

The problems of report writing stem primarily from lack of clarity of thought. So, for an assignment report, for example:

- Will the report satisfactorily meet the terms of reference? (You should refer back to the original proposal.)
- Are you identifying and addressing the really important relevant issues (which may only partially be covered by the terms of reference)?
- Are your recommendations sound? Do they follow from your assessment of the situation? Do they make sense (ask a colleague) and are the priorities balanced correctly? Are they feasible – what is sound for one enterprise may be impossible in another?

Do not gloss over these points of self-examination; a little time invested here can save time later. (Too often however, this point is usually acknowledged only after bitter experience, having failed to do it.)

Step 5: decide what is to go into the report

The last stage is about deciding what is to go into the report – and what is not. Sometimes there is some confusion between a report and a record; a former colleague of mine had not made the distinction and as a result his reports were diffuse and full of extraneous details. They became a lot better once he used the report as a means of conveying selected information rather than a total record.

What must *not* be put in the report is material which should not be committed to paper. This in particular covers criticisms of individuals; remember that unless special precautions are taken, people other than the intended recipients will have access to your report in the client organisation. So do not needlessly commit confidential information to paper.

It is also important that there is a homogeneous level of detail in the report; it would be inconsistent in a report on corporate strategy to deal with details of canteen menus (and vice versa). Similarly, the nature of the reader for whom you are writing should be consistent throughout in terms of assumed knowledge and the level of treatment of the subject.

The appendix is a useful way of dealing with details. In deciding whether material should be in the body of a report or in an appendix, consider, does the reader need to study these facts now, or can he take them on trust for the time being? If they can be left, then they are material for an appendix. For example, statistical tables may be summarised in the text to support the main conclusions with the full data reproduced in appendices. On the other hand, do not condemn all information to the appendices; it is very irritating to have to turn continually from the body of a report to refer to a table in an appendix.

By the end of this step you should have completed the preparation for your report. You should have decided on its major divisions and sub-divisions and the main points you will make in each.

It may seem that the preparation outlined above is laborious; so it may be, but it is not unduly time-consuming and can save a lot of time later. It can be completed in an hour or so for short reports and even for major reports I have found it takes rarely more than a day. It is brief compared with actually writing a report, because writing entails not only considering *what* to say but also *how* to say it. Deciding how to express a particular point well can be time-consuming and is time wasted if the point does not merit inclusion in the report.

Inexperienced consultants (and experienced ones too) may find the completion of the preparation stage a good point at which to discuss the structure and content of their report with a colleague.

After this comes the time-consuming part – writing the report.

Writing the report

By the end of the preparation stage – organising and structuring the material – you should have decided what it is you want to put across and in what order you are going to do it. Now, this is not a book about style or grammar (there are plenty of books about those) but there are some important points for consultants to consider in expressing themselves on paper.

Is there a consultancy style of writing?

Inexperienced consultants sometimes think there is a peculiar style of expression which they should use when writing as a consultant. I have come across reports constructed to include a particular turn of phrase because the writer considers it compelling. The rule is, however, write to express, not to impress.

If there is a consultancy style of writing, it is a style of great clarity. The task of a consultant in communicating with clients is to clarify rather than to obscure.

As with all communication, writing has to be attuned to the receiver; this does not mean that it must be written in the same way that the client would write it, but it must be comprehensible if it is to serve any purpose.

By way of example, Figure 6.4 illustrates alterative section headings for the same report, geared to different audiences. The first is perhaps more suited to a staid, traditional organisation; the second style might appeal to more radical clients.

Figure 6.4 *Alternative titles*

A study of the feasibility of introducing a performance appraisal system	*Performance appraisal: a management priority*
1 Introduction	1 A history of impoverished performance management
2 Findings of this study	2 Views of the executives
2.1 The need for performance appraisal	2.1 We need to manage our people better
2.2 The acceptability of a formal appraisal system	2.2 We don't like appraisal but we ought to do it
2.3 The design of the system	2.3 Use appraisal for taking salary and development decisions
3 Recommendations	3 The way ahead
3.1 Design of a new system	3.1 Introduce a new appraisal system
3.2 Implementation plan	3.2 Do it now

Phraseology and expression

These ought to be controlled to reinforce the message. It does not always do to call a spade a spade. I have even come across a client who, in effect, said 'We recognise our performance in this area as appalling; we don't need you to tell us this and we do not wish to see a report cataloguing our failures. We are confident in your judgement and want only your recommendations'.

I have always tried to use a delicacy of phrasing when referring to a client's deficiencies – part of the skills of regarding a half-empty bottle as being half-full. (Although a cynic has commented that a consultant would never say this, but conclude that the bottle was twice as large as it should be.) So, instead of weaknesses, one refers to 'areas where there is scope for improvement'. Weasel words, perhaps, but ones which convey the same meaning without loss of face to the client.

On the other hand, there are a few clients who take an almost masochistic pleasure in being told how awful they are.

Language

Language – the words that you use in writing – must be used well. Short words are preferable to long, if they are equivalent, but use the language which comes most easily to you. It is probably easier to get the points down on paper first, in a way which you find comfortable, and subsequently check that the language is clear and simple, rather than strain for a different writing style. Practice should aid improvement.

Figure 6.5 shows the well-known formula to determine the so-called 'fog factor' in writing. What this shows is that the more words used on average per sentence and the longer the words used, the more difficult it is to comprehend what has been written.

Figure 6.5   *Fog factor*

An empirical formula used to assess the complexity of writing measures the so-called 'fog factor' of a piece of writing:

$$0.4 \times (W + X) = Y$$

where:

W = average number of words of three or more syllables in a sentence.
X = average number of words in a sentence.
Y = number of years of full-time education required to comprehend the writing.

Every business, industry, or profession has its own language to describe specialist aspects of it; this *jargon* (and I am using the word in this particular sense) is helpful to those in the know but can be unintelligible to the outsider. (Some examples are given in Figure 6.6.) It would be laborious to have to express everything in layman's terms – just imagine how difficult hospital doctors would find discussion without using the specialist terms they are taught. I therefore do not believe that the use of jargon is a bad thing.

Figure 6.6   *Examples of jargon*

Business/specialism	Special terms
Printing	Flong
Haematology	ESR phagocyte
Banking	Zero coupon instrument
Accounting	SSAP
Pharmaceuticals	Elixir
Electronics	Gate array

Indeed, for consultants one of the signs of proficiency in a business sector is that they learn its jargon, and can therefore use it with their clients. The use of jargon is wrong when it does not apply to the client's business and particularly when it is used as a smokescreen to try to impress. Fortunately, most clients have the sense to cry 'Foul!' in the latter case and the consultant hopefully learns the lesson.

Finally, on the subject of language, is the use of verbs in the active or passive voice; the difference is illustrated below:

- Active: 'We carried out a survey';
- Passive: 'A survey was carried out'.

Those with a scientific schooling will have been strongly influenced to use the passive voice ('a test tube was taken ...') in reporting their experiments, but the constant use of the passive voice makes for dull reading. Figure 6.7 illustrates the same passage written wholly in the passive and active voices.

Normally, this is dealt with by using 'we', even when a single individual only was involved with the work. The danger then is too many 'we's – we this, we that, etc. So a balance between active and passive voices is desirable. A feature of the passive voice is that it is impersonal – 'a survey was carried out' – we need not say by whom. Conversely, the active voice is not impersonal – we need to say who carried out a survey.

Figure 6. 7 *Active and passive voices*

Passive: 'At the start a survey was carried out. Respondents were asked to complete a questionnaire. Key features of the product were listed in the questionnaire and had to be placed in order of attractiveness by respondents. Design and colour were considered most important.'

Active: 'At the start we carried out a survey and asked respondents to complete a questionnaire. We asked them to place key features of the product, listed in the questionnaire, in order of attractiveness. Respondents considered design and colour most important.'

The use of illustrations

Although a cliché, a picture *can* tell a thousand words. So it is worthwhile thinking how you can illustrate the points you are making in a report. There are a host of ways of doing this, but remember that illustrations are meant to help rather than hinder understanding. The most frequent cause of the latter is presenting too much information or irrelevant data. The key question is, 'Does this illustrate the point I am making, simply and clearly?'

Illustrations are often used to make qualitative points – to show trends, relative sizes or relationships – and thus great precision is not required. A *bête noire* of mine is the use of numbers to six significant figures – rarely needed – and even more heinous is to derive those figures from ones which are not as accurate themselves. (For example the average of 55, 57 and 58 is better presented as $56\frac{1}{2}$ or 56.7–56.6667 implies accuracy to the fourth decimal place, which may not be true at all.)

Revision

When you have written the report, read it through. This is not just to check grammar and spelling; it is also sensible, metaphorically, to step back to examine your handiwork. Provided the preparation has been done well the contents should be all right, but revision should include cutting verbiage, and simplifying wording. Above all, ensure that you have expressed simply and clearly what you are trying to convey in your report.

Report production

As part of a consultant induction training course, I used to run a business appraisal case study, which required consultants to prepare a project plan for a hypothetical assignment. Without fail, they always forgot to include the time for producing the final assignment report in their plans.

It is as well to remember that there are several stages between completing the *magnum opus* and its delivery to the client:

- typing;
- proofreading and correction;
- quality assurance;
- amendments and approval;
- preparation of final typescript;
- printing;
- binding.

So the first important lesson about report production is that it needs *time*, and sufficient time should be allowed for it.

The list above also shows quality assurance and it is vital it happens – at the very least on the physical production of the report. So it is worthwhile asking a colleague to read through the report for typing errors and for comprehension. A consultant close to a particular problem can easily fall into the trap of believing that others will see things as they do. The consequence could be passages in a report which are at best ambiguous or at worst incomprehensible or libellous. A colleague who has some understanding of what you are writing about should be able to point these out. (If you are a sole practitioner it is still worth getting someone – your secretary, spouse or a professional colleague – to help out if at all feasible. As an alternative, you might get a friendly member of the client's staff to look through it.)

In large firms, quality assurance may go beyond this, covering the structure, content and writing in the report as well as its presentation. If this is the case, it is sensible to start the quality assurance process before setting pen to paper – get agreement to the structure and content of the report in principle before writing it. Alterations at an early stage are far easier to accommodate and less time-consuming than are attempts to recast the 'finished' product.

Finally, there is the question of presentation of the report itself. Quite a lot of expense may be justified in the case of an assignment report which may be the only tangible evidence of the work the consultant has done.

Large firms may have a house style – a typeface, paragraph numbering, report covers and so on which are standard. Small firms or sole practitioners may have a *de facto* house style. In any case, I would suggest the following priorities for production of an assignment report:

1 The content of the report. Irrespective of how glossy the report is, if the content is obviously poor, then you have failed.
2 The editing of the report: it should be laid out well and free from typographical errors.
3 It should not be delivered late. The delivery of a report is a very clear manifestation of the performance of a consultant, and late delivery counts against you.
4 Packaging and presentation: a good typeface, and high-quality paper (not an obvious photocopy), robustly bound and with an attractive cover can help a lot.

A concluding note on report writing

Report writing is a skill and, like most skills, improves only with practice. It is unrealistic, therefore, to imagine that on concluding this chapter you will write reports which are a vast improvement on what you have achieved in the past. There are a lot of pitfalls in writing, however, and avoiding those I have highlighted should create some improvements.

The other major means of improvement will come about by adopting a careful work plan in producing a report. This chapter has suggested one and it is summarised at the front.

7 Making presentations

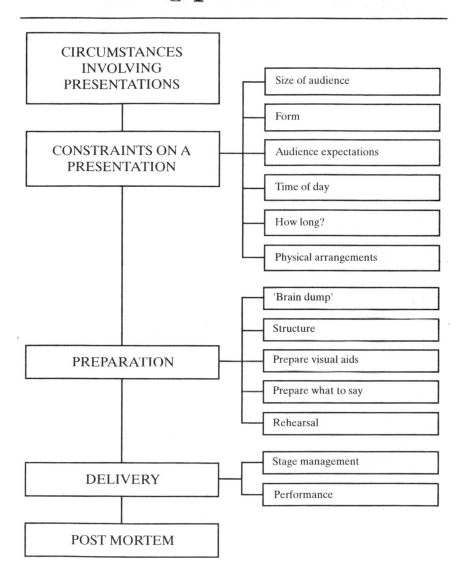

7   Making presentations

Sometimes when a speaker has his audience on the edge of their seats, they're trying to muster the nerve to get up and go home.

Anon

- One of the most brilliant presentations I have ever seen was during a training course for consultants. Each had to make a five-minute presentation on the subject of his choice. Gerald's was on the economic cycles following decolonization in Africa – an impossibly large subject to tackle in the time. He illustrated his talk with sheets of scrappy flip-chart paper spread round the room; his delivery was a sustained gabble; his language was from a political stance slightly right of the *Daily Telegraph*. Despite these apparent offences against the 'rules' of presentation, his was a *tour de force* which I remember years after the event.

Why does this presentation stick in my mind? Despite breaking the rules of presentation it had style; it was informative and humorous. It kept our interest and was memorable, and this style was appropriate for the occasion – a training course, when many of the other presentations were simply worthy. So, despite the apparent breaking of the rules, it achieved the main objectives of a presentation.

Of all the topics in this book, making presentations – public speaking – is therefore the one about which it is least advisable to be doctrinaire. Part of the art is entertainment and stage management: the aim is to attract and retain the interest of an audience for a period of time and leave it with a favourable impression. As with entertainment, there is scope for considerable variation in making presentations, and it is a mistake to force people into the wrong style of presentations. I remember one individual whom I persuaded to use very conservative slides for a presentation. The next time I saw him present he used his own highly-stylised slides: not only were the slides better but they also improved his presentation and it was far more memorable.

So, regard this chapter as a primer only. It will not teach you to make brilliant presentations, but it should provide a guide to making satisfactory ones and help you to avoid the more dangerous pitfalls. With growing confidence and experience you will be able to decide which techniques are most helpful – and which to disregard – in your own presentations.

In our private lives we may be called on to make speeches – after dinner, at weddings and other family occasions or in some capacity in a society or in public office. Practice and experience of these stand the consultant presenter in good stead, but there are special occasions peculiar to his profession. One has already been mentioned – the training course. Some of the other frequent circumstances are set out in Figure 7.1 opposite.

Chapter **8** deals with designing and presenting a training session. The reason for segregating training as a special form of presentation is because the trainer usually has far more freedom in determining structure, timing and so on than in other types of presentation, and can control these to his advantage.

The importance of presentations to management consultants is that their business success can depend on how well they are done. The most significant occasions when a consultant needs to make a presentation in this context are:

- a sales presentation at the beginning;
- a concluding project presentation.

In both cases, the object is that the client will accept the consultant's recommendations: to proceed with the project using the consultant's support (in the sales presentation) or to proceed with the next stage of work (in a concluding presentation).

Presentations may also be needed during the course of a project for disseminating information, reporting progress, and so on. The content of all of these may be the oral presentation of cases that in other circumstances may be covered on paper (see Chapter **6** on Report writing and Chapter **9** on Rational persuasion), but in all cases, the client will be influenced not only by the validity of the consultant's arguments, but also by the quality of the presentation. It is essential therefore that a consultant learns the mechanics of making good presentations at an early stage.

Constraints on a presentation

There is rarely complete freedom in making presentations, however; as shown in Figure 7.2 on p.148, the typical consultant's presentation can be hedged around with many constraints over which he has little or no control.

Before beginning to prepare your presentation, it is therefore worth-while thinking about the constraints and how you can work effectively within them.

Figure 7.1 *Circumstances involving presentations*

Content	Audience	Comment
	Client	
Proposal for a project	Decision influencer Decision maker	The decision influencer may select for a shortlist; the decision maker takes the final decision
Programme of work	Client staff	Next step after proposal accepted
	Trade union or other rep- resentatives sentatives	May need to be informed about project
Progress review	Client	
Recommen- dations	Client	Presentation equivalent of an assignment report
	Public	
Conference		Very wide range of possible circumstances
Training course		
	Internal	
Project review	Colleagues	Do not underestimate the importance of these events
Operating technique	Colleagues	

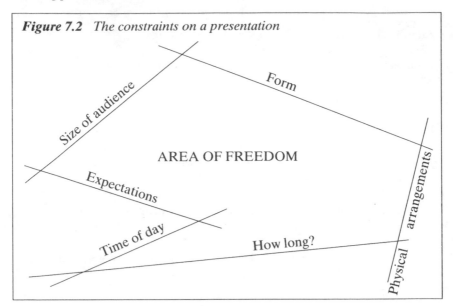

Figure 7.2 *The constraints on a presentation*

Size of audience
Form
AREA OF FREEDOM
Expectations
Physical arrangements
Time of day
How long?

Size of the audience and interaction with it

Large audiences make for more formal occasions. The conference presentation to 250 delegates has to be different from the boardroom presentation to three directors. The size of the audience determines the nature and extent of the interaction you can have with each individual – for example, on the simple matter of eye contact. It is a good thing to establish eye contact with individuals in the audience, but with an audience of 250, all you can do is let your eyes range over them.

The larger the audience too, the more inhibited most people will feel about asking questions or making points from the floor (leaving aside hecklers at political meetings!). Although you have greater control as a presenter, the amount of two-way communication will be very limited. The size of the audience will therefore condition the form of the presentation.

Form

By the 'form' of the presentation I mean the proportion of time you are expected to speak continuously without interruption and the degree of control you have over the content. Figure 7.3 illustrates a spectrum of occasions – both social and working – which have different forms.

The spectrum runs from presenter-orientated to audience-orientated. In the former, the onus is on the presenter to keep things going; in the latter, they

---

Figure 7.3   *Form*

↑ PRESENTER ORIENTATED

Lecture
After-dinner speech

Formal presentation
Informal presentation

Discussion session on training course
Everyday conversation
Questions after a presentation

'Any questions'/panel session
interview

↓ AUDIENCE-ORIENTATED

---

are much more at the dictate of the audience, perhaps under a chairman, as exemplified by a panel session in which he must respond to the audience's questions.

Working at either extremes of the scale of form is difficult; a lecture may require careful and extensive preparation for fluency, but equally, responding to questions needs the ability to put your thoughts in order very rapidly and to be able immediately to express them well.

The middle of the scale is easiest – everyday conversation in which we all engage – so if you have any control over form then it is worth pushing the form of the presentation towards the centre of the scale where it is easiest to operate. Many presenters do this instinctively; for example, the management trainer may choose to have a participative discussion session on – say – 'skills of recruitment interviewing' rather than deliver a lecture. (There are other reasons, of course, for encouraging participation – see Chapter **8**.)

Audience expectations

Consultants' presentations are almost all subject to the expectations of the intended audience – often a client. Expectations may be partly logistical – e.g., what time the presentation will start, how long it will last, the supporting documentation – and partly to do with the presentation itself – its purpose, content, form and so on.

Of course, some presenters engage their audiences' attention by deliberately *not* meeting their expectations. It is probably unwise to contravene logistical expectations (no point arriving on the wrong day or speaking for three hours when only half an hour was required), but you perhaps have rather more latitude as far as the content and delivery of the presentation are concerned. Even so, consultants have less freedom than others. (Some time ago I heard a certain member of the House of Lords speak after dinner and he gave an amusing account of life in the Upper House. Six months later I heard him again, when he was billed to discuss the attitude of central government to a particular aspect of business. He gave the same speech as before and it was equally well received.)

Time of day

It is curious that after lunch or dinner are regarded as appropriate times for speechmaking, but are avoided by formal presenters. Maybe that is because the average presenter, assisted by audiovisual gadgetry, is not half as interesting as a good after-dinner speaker.

Sometimes scheduling a presentation at an unusual time may cause interest. Breakfast meetings are not unknown, but the only time I have been invited to make a presentation at midnight was to a team of nightshift workers.

If you want to limit the amount of time spent on discussion (in circumstances when discussion might expand to fill the time available) you could schedule the presentation the necessary time before lunch or finishing work for the day.

A frequent question is, if involved in presenting a proposal for new work in competition with other firms, is there any advantage in presenting first or last? The advice of an experienced (and successful) consultancy salesperson to me was 'Don't be first. Aim for last, but avoid the end of the day'. Other factors, however, such as the quality of the proposal and its presentation and the rapport struck between consultant and prospective client will probably influence the outcome far more than the timing of the presentation.

How long should you speak for?

Ideally you should be able to have the time you require to make a presentation, but often you will have to present within a given timetable. For example, if competitive presentations of bids for a particular project are scheduled at 90-minute intervals you will need to work within this limit. If no timescale is given, it is worth a telephone call in advance to find out what is expected. If presenting to a board of directors, say, it is likely that your sponsor's secretary will know the amount of time to be put aside for the presentation. If no time limit has been proposed, you will have to work to your own timetable. My experience is that presentations of proposals for prospective work usually last between one and two hours; progress reviews can vary considerably, as can the presentation of recommendations at the end of an assignment. In these latter cases, the length of the presentation has to be determined by the material you are trying to put across.

Remember that the structure of a presentation should allow time for questions and discussions as well as your delivery. Remember, too, that the audience will lose interest if a speaker goes on a long time without interruption.

Some clients take a while to get organised. It is not unusual to go to a client's office and have to wait 15 minutes whilst the audience is rounded up. This does have its advantages – it gives you a chance to familiarise yourself with and relax in the surroundings where you are to make the presentation and to get your notes, visual aids, etc., organised. You can also be introduced to the audience as they arrive. So, though tardiness on the part of the audience can be irritating, it can have its advantages over walking into a strange room, facing a sea of expectant and unknown faces, and having to jump straight into a presentation.

Physical arrangements

You will rarely find yourself presenting in the ideal setting. When speaking at a conference, with luck you will have good facilities, but when presenting on a client's premises the chances are that you will present in an office or meeting room. You will have to make the best of it. There may be little flexibility in arranging where people sit and the scope for visual aids will probably be limited.

Every consultant has their own particular horror stories about disasters with visual aids; almost everybody has suffered because an overhead projector bulb blew and there was no spare. One of mine was the occasion we were bidding for a particular project and had some 35mm slides prepared at short notice (and great expense) to illustrate our presentation. We were assured that a 35mm projector would be available at the hotel where the presentation was to be made. To be on the safe side, however, we decided to take a projector of our own too. As we went to the taxi, laden down with briefcases, slides and projector, we took a last-minute decision not to take our projector. Needless to say, the one promised was not available and our presentation therefore suffered. So with media, remember Murphy's law – if anything can go wrong, it will.

Preparation

As with other forms of communication, preparation is a large determinant of success. A good presentation is like an iceberg – the bit you see is supported by a vast amount of preparation you do not see. So do not stint on preparation. Almost certainly you will need to spend more time on preparation than the duration of the presentation; some consultants use a rule of thumb which allows an average preparation time three times the length of presentation. If the material is in readily presentable form (the contents of a report which has already been written, say) or the content is very familiar, then the time required will be less. On the other hand, the rule breaks down, in my experience, for short presentations; a first-class 10 minute presentation may take several hours to prepare!

Many of the comments about the structure and content of reports (see Chapter **6**) apply to making presentations. The main difference lies in the capacity of the audience to absorb what is being presented. Harold Macmillan was disappointed with the reception his maiden speech received in the House of Commons when, as he commented to a fellow member, he had included 14 good points in it. He was told that any good parliamentary speech would have only one point in it, if it was to have any impact.

It is difficult to follow this dictum as consultants, but the principle remains that it is generally more difficult for an audience to absorb orally presented information than written; similarly, most people retain what they see rather better than what they hear. So why bother to make presentations at all?

Firstly, the personal contact enables two-way communication to take place; you cannot ask questions of a book.

Next, it allows you to invest the content with light and shade – you can emphasise important points in a way which is not possible in the written format.

Finally, it allows you to bring the force of personality to the persuasion process – charisma if you like.

- I would never have accepted the last point until an occasion when I lost my voice. I was running a series of one-week long courses for a particular client's managers, Monday to Friday. Arriving at my hotel one Sunday evening I found the cold I had had eventually caused me to lose my voice completely. I telephoned the colleagues who were sharing some of the sessions with me and told them (in a soft croak) of my difficulties.

  They were not able to reschedule their sessions to the beginning of the week, so there I was, at 8.30 am on the Monday morning with a new group of managers, about to start the course. Fortunately, the lecture room was equipped with a microphone through which I was huskily able to outline and start the management course. But I felt divested of power; it was not until then that I realised how much I depended on the use of my voice to project personality and hence to compel attention, to start to unfreeze course participants, to establish the right relationship between me and the managers, and the 101 other things that one has to do on a course, other than simply presenting the material, to make it work effectively. I got my voice back later in the week, but the course had one of the poorer ratings at the end of it.

As mentioned above, the preparation of a presentation is similar to that of a report. In preparing a presentation from scratch, the following steps can be followed:

(i)   Brain dump.
(ii) Structure the presentation.
(iii) Prepare the visual aids.
(iv) Preparing what to say.
(v)   Rehearsal.

Brain dump

The brain dump for a presentation is much the same as that for a report (see p. 130) – it consists of notes, jottings and so on. This can be created by reviewing material around the topic, notes from previous talks made on similar topics and so on. From this series of notes will come a number of themes – in the same way as preparing a report – and you may want to group the material relating to each theme together. From this, by putting it in an appropriate order you will work towards a structure for your presentation.

Structuring the presentation

A good structure is vital for a good presentation. Bearing in mind the difficulties of oral as opposed to visual communication, good structure is even more important to a presentation than it is to a report. It is like telling a story, and the reason structure is so important is that, unlike a report, in which a reader can flick back to check a point or re-read something they have found difficult to understand the first time, a presentation is in 'real time'. Once you lose the comprehension of your audience you will have lost their interest. So it is important to start off from what they know or can reasonably be expected to know – and develop from there.

An old adage is, 'Tell them what you're going to say, say it, and then tell them what you've said'. There is some merit in this advice if used carefully; presentations should seem natural rather than overly prepared and an undue emphasis on technical structure detracts from professionalism.

Making presentations

- A former colleague of mine suffered from this; his presentations were faultless – and boring. They were carefully structured and meticulously prepared – but they were tedious. What had happened was that he had effectively removed any imprint of his own personality from the presentations, so they were lifeless. On the other hand, there are entertainers who can make a recitation of the London telephone directory exciting.

Notwithstanding these reservations the adage does remind us that presentations have a beginning, middle and an end. For the time being I will concentrate on these and then come back to opening and closing presentations.

The beginning

At the start of a presentation it is worth making some allusion to what is to come. I often do this by using a slide of the structure of the presentation – for example the topics to be covered. Figure 7.4 illustrates such a slide for the contents of this chapter, but an alternative might take the form of an agenda or programme, involving different speakers, as shown in Figure 7.5.

Figure 7.4   *Contents of this chapter*

Situations requiring presentations
The constraints on a presentation
Preparing for a presentation
Delivering the presentation

Figure 7.5   *Example of presentation content**

Results of the market research programme	John
Marketing strategy proposed	Bill
Production plans	Maria
Financial forecasts	Bill
Proposals for next phase	John

* We are often encouraged to be more informative in our titles, and alternatives might be:

- Why product X represents the best choice
- Plan to raise product X sales to £_____ pa by 19__
- Putting X into production
- What it all costs
- Next steps to implementation.

It is sometimes helpful for the listener if you recap where you have got to in the presentation between major topics. Thus, taking the example in Figure 7.5, John might finish his initial presentation by showing the slide again to introduce the next speaker, Bill, and the topic he will cover.

Another major function of the beginning is similar to the introduction at the start of a report – the aim is to bring everybody to the same starting point. How you do this depends on the audience and purpose of the presentation. If, for example, you are reporting progress to a client whom you see routinely, the nature of the introduction will be different from a sales presentation to a group of strangers.

Finally, your introduction should make clear the ground rules for the audience. Are you expecting them to participate, interrupt, ask questions, keep silent until permitted to speak, or what? You can deal with this by explaining how you wish to handle questions.

The choices are:

- as you go along;
- at the end of each section;
- at the end of the presentation.

Which you pick depends on the circumstances. For example, if there is the risk that questions simply anticipate material to come, then it might be sensible to defer them. Allowing questions as you go through helps comprehension better, but has the risk of disruption; it can play havoc with time management as it can be very difficult to keep questions and answers within the time allowed.

Much also happens in terms of group dynamics at the start of a presentation, and this is covered under 'Opening and closing', below.

The middle
The middle of the presentation is its core. Structure here applies both to selecting the content and to the order in which it is delivered.

Communication is for a purpose and it helps to have some definite ends in view in selecting the material to be delivered. For example, at a sales presentation, an objective might be to convince the prospective client you have sufficient experience to undertake a particular project. You then have to select from the material in the brain dump to give the key points to support this objective.

The best way of structuring the delivery of presentation is as a story.

155

Making presentations

A novelist does not introduce significant characters without at some stage explaining (or at least enabling the reader to infer) who they are and their relevance. The writer of 'whodunnits' would get short shrift from readers if, on the last page, the culprit was an individual unmentioned before. The same principle applies to a presentation: the audience must understand not only what you are saying, but also why you are saying it and what they are to make of it.

A good structure is half the battle in doing this, but beware: the same structure may not work for a presentation as for a report. For example, it may be better to announce a recommendation at the start of a presentation than wait until the end. An introduction to a location study which starts, 'Following our study, we recommend that the new plant is located in Liverpool', may help the audience to understand the intermediate argument rather better than if there is a cliffhanger until the end. In the context of, the *rules* of structure set out in Chapter **6** this is equivalent to the summary preceeding the body of the report.

It is important not to forget that you are engaged in a persuasion process when you are making a sales presentation; you should therefore refer to Chapter **9** on rational persuasion in structuring your presentation.

There will, of course, be many presentations which are oral reports, and you can therefore structure these in the same way as the written report.

The conference presentation is often akin to a lecture; there is usually a continuous presentation from the speaker rather than one punctuated by interruptions and questions. The presentation must again be logical. In many respects the conference presentation demands even more care than the others: you know less about the audience – it is likely to have varied starting points of interest, knowledge and ability – and you are less likely to get feedback on the clarity and quality of your presentation, as questions may be less forthcoming.

The end
The end of the presentation is often used to recap on what has been said and in particular to re-emphasise the main points made. The end of the presentation will have more impact than the middle (and sometimes adroit speakers claim attention by indicating the talk is about to finish, by phrases such as, 'In conclusion, then . . .'). If there has been some discussion during the course of the presentation, a skilled presenter may include some relevant points arising from it in the conclusion.

Do not neglect the end of a presentation. The whole presentation can be thought of as being like a piece of orchestral music, with an introduction, middle and end. An orchestral piece does not simply fade out – it has a clear and deliberate end. It may even have a grand finale.

Preparing the visual aids

It would be nice to think that presentations are prepared in a totally logical order; in practice, however, the process is iterative, as shown in Figure 7.6.

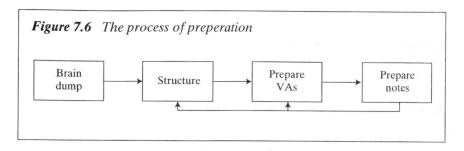

Figure 7.6 *The process of preperation*

What this shows is that during the course of preparation other ideas may emerge which affect earlier stages. Indeed, for presentations which are repeated (as in a training course) there will be further refinement following the delivery of the first one or two presentations.

In theory then, you should decide what you want to say, then decide which bits need illustrating. Some people may even prepare good presentations like this; but the practical fact is that consultants are working under time pressure and have to take a few short cuts.

One such is to prepare the visual aids first and use them as a framework. You can use the visual aids as a basis for speaker's notes by annotating a series of photocopies of them with the comments you wish to make about each. Do not do the reverse, however, representing your notes as visual aids – the only person they will be aiding is you! Figure 7.7 illustrates what *not* to do.

Figure 7.7 *What not to do!*

- Why we were invited to bid

- The difficulties in bidding

- The method of approach proposed
  - tackles more than the terms of reference
  - less risky
  - more cost-effective

- Conclusions

Appendix **4** covers the main types of visual aid and pros and cons of each. But there is one vital thing to remember – that visual aids are meant to be aids. Too often presentations are supported by visual handicaps. Most visual aids used are screen projections (slide, foils, etc.) and the common failings of these are lack of visibility – the audience is not able to read what is on the screen – and too much information being compressed on a single slide.

Preparing what to say

Speakers' practice varies from using no notes at all to using a complete script. Which you choose will depend on the circumstances and your own personal preferences.

The *circumstances* influencing the choice of detail on notes are:

(i)   The formality of the occasion: if you are making a speech, for example, which is likely to be recorded or widely quoted, you may prefer to use a script or detailed notes. Unless you are very skilled, however, a full script means gaining precision at the expense of spontaneity. Rarely is the trade-off worthwhile. Consultants often use brief headings as a prompt – it is rare to need a detailed script or (in a client presentation) to use no notes at all. (Although, the appearance of using no notes at all can be given if the visual aids are used as a prompt.)

(ii)   Coordination with visual aids: it may be necessary to work on cues if control of the visual aids is not in the hands of the speaker; this can be better done by using a script.

(iii) The lighting: I once had to make an internal presentation at short notice to substitute for one of my colleagues. It turned out that the arrangements were such that the lecture room had to be in darkness to see a TV projection so I could not see my notes – I had to make the presentation from memory!

Personal preference will depend on:

(i)   Familiarity with the material: you may make a presentation on a particular topic on more than one occasion and, although the context may be different, as you gain greater familiarity with the material you will need less extensive notes on later occasions.

(ii)   Your experience and confidence in making presentations. Less experienced or less confident presenters may prefer more extensive notes. A word of warning, however: spoken language is not the same as written and what looks good on paper does not sound so compelling when spoken.

(iii) Your fluency: some individuals have great skill in speaking to few notes – others need more prompts. At the other end of the scale, there is the need to have a certain acting ability to impart life to a full script.

The use of humour

The person who makes a living telling jokes is called a comedian. Unless you are a comedian, there is no need to make a presentation entertaining by telling jokes. Humour, however, is quite different from telling jokes, and it is more appropriate to consider the use of *wit*.

A good rule is that if you cannot think of something humorous to say – then don't say it. In a presentation you are presenting something of yourself, and an audience is quick to spot someone who is attempting to be something different from what they truly are. So, if it is in your nature and ability to tell a good joke, then you can do that in a presentation; if you are not a natural humorist, it will stick out like a sore thumb and your audience will be embarrassed to have to respond to a poorly told joke. (All of us have been part of an audience on some occasion when this has happened – so we know how embarrassing it can be.)

The subjects about which to be humorous need to be chosen carefully. The presenter has the privilege of the attention of an audience and has an advantage over them. The poor use of humour abuses that privilege, and tempts the reaction, 'Why do we have to waste time listening to this?' So humour should at most be a leavening to the presentation, not a major part of its content.

Opening and closing

The opening and closing of a presentation have particular features unrelated to content.

The opening is the more important; it is the point at which the audience is forming an impression of the speaker, which will affect their reception of the content of the presentation. It is important therefore to be in control of this process.

The first thing to consider is your appearance – what you wear and your grooming. It is not unlike a job interview, when again you are trying to create a favourable initial impression. As a consultant, you need to look smart and businesslike. It is a debatable question what you should wear: it is not always a good idea to dress as your clients do, because they may expect you to look the part of a consultant.

Next, remember that the audience is assessing you, and thus may not be paying as much attention at the start of the presentation as later on. It therefore pays to start at a slower pace and increase as you go on. It also makes sense to defer getting right into your presentation at the start; it is better to concentrate on putting the audience at their ease and arousing their interest. Many speakers do this by introducing their presentations by a relevant anecdote or story.

Some presenters do the opposite of making the audience relaxed. I attended a conference at which a noted QC and parliamentarian began by asking delegates questions in a very aggressive fashion. His questions were akin to a cross-examination, and good answerers were awarded a House of Commons key ring. He kept everyone's attention, it was instructive and entertaining, but it would be untrue to call his session relaxing!

Closing is important because it leaves a final impression with the audience. It does not have to be a climax, but the most common difficulty of inexperienced presenters – especially at conferences – is running out of time. This can give the appearance of a hasty or ill-thought-out end to the presentation. It is as well, therefore, to pace yourself through the presentation – to have some idea of at what point you should have half your time allocation left, and so on. (Pacing is far more difficult during an informal presentation when questions may interrupt and disturb your own time schedule.)

To this end when preparing your speaker's notes it is useful to consider your material as shown in Figure 7.8. This represents a target, and you should divide your material as follows:
Must: vital to the argument.
Should: important supporting material.
Could: useful padding (e.g., humour or anecdotes) but no harm if not
         included.

If you are running out of time, you can then concentrate on the 'must' items.

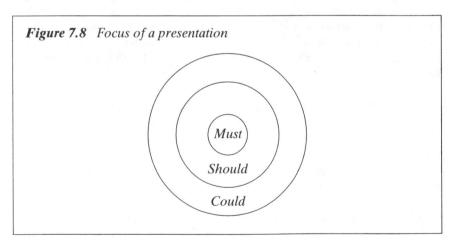

Figure 7.8 *Focus of a presentation*

Rehearsal

In theory, all presentations should be rehearsed; in practice, time has a measurable cost to consultants and therefore the practical opportunity for rehearsal will often be limited. Figure 7.9 suggests a rule of thumb to decide whether to rehearse or not.

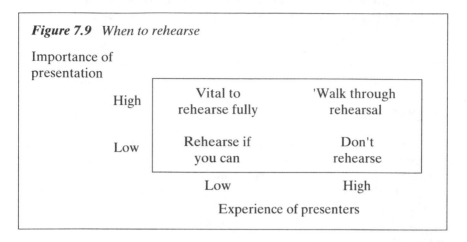

Figure 7.9 *When to rehearse*

Importance of
presentation

	Low	High
High	Vital to rehearse fully	'Walk through rehearsal
Low	Rehearse if you can	Don't rehearse

Experience of presenters

There are different degrees of rehearsal and the most comprehensive is the dress rehearsal when the presentation is made as it will be 'on the day'. Dress rehearsal is vital for an important presentation with inexperienced presenters, and is desirable in all cases where the presenters are not experienced.

Experienced presenters, however, are less likely to need a rehearsal, but on important occasions a 'walk-through' rehearsal is useful. This checks the stage management and is particularly helpful on those occasions when a team is presenting. During the walk through, you can agree on the programme and how questions will be handled, ensure that visual aids are used consistently and so on, i.e., make sure that the details run smoothly.

In rehearsals of all presentations you should check:

- timing: not only the duration of the whole thing, but the balance between sections, too. Remember that presentations almost always take longer on the day than in rehearsal;
- the visual aids: they are available, work and can be seen;
- continuity: between the sections of your own presentation or those of colleagues, if presenting in a team.

If you are rehearsing a presentation, it is as well to do it with an audience. An audience helps to supply a degree of realism (which mirrors the real thing) and they can often make helpful suggestions afterwards for improvements.

Delivering presentations

You have prepared what you are going to say and rehearsed it. The great day (or, more likely in the case of a consultant, the day) has arrived: what now?

Whether you like it or not, presentations are a form of entertainment; on the day you have to think about *stage management* and *performance*.

Stage management

Stage management is visible only when something goes wrong. At the theatre, stage management goes unnoticed unless the safety curtain refuses to rise, the lights fail or some similar disaster strikes. The same applies to presentations: the horror stories told by consultants almost invariably involve some failure of stage management. It is very evident if a projector breaks down or you arrive late. So what follows is a checklist covering points of stage management before and on the day.

Before the day:

(i)   Be sure you know where the presentation is to be held, when and for how long.
(ii)   Ensure that any equipment you need (projectors, etc.) is available if being supplied by the client. With projectors, also remember you need a screen (not always remembered by client's staff). If you are taking your own equipment, you can be sure that if you do not take an extension electric cable, the one on your projector will not reach the electric point.
(iii)   If you are using 35 mm slides or video, you will need subdued lighting to see them clearly. If so, check that the room can be darkened.
(iv)   Check how many people are coming; this will affect the number of hand-outs required (if you are using them) as well as the form of the presentation.

On the day:

(v)   Arrive early. This allows time to organise yourself and visit the toilet.
(vi)   Try to get to the presentation venue before the audience (not always possible, particularly if the presentation is at a conference). This will give you a chance to reorganise seating arrangements if you need to (so that for example, everybody has clear sight of the screen).
(vii)   Check that all equipment is working: that slides are loaded correctly in the carousel and that foils are in the right order. If using a flip chart, check there is clean paper on the stand (I have known occasions when

you may be given a pad with only two clean sheets on it), and that you have markers which work. (A favourite trick of presentation course tutors is to put the caps so tightly on flip chart pens that they cannot come off. This certainly reinforces the point to students.)

(viii) Make sure your speaker's notes are to hand and in the right order. If you are using cue cards, then make sure they are tied together in some way. (If not, you could have considerable difficulties if you drop them.)

Performance

Some years ago I came across a consultant who had a monotonous voice. He knew his voice was monotonous, but it was the way it came out and there was nothing he could do about it. He could give witty and entertaining presentations, but his voice remained a distinct disadvantage.

By the time you become a consultant, your speech and accent are probably set; besides, the attempt to make them something other than they are will be transparent and to your disadvantage. So this section deals with delivery as a series of simple rules. They will not make you a good presenter, but they help you to avoid most common pitfalls.

(i) Speak so that you can be heard. This will sometimes require you to raise your voice. You can ask your audience if they can hear you.

(ii) Speak naturally. Rhetoric is rarely appropriate or necessary in business, so use the tone and language with which you feel comfortable. For most people, however, it is worth slowing down the speed of delivery.

(iii) Look at the audience – which is more difficult with a fully scripted presentation. Eye contact helps to make people feel included; looking at the audience enables you to observe their reaction. Do let your eyes move from one individual to another – continuously looking at one member of the audience can make them embarrassed and cause the rest to wonder whether you have a special relationship! Similarly, do look at members of the audience – not over the top of their heads. You may be trying to communicate a vision, but do not pretend it is behind the audience. If you are holding your speaker's notes, hold them well up, so that you keep your head up. (We all know people who make presentations to the floor.) If you are using visual aids, avoid spending long periods turned to the screen.

(iv) Control what people see. This does not mean only visual aids but keep them visually interested. When you watch a play, you will see that the actors on stage other than the one speaking will remain still – particularly during a long speech; then, when it is time for another to speak, they will move with a flourish to attract attention. So it is with a presentation – your movements will attract attention (so will the movements of members of the audience and the tea-lady, coming in or out of the room.) If you want people to concentrate on a picture, keep still; move when you want them to pay attention to you. Again, if you are holding your notes, do so in your less dominant hand, to avoid waving them around.

(v) Do not devote great chunks of your presentation to explaining how you come to be giving it, commenting on its mechanics or the process of its creation ('When I was asked to give a presentation on "congenital idiocy" I looked it up in my dictionary . . .') or apologise for being there. These will make the presentation seem amateurish in the hands of anyone but a talented professional.

(vi) Prepare for questions. In some presentations, it is possible to have a few 'planted' amongst friendly members of the audience, so that you can shine by your prepared response. The audience at a rehearsal can also be used to identify questions which might be asked.

Obviously the best technique is to answer questions honestly and say when you do not know the answer. Sometimes you may need to buy time whilst you think of an answer, and a technique for doing this is to ask a question in return ('I wonder if you could elaborate on that a little . . .'). A further technique, much favoured by politicians, is to answer a different, more easy, question.

If you are faced by a hostile questioner, do your best not to be more aggressive in return. If anything, try to be demonstrably helpful and courteous; at best it may mollify their hostility. There is a good chance that many in the audience will sympathise with you, but you will lose that sympathy if you respond aggressively.

Post mortem

The greater part of this chapter has been given over to the preparation of a presentation. This is because preparation should take more time than delivery, and the knowledge that you have prepared well will boost your confidence. But as with all communications, improvement only comes about through analysing carefully after the event:

- what went right;
- what went wrong;
- what will I do different and better next time?

It is best to do this analysis shortly after the presentation. If it has been notably good (or bad) then it will be self-evident, but most of the time your performance will be mixed. Comments can be solicited from colleagues and informally from individuals in the audience. The latter, however, are more likely to criticise the content of the presentation rather than the quality of its delivery.

It is worth distinguishing between content and delivery in your own critique. If your presentation went wrong, was it because you delivered a brilliant presentation of irrelevant material, or did the presentation fail to do justice to the material? There are different lessons to be drawn in each case.

Either way, it is sensible to try to limit your personal improvement plan to a few tasks which you consider are important and achievable. Figure 7.10 shows an example of one such plan.

Figure 7.10   *Presentation improvement plan*

At my next presentation I aim to:

Aim	Action
• Avoid jangling coins in my pocket	Remove coins and keys to my briefcase beforehand.
• Prepare clearer visual aids	Use larger typeface
• Keep to a timetable better.	1 Reduce the amount of material I try to put across. 2 Pace myself – have ⅓ and ⅔ marks as well as half-way points. 3 Put watch on table so I don't feel inhibited about glancing at it.

---

8 Designing and presenting training sessions and workshops

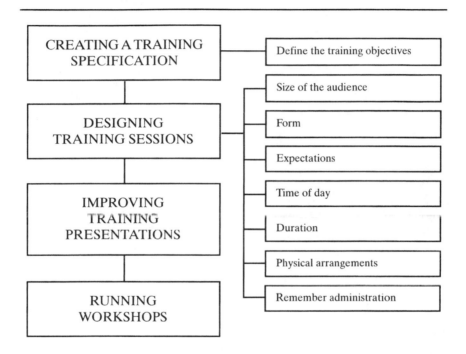

CREATING A TRAINING SPECIFICATION	Define the training objectives
DESIGNING TRAINING SESSIONS	Size of the audience
	Form
	Expectations
IMPROVING TRAINING PRESENTATIONS	Time of day
	Duration
	Physical arrangements
RUNNING WORKSHOPS	Remember administration

8 Designing and presenting training sessions and workshops

Education is an admirable thing, but it is well to remember from time to time that nothing that is worth knowing can be taught.

Oscar Wilde

Most consultants have to run a training session at some time. This chapter is thus not aimed at the professional trainer – or the consultant who regularly presents training courses – but at the consultant who has to run a training course as an adjunct to the project being carried out. Instances when training might be required could be on introducing new systems (computer or manual), teaching client staff new specialist techniques and so on.

There are two key differences (at least two) between presenting a training session and presenting in the other contexts described in Chapter **7**:

(i)   Training is directed towards enhancing a skill so that individuals should be able to do something different or better as a consequence. By contrast, other presentations could be aimed more at informing or persuading.
(ii) You should have fewer constraints on training than on a presentation. More flexibility enables you to fashion the session so as to be able to achieve the training objectives better.

A lecture at a conference could be construed as a form of training but I have in mind, however, the occasion when you have a small number of people – up to about 25, but often a dozen or even fewer – whom you have to train, and it is up to you to decide how you will do it.

Workshops are yet another kind of gathering aimed at developing performance. They have many characteristics in common with training sessions, but some important differences too. These are covered at the end of the chapter.

Creating a training specification

A training specification is a useful bridge between the outline of a training programme and its detailed design. If you are designing a training programme for a client, you can use the training specification to get client input or agreement at an intermediate stage. The contents of a training specification are:

(i)   Description of the programme:

- the training objectives;
- the number and nature of participants for whom it is designed;
- its duration and structure (e.g., four days, two two-day seminars, residential or non-residential);
- its style (e.g., a series of exercises based on a case study; a participative workshop, etc.);
- the resources required (trainers, equipment, films, etc.).

(ii)   Timetable, setting out the timing of each session.

(iii) Session outlines: for each session:

- rationale: why this session is included in the course;
- objectives: the teaching objectives for the session:
- key learning points to be covered in the session;
- session outline, describing what will happen in the session.

(iv)   The basis on which the training is to be evaluated.

Define the training objectives

You must start off by deciding what the purpose of the training is: what participants should know or be able to do at its conclusion.

It is particularly helpful to think about objectives in terms of behavioural or testable outcomes. Figure 8.1 shows the objectives for a session on the techniques of 'brainstorming'.

When you are dealing with easily testable skills or outcomes – such as those illustrated in Figure 8.1 – then the need for the training should be fairly clear, as should be the method of carrying it out.

Where training is less specific – for example, management training – there is often a 'syrup of figs' mentality: participants are subjected to it on the grounds that whatever it is, it will probably do them some good! This is probably true, but it does represent an ineffective use of time and resources. In these circumstances it is sensible to carry out some detailed training needs analysis. This might be carried out by getting precise answers to the questions:

(i)   In what way are we trying to improve business performance?
(ii) What requirements does this place on improving individual or group performance?

(iii) What do people need to do differently or better to achieve this improvement?

(iv) What support do they need to accomplish this?

(v) What role does training have in this?

(vi) How should this be delivered?

(vii) What conditions need to be created so that the training is applied effectively at work?

Figure 8.1 *Objectives for a brainstorming session*

At the end of the session participants should be able to:

1 Define brainstorming

2 List the characteristics of a brainstorming group

3 Identify the guidelines for a brainstorming session

4 Participate constructively in a brainstorming session

5 Recognise possible applications of brainstorming back at work.

Very often the consultant is invited in only at stage (vi). This is not necessarily a problem provided the causality back to stage (i) is clear. If it is not, then perhaps this indicates some work that the consultant needs to carry out beforehand, to clarify the model of performance applying to the business.

If the subject you are teaching is complex it may need a series of sessions to put it across – in other words, a training course.

You will then need to define the objectives for each session.

Designing training sessions

Having defined learning objectives, you will need to design a session to achieve them. To this end you need to have some basic guidelines on how people learn.

There is a saying often quoted by trainers:

'Hear and forget,
see and remember,
do and understand.'

It underscores the points that *in general* people's visual memories are better than their aural ones, but personal experience has a more profound effect than either. People have different preferences in the way they learn. Some learn best by observation; some by actually doing. Some like to understand the theory and others the practical application of what is being taught.

Groups of people being trained will have a mix of these preferences and so a mix of activities is used. Inevitably, therefore, sessions popular with those who have one preference will leave those with another indifferent.

The choice of method of putting material across also depends on what is to be learned.

Figure 8.2 illustrates a relationship between the nature of what is being taught, and the method used.

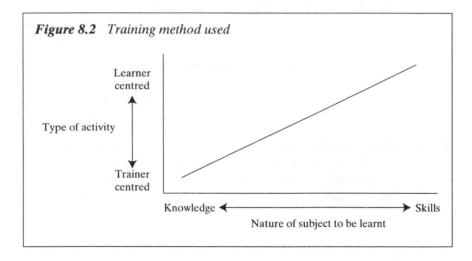

Figure 8.2 *Training method used*

Knowledge-based learning is – as the name suggests – directed towards increasing a participant's knowledge. An example of this end of the spectrum is training client staff in, say, the implications of a new piece of legislation. A skill-based subject is related to doing something. This covers all operative skills – for example, how to operate a new PABX – but it also covers a lot of managerial skills (for example, making a presentation.)

A trainer-centred activity is focused on the trainer (e.g., a lecture) whereas a learner-centred activity is based on the trainee (such as a practical exercise).

Skills training is effective when done on the job, as well as away from work. In this chapter however, we are concerned with making a training presentation and therefore are concerned only with training away from the job; Figure 8.3 lists some of the most used methods of training. Also shown is the relationship between the type of subject to be learnt and the training method most appropriate. If the trainee has no knowledge of a subject, it is probably best for the trainer to tell them about it first, and thus the trainer-centred approach is appropriate. On the other hand, the use of – say – a new computer system is best learned by practice.

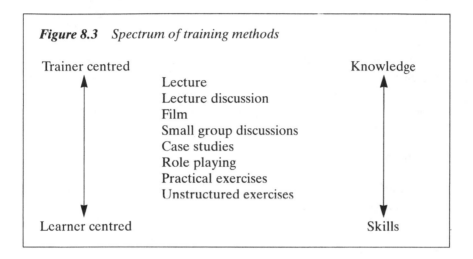

Figure 8.3   *Spectrum of training methods*

It is essential to remember that 'learner-centred activities' involve the trainer in different forms of activity rather than sitting back and watching what happens.

With learner-centred training you should consider how trainees are to get feedback. If they are undertaking a practical exercise, for example, how will they know what they are doing right or wrong and how will they judge the quality of their performance?

The trainer has therefore to organise the feedback process. It can be done by the trainer or through other members of the group. If the latter, group members must feed back only that data which they can reasonably be expected to be able to collect. (For example, in training in recruitment interviewing, trainees may take the roles of interviewer and prospective recruit: the 'recruit' could quite legitimately comment on how they felt during the course of the interview.) Group members should be coached in the skills of observation, if they are to give feedback, and they need to be able to recognise the difference between effective and ineffective behaviour or performance. Closed circuit TV recordings can often help in the feedback process.

The amount and rate of feedback must be regulated; too much feedback is indigestible and can result in a deterioration of performance.

So, in designing a training session you should consider the structure of the topics to be taught and where they fall on the 'knowledge-skills' spectrum. Almost certainly there will be a mix and you should use the appropriate method for putting across each element. In my experience, consultants tend to err towards the 'trainer centred' end of the spectrum in terms of the content of a training session. There is usually more scope for learner-centred activities – and it makes it more interesting for participants, too.

At the beginning of Chapter **7** we reviewed the constraints which surround a presentation and their influences on it. Constraints are usually fewer in a training session as the consultant has more control. In this section we consider how they might be arranged so as to meet the training objectives best.

Size of the audience

The size of the audience you choose should be a function of administration, organisation and the need for personal interaction. So it will depend on:

- How many people are to be trained?
- How many can be spared for a training session at a single time?
- How many can be comfortably accommodated in the training room?
- How are they going to be involved? (If, for example, you want people to join in a discussion, the average 'air-time' available for each participant in a group of 30 is two minutes per hour.)
- What constraints are there on the physical facilities? For example, if trainees are to use microcomputers, how many are available?
- What are the constraints imposed by your teaching structure? If there are practical exercises involving sub-groups, how many people should be in each? Does this put a minimum number on the course participants? Similarly, if groups are to work in separate rooms, how many can be accommodated and does this place a maximum number on the participants?
- What is the need for interaction between you and each participant? If individual coaching is required in part of the session, how many people can you deal with? If this is a major limitation, is it worthwhile having a colleague available for this part so you can have more people on the course as a whole?

Project management or commercial constraints will often influence a training session as well and cause departures from the 'ideal' approach.

Form of the presentation

A lecture is only rarely an appropriate form of training. Almost always some form of audience participation is necessary to maintain interest. It has been said that people can concentrate only for eight minutes at a stretch without some involvement. I am not convinced that eight is the right number, but I do believe that audience participation enhances interest and learning.

Audience participation can be achieved by asking questions, soliciting opinions, and allowing people to air their knowledge. Answers can be posted on a flip chart (and the sight of a trainer poised, ready to write down comments on a flip chart, often can help to elicit responses from an audience). Remember that open-ended questions (starting with how, why, where, etc.) will prompt more comment than close ended questions (starting 'do you . . .', 'have you . . .', etc.) which simply invite a 'yes' or 'no' answer.

Expectations of the audience

It is the trainer's job to fashion the expectations of the audience. The trainer may have been responsible for initial briefing beforehand – perhaps by a letter and outline of the course content – which will influence expectations before arrival.

The first part of a training course (or session within it) will set the tone for the whole. At the start of a course a trainer may give a short briefing about what is to come, but will usually be giving a lot of verbal and non-verbal signals about the style of the course. Typically, nowadays, the style of a training course will be:

- *informal*: it is not run as a formal conference or meeting;
- *relaxed*: allowing participants to behave naturally rather than being on their best behaviour;
- *low-risk*: it does not matter if participants make mistakes or are wrong;
- *businesslike*: notwithstanding the comments above, participants are there to learn and this involves hard work and effort.

A technique I use at the start of a training session, which helps to unfreeze groups, is to get them to do something counter to their expectations. For example, if they expect a lecture, with their bottoms stuck to their seat for half the day, try to start with an exercise in which they have to move around the room.

The trainer will set the norms of behaviour for the session. For example, sitting behind a desk with your jacket on will convey a completely different impression than sitting on the edge of the front of a desk (nothing between you and the audience) with your sleeves rolled up.

Again, the way you talk to the audience will influence their attitude; making fun of questions may inhibit other questioners; criticising their contributions may create an adversarial attitude.

Thus the presenter's behaviour, although nothing to do with the content, can profoundly influence the quality of a training presentation; controlling behaviour carefully leads to better sessions.

What time of day should you choose?

More often than not the time of day chosen for a training presentation will depend on administrative limitations.

Consider whether the training is best given at a single session or two (or more) sessions. It might be better, for example, to have two half-day sessions than one whole day.

If the session is not to last a whole day, the timing may be constrained by the availability of participants. It may be easier to release them at one particular time than another.

It is important that a consultant considers the implications of timing on participants' perception of the importance of training. If it is clear that it is being squeezed in around a host of routine matters then it will not be rated as very important. On the other hand, if participants have a three line whip to attend (from their bosses – not the consultant) then they will rate the importance of the training more highly.

Duration of training

Training should take as long as it needs; a training session, however, will need in most cases to allow for breaks in mid-morning, lunchtime, and mid-afternoon unless there are strong reasons why it should not. The ability to judge how long a session should last comes with experience, but making a session plan helps. Figure 8.4 illustrates this for a half-day training session on presentations.

Remember to pace yourself through a training session. If you are falling behind, you can perhaps cut some of the 'could' or 'should' material from later sessions. Work longer hours and have shorter breaks only as a last resort.

Figure 8.4   Timetable for training session on presenting

Time

9.0am–9.30am	PLENARY:	Lecture/discussion: 'Presentation – preparation and delivery'
9.30am–9.55am	INDIVIDUAL:	Put finishing touches to five-minute presentations (prepared in advance)
9.55am–12.00pm	TWO SYNDICATES:	Individual presentations, video recorded (inc. coffee break)

5 min presentation
5 min discussion
3 min replay
2 min contingency

15 min total per person

7 people in each syndicate

| 12.00pm–12.30pm | PLENARY: | Film – 'Making presentations' |
| 12.30pm–1.00pm | PLENARY: | Discussions of key learning points arising |

Physical arrangements

The first requirements of the physical arrangements are that they should be comfortable and free from distraction.

Taking participants away from their place of work is worth considering – for example to a hotel or preferably a specialist training centre – for longer training courses, to avoid interruptions, but has the disadvantage of cost.

Room layout can also be managed to good effect. Practical considerations such as being able to see visual aids, will strongly influence layout, but tables and chairs can be arranged in different ways. Figure 8.5 shows the main layouts.

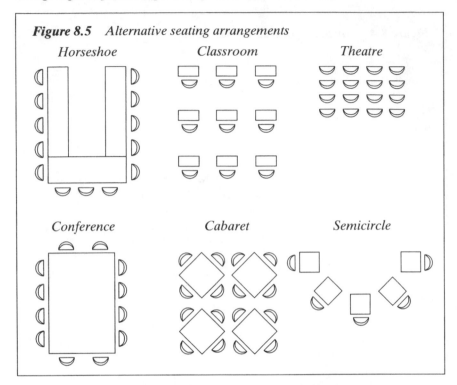

Figure 8.5 *Alternative seating arrangements*

Remember administration

If you are running a training course, the administration of the whole course may be your responsibility. If this is the case, then give it the high priority it deserves. My experience is that delegates on a course will put up with poor trainers, but not with poor administration. Failures of administration are far more apparent than those of training, so do make sure that the administration works. A poor speaker will create far less havoc than no lunch!

Improving training presentations

You can use the same approach to improving a training presentation as for any other. On formal training courses, however, there is usually some attempt to collect participants' views at the conclusion and this can provide helpful feedback on the quality of presentation.

The quality of the training, however, is often more difficult to assess. Some aspects will be easily assessed but others will be less susceptible to assessment, and may require some time to become apparent. If you are making a training presentation as part of a larger project you may be able to follow up to see how effective the training was.

The question to be answered in any assessment is, did the training achieve the desired objectives? Remember that a highly-rated presentation does not mean that the training objectives were necessarily achieved. But you can be fairly sure that a bad presentation will lead to poor training.

Running workshops

A simple distinction between a training session and a workshop lies in the role of the consultant. The consultant as trainer is required to be fairly directive – the trainer has the information, skills or knowledge and needs to impart it to the trainees and is therefore in the best position to define how it must be done. This does not necessarily apply at a workshop, and so the consultant has to act more as a facilitator. These two roles are therefore at different places in the spectrum of consultancy behaviour defined in Chapter **4.**

A workshop none the less has to be planned as carefully as any training session. Amongst the points you should consider are:

1 What is the purpose of the workshop? You might also consider whether the first item on the workshop agenda should be to reaffirm its purpose, its importance, and to define some criteria of success at its completion.
2 Who should attend? What agendas are they coming with, and what processes will need to be put in place to deal with these?
3 What should the workshop agenda be? In a training course, the trainer can set an agenda in some detail; by contrast, in a workshop the participants may well have strong views on the way the agenda is to develop. Even so, you will need to think through each item on the agenda. Training might feature on it – e.g., teaching participants a problem solving technique applicable to the work being done. You may also need to have contingency plans to cater for the different directions in which the workshop might properly go.
4 What logistics should be put in place? For example, a one-day session on creating a new strategy might work better if people are away from work, in an unusual environment, wearing casual clothes etc., as these differences may prompt them to think in different ways.

In many ways, a workshop is a halfway house between a training session and a meeting; a consultant must be competent in handling all three to be effective.

9　Rational persuasion

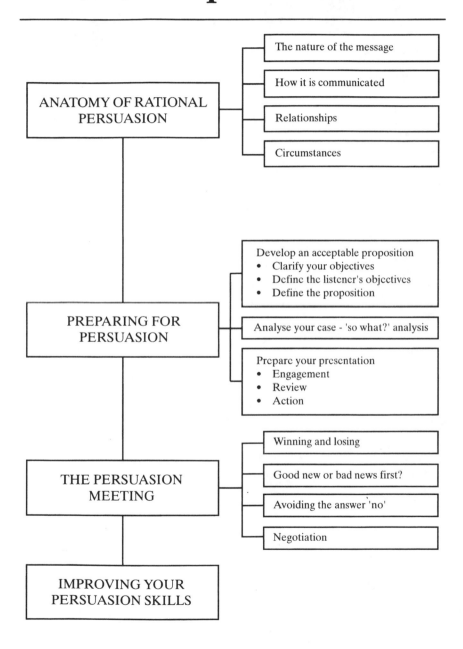

ANATOMY OF RATIONAL PERSUASION
- The nature of the message
- How it is communicated
- Relationships
- Circumstances

PREPARING FOR PERSUASION
- Develop an acceptable proposition
  - Clarify your objectives
  - Define the listener's objectives
  - Define the proposition
- Analyse your case - 'so what?' analysis
- Prepare your presentation
  - Engagement
  - Review
  - Action

THE PERSUASION MEETING
- Winning and losing
- Good new or bad news first?
- Avoiding the answer 'no'
- Negotiation

IMPROVING YOUR PERSUASION SKILLS

9   Rational persuasion

Persuasion: a species of hypnotism in which the oral suggestion takes the hindering form of argument or appeal.

Ambrose Bierce

In Chapter **4** we considered the subject of change: how it could be created within organisations and how they could be rendered more receptive to it. The approaches suggested were aimed at influencing groups; in this chapter, by contrast, we look at influencing an individual.

Persuasion is how we get other people to undertake an act or a decision that we want and is required in situations when the person you are trying to persuade – the listener – has the option of saying 'No'. Whatever the input or the process, the output is (or should be) clear. There are numerous occasions when a consultant attempts to persuade a client, from the mundane to the momentous:

* to adopt particular recommendations;
* to fix a meeting on a particular day;
* to second a member of staff to a project;
* to agree to extending a deadline;
* to sanction additional expenditure.

Of course, persuasion is an art we use throughout our life, with family, friends and colleagues, and much of the time we use persuasion unconsciously. We encounter different styles of persuasion every day:

* the six-year old child who says, 'If you won't let me play with that toy I won't be your friend', is using an emotional threat in order to negotiate. Adults do the same but (usually) rather more subtly;
* individuals may compel acceptance of their views simply through their status, force of personality, or another sort of power (see Chapter **4**);
* our relationship with an individual may be very trusting; they have been sympathetic and supportive to us in the past, and we will agree with their proposal simply because we trust them;
* we are influenced by other's opinions and actions; if common behaviour in an organisation is to work on a Saturday (even though it is not a working day) we may feel compelled to do the same;
* we can be inspired by someone communicating an appealing vision (a method often used by orators).

All of these are effective methods of persuasion but they depend on the use of emotion or power. Rational persuasion, however, depends on reason –

on logical argument. It is the process of rational persuasion with which this chapter is concerned.

The anatomy of rational persuasion

Rational persuasion is the basis which consultants use most often to analyse and present a case persuasively. The key elements are shown in Figure 9.1.

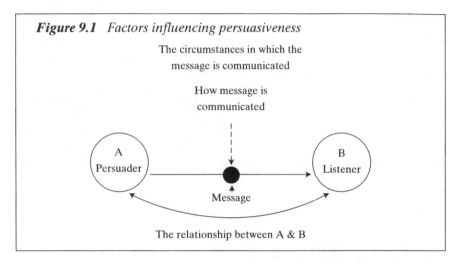

Figure 9.1 *Factors influencing persuasiveness*

The circumstances in which the message is communicated

How message is communicated

A Persuader

B Listener

Message

The relationship between A & B

- The *message* will affect the reaction of the listener. Any message which B perceives as having a bad net outcome is going to be poorly received. Such messages might be:

  – 'Please work late tonight';
  – 'You owe me £2,000';
  – 'We want you to work in our Timbuctu office'.

- *How the message is communicated* will affect how it is received. There is an old joke about the Army sergeant who was asked to break the news to Smith, one of the corporals in his platoon, that his father had died. After some thought, the sergeant formed up the platoon on parade and gave the command 'All those with fathers, one pace forward ... where do you think you're going, Smith?' Insensitive communication can create resistance to a persuading message; for example, contrast the appeals:

  – you will work late tonight;
  – could you please work late tonight?

  Both of which (despite the apparent diffidence of the latter) could be orders.

- The *relationship* between the persuader (A) and listener (B) is crucial and will depend on B's perception of A. At an extreme, if A is an untrusted enemy of B, it will be very difficult for A to persuade B of anything, but there does not need to be a historical relationship between A and B for there to be difficulties. For example, if B has a totally irrational and base-less dislike of red-headed Glaswegians and A happens to be one, then A will start with a disadvantage.

- The *circumstances* in which the message is communicated. We are much more likely to be persuaded to climb down a drainpipe from a third-floor window in the event of a fire than simply for the sake of it.

It is unlikely that you will have total control of all these items; none the less, there will be occasions about whose outcome you may be particularly anxious, and in which you wish to maximise the chance that your persuasive attempt will be successful. In this chapter we concentrate on the first two items above – namely, the nature of the message and how it is communicated. With most communication the basis of success starts with careful preparation. The issue for a consultant is therefore how to present a proposition in the most persuasive way.

Preparing for persuasion

Outlined below is a practical approach to preparation which has three stages:

(i)   develop an acceptable proposition;
(ii)   analyse your case;
(iii) prepare your presentation.

Developing an acceptable proposition

If the proposition you are making is totally unacceptable, persuasion will not be successful. Conversely, if the listener is likely to be totally agreeable to the proposition, then there is little point going through an elaborate routine of preparation.

There is little chance of acceptance of an unacceptable proposition except by misrepresentation or manipulation, both of which involve deceit. For example, a confidence trickster uses deceit to persuade someone to part with money for nothing in return.

There are three steps to developing an acceptable proposition:

- clarify your objectives;
- define the listener's objectives;
- define the proposition.

Clarify your objectives

The first step is to know what you want to achieve. Simple persuasion objectives for a consultant in the course of operating might be:

- to defer the progress review for a week;
- to accept Tom instead of Dick on the assignment;
- to start work on Phase 2 in February.

It is also important to know *why* these objectives are necessary, i.e., the ends to which these are the means. The reasons, related to the examples above, could be respectively:

- to complete more work prior to the next progress review;
- to provide Dick with sufficient time to undertake a new assignment which requires his particular skills;
- to allow sufficient time for this phase to be complete by July.

Having defined these ulterior objectives, alternative means of meeting the same ends could be defined by asking 'how' of them. Taking the first example, asking 'how?' of 'to complete more work prior to the next progress review' could lead to the alternatives of:

- work weekends and evenings;
- add additional people to the team; as well as the original proposition of 'to defer the progress review for a week'. Pictorially the process is illustrated in Figure 9.2.

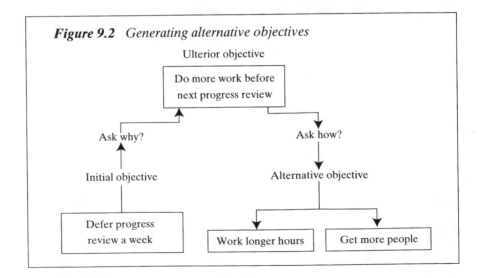

Figure 9.2   *Generating alternative objectives*

If the first proposition is not acceptable, this process could lead to alternatives which are acceptable. It is also a useful process in deriving alternatives if negotiation is to take place.

Define the listener's objectives

You will have noticed that each of the ulterior objectives shown on p. 186 has benefits for the consultant. Although the client may be sympathetic to these, they are in themselves unlikely to be persuasive. Persuasion is listener oriented, and the process that has to be followed is to show how the required act or decision can help the listener meet their *own* goals. This is depicted in Figure 9.3. This means that the persuader has to have some idea of what the listener's goals might be.

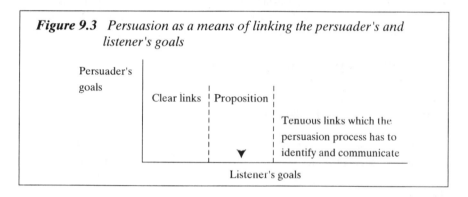

Figure 9.3   *Persuasion as a means of linking the persuader's and listener's goals*

If we know him, then we will probably have some idea of what his goals might be in both general and specific terms, for example:

– to avoid risk taking;
– to go home at 5pm on Tuesday;
– to complete the project before the end of the year;
– to keep control.

- Some time ago the tutors in a training college had to convince two directors to sanction expenditure on an interactive video system. One – Barry – was keen on anything new, whereas Alan – the other – was very conservative. The tutors knew that they would have to appeal to them separately. With Barry, it was along the lines, 'Barry, interactive video is new in training. If we want to be ahead of everybody else, we've got to have it.' Barry's reaction was 'That's exciting – let's have it! '

With Alan, the presentation was different. 'Alan, interactive video has been around for some time now; it represents the next natural step from the investment we have made already in computers and video.' Alan's reaction was, 'That doesn't sound revolutionary – why don't we go ahead?'

It would have been impossible to appeal to their contrasting innovative and conservative motivations simultaneously, but tuning the approach separately worked.

How do you infer the objectives of a listener you have never met? One way is to be briefed by someone who knows them already. For example, a client's subordinate can help you to work out their boss's objectives. Other than this, you have to guess, but this is not difficult as most people's general objectives are those of self-interest or the interest of groups or institutions to which they belong. In these cases, it is probably worthwhile assuming fairly general objectives until the initial conversation with the listener gives you more clues. You therefore have to listen very carefully at the start of the conversation to what the listener says to pick up any clues about their goals.

Define an acceptable proposition

Having clarified your own and the listener's goals, you need to define a proposition which meets them both.

Take the example given earlier: to defer the progress review by a week. This may be totally acceptable to the client, so there is no problem – they could not care less. But if they had to make a report on the assignment to their board of directors the day after the scheduled date they will be averse to any deferral. The proposition would not be acceptable and an alternative should be sought.

Whereas persuasion is a process whereby the listener accepts a particular proposition in preference to all others, negotiation is more complex. It involves a number of propositions, *quid pro quo*'s, bargaining and so on. A model often used by negotiators to describe the negotiation process is illustrated in Figure 9.4. It shows the range of propositions on a spectrum of best, expected and least acceptable results from our point of view. Likewise, the other side may also have a rank order of attractiveness – but in the opposite direction from us.

Take a simple example – bartering in a middle eastern bazaar for a carpet. The positions may be as shown in Figure 9.5.

In the example, we reckon on a price of up to a 1000 rials for the carpet; the carpet seller will not accept less than 800. Fortunately there is some overlap, and the final price settled on will be a result of the relative bargaining skill of the two parties. (Of course, the matter is made more complicated because we do not necessarily know the range expected on the other side. The first time I went into a middle eastern bazaar, I didn't bargain – I paid the price asked. The shopkeeper looked amazed, and a little disappointed.)

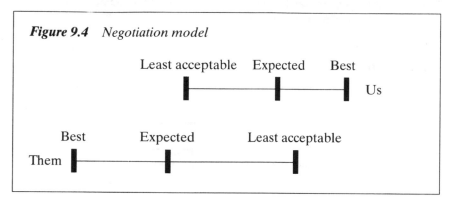

Figure 9.4   *Negotiation model*

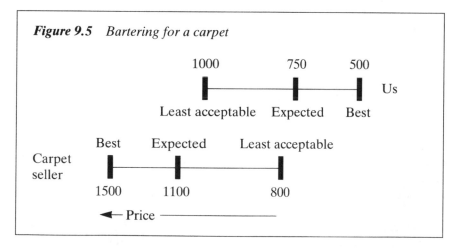

Figure 9.5   *Bartering for a carpet*

If the two ranges of position do not overlap, then it may not be possible to resolve matters by negotiation. In a shop, this may not matter; in business if a resolution is needed, the conflict analysis model given in Appendix **2** can be helpful in planning a resolution strategy.

Analysing your case

Insurance salesman: 'Dick, this is a really good policy. I recommend it to you whole-heartedly because it gives me the best commission.'

Not a particularly compelling sales message, is it! It aims to persuade by showing how the listener can help the persuader achieve their objectives.

Rational persuasion

Persuasion must be listener orientated and needs to show how the proposition can help the listener achieve *their* own objectives.

A form of analysis similar to that used for selling products can be used in selling ideas, and is shown in Figure 9.6.

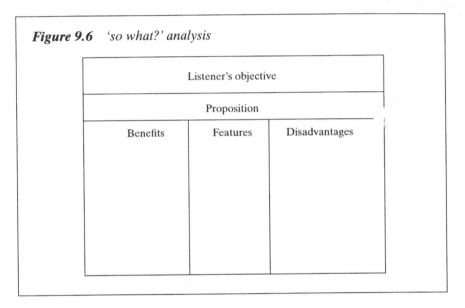

Figure 9.6 *'so what?' analysis*

It is sometimes called a 'so what?' analysis. The listener's objective (relevant to this case) is written at the top, so as to keep it in mind. The 'so what?' analysis is of our proposition and the principal alternative. The alternative may often be, 'do nothing', or there could be several.

In each case, the analysis is the same; a list is made of the principal features of the proposition, in the centre column. Features are the objective facts about the proposal:

- it is eight feet long;
- it is red;
- it costs £27;
- it will take seven days.

A recital of facts about a proposal is not compelling by itself; what is more attractive is interpreting the facts in the context of how they will help achieve the listener's objective or not. These are the *benefits* and *disadvantages* of the proposal. Benefits and disadvantages of the features listed above might be:

Benefit	(Feature)	Disadvantages
It will fit in	(It is eight feet long)	It's too big
It will go with your dress	(It is red)	I wanted green
It is cheaper	(It costs £27)	It's more expensive
That will be in time	(It will take seven days)	That's too late

Each benefit or disadvantage above relates to a hypothetical listener's objective. In the first example, therefore, if the objective is to find a car that will fit into a garage nine feet long, then the feature is a benefit. If on the other hand, the aim is to find a sofa to fit into a space six feet wide, then the feature is a disadvantage.

If you want to translate a feature into a benefit or disadvantage, you ask 'so what?' of it (and hence the name of this form of analysis).

For example:

- It is eight feet long.
- So what?
- It is less than nine feet long.
- So what?
- It will fit in my garage which is nine feet long.

Figure 9.7 *Example of 'So what? ' analysis*

Listener's objective: To ensure the project is completed on time.

Proposition: To put back the progress review meeting by a week.

Benefit	Feature	Disadvantages
Recognise that consultant is being honest with him	Client is told of need to put back meeting by a week	
	Later than planned	Seems as if the project is falling behind
More progress to report at review	Allows more time for work prior to review	
	Other members of the review panel will need to be told	They will wonder if there is a problem

Rational persuasion

This approach is more straightforward for material items than for ideas or concepts, but is applicable to the latter. There may also be a complex mass of objectives, too, so the first step must be to simplify objectives and features. This is done in the example in Figure 9.7, which illustrates the analysis for the proposition given in an earlier example. Once completed for the objective quoted, there may be other objectives which are also relevant; the first feature is also relevant to the (client's) objective 'to be able to trust the consultant'.

Once complete for the proposition, a similar analysis could be done for any alternative propositions, the most likely of which is 'keep the meeting at the same time'. (This is not quoted here because it is in the main simply a reversal of the benefits and disadvantages shown in Figure 9.7.)

This form of analysis helps you to look at your proposition – and the alternatives – from the listener's point of view. Remember – persuasion is listener oriented communication.

Having analysed your case, you have then to decide how to present it.

Preparing your presentation

Persuasive presentation needs to be structured in the order:

(i)   engagement;
(ii) review;
(iii) action.

Engagement
Initially the listener needs to be convinced that there is a problem which merits their attention and needs action – or a decision – from them now. You have somehow to engage their attention and to do so:

- the problem or issue must be recognised and accepted as such by the listener;
- the solution of the problem must be a matter of priority for them;
- they must believe that a solution *is* possible.

In matters of complex persuasion, the process of engagement – getting the listener to 'buy into the problem' – may be a separate step in the persuasion process.

- A personnel manager was having great difficulty in administering the company's car scheme. The boss, the personnel director, whilst accepting the problem, did not accept the personnel manager's view of its nature and urgency. What the personnel manager then did was to stop protecting the boss from all the queries and problems on the car scheme.

Soon thereafter, the personnel director began to see the problem from the personnel manager's point of view.

Attempts at persuasion will be successful only if the engagement step has been completed. Failures in persuasion are often due to entering at the review or action stages without having completed the engagement stage satisfactorily. Thus, for example, starting the discussion on the proposition 'put the review meeting back by a week' with a question about to what date it should be postponed, is starting at the review stage.

Review

Having accepted there is a problem or issue, which must be addressed now, the listener's next question may be, 'Well, what do we do about it?' Indeed, they may immediately put forward propositions of their own. (Incidentally, this latter behaviour is a sign that the engagement stage has been satisfactorily completed.)

This is where the preparatory analysis is used. In describing your proposition you highlight its benefits and the disadvantage of the alternative. Thus:

- *Consultant*: 'By deferring the progress review meeting by a week, we shall be able to report much more significant progress than if we held it as scheduled.'

The client may respond with objections; these will be based on the disadvantages of your proposition and the benefits of the alternative, thus:

- *Client*: 'Deferring by a week will create some concern among panel members that the project is falling behind schedule.'

The preliminary analysis will have shown up this as a potential objection and you should be prepared to deal with the most likely objections. A possible response is:

- *Consultant*: 'It may cause more concern to have the meeting at the original time if we have not completed the action agreed at the last meeting'.

Note in this exchange that they are talking about how to avoid creating concern among panel members – *not* whether the meeting should be deferred. This could be because either the client is representing the other panel members to articulate his own concerns, or has accepted the consultant's proposal and is now thinking how to implement it to best effect.

The consultant might confront this by using a technique known as a 'trial close':

- *Consultant*: 'Are you willing to put the meeting back a week if we can put the other panel members' minds at rest?'

The response to this will help direct the subsequent discussion; is it concerned with convincing the client to defer the meeting, or is it about helping him to implement it effectively? Further trial closes can be used to identify other objections or concerns the client might have. If the consultant cannot find the answer by using the trial close he must still try to find out from the nature of the discussion, so he can direct his efforts in the most effective way.

I have dwelt on what may seem a trivial point because in my experience it crops up over and over again; the barriers to a proposal are often not those of 'why' but 'how? In other words, there is a concern about means rather than ends.

So review consists of the debate about the possible ways in which the problem or issue might be addressed and the pros and cons of each. This should culminate in an agreement on action or a decision – hopefully the one you wanted.

Action

Action, however, does not automatically follow from review. You may have taken the horse to water, but it will not always drink. The ideal response might be:

- *Client*: 'OK, I'm happy to postpone the meeting by a week. I'll call up the other members of the panel to let them know and make sure they don't get worried'.

In practice you might get responses like:

- 'I'd like to think about this'
- 'I'd like to talk this over with . . .'
- 'Let's stick with the original date for the time being and review closer to the time.'

Now, the face value of these statements may be what is meant, and if it is you have to treat them as such. Alternatively, what is being said might mean 'I'm still not convinced but don't want to continue this conversation'.

Another possibility is that the client does not like to commit themself to a decision. In both the latter cases, they may need further pushing.

The techniques you might use when being put off are:

- If the listener is putting you off for *genuine reasons*, you have to respect them: further pushing would simply irritate them. What you can do, however, is to confirm what happens next. A response such as, 'Fine; when should we get together again to decide what to do?' gives you the chance to try again if you have heard nothing. So, although you do not have a firm commitment to the action or decision you want, the steps leading to it will be clear.
- If the listener is still *unconvinced* you need to find out what is bothering them. There may still be a misapprehension on their part which you have failed to address satisfactorily, or they have a piece of relevant information unknown to you, which is their reason for procrastinating. You have to run over the steps in the persuasion process to find out what the sticking points are:

  - 'we agreed this was a problem which required a decision now';
  - 'we have reviewed the range of possible solutions';
  - 'we have agreed that this is the best solution';
  - 'so, let's go ahead.'

- Some people *dislike taking decisions*: a favourite ploy for avoiding decisions is to seek further information. Again, it is essential to distinguish circumstances in which more information is truly required from those when it is a procrastination ploy. In these latter circumstances, you need to emphasise:

  - the adequacy of the data already available;
  - the urgency of taking a decision.

Once the listener has agreed with your proposition, close the discussion. Continued discussion may result in their rethinking their position, and you will have gone backwards in the persuasion process.

The persuasion meeting

In this section we consider some of the features of a persuasion meeting and some of the techniques you can use to increase success.

Winning and losing

What are your feelings about being persuaded? Are you easily persuaded? If so, are you a person of little strength of character or have you taken to yourself the wisdom of Andrew Carnegie, whose epitaph on himself was said to be, 'Here lies a man who knew how to enlist into his service better men than himself'?

Difficulties arise in a persuasion event when it is seen by either side as a contest in which the winner will be the one whose view holds sway at the end of the day. The danger of persuasion becoming a contest is that the listener can always win: they can say 'No'. So as a persuader you need to avoid circumstances in which it becomes more important to win the debate than discuss constructively. The route to win/lose comes from a polarisation of views and is like an oral tennis match with two sides hitting the conversational ball at each other from opposite sides of the net. It is characterised verbally by a lot of 'Yes, but . . .' statements as each protagonist puts their point of view counter to the other. Argument usually reaches an unsatisfactory conclusion.

A technique to deal with this is to ask 'Let me see if I understand what you are saying' and going on to summarise your understanding of their position. This has the benefits of demonstrating listening, checking comprehension and breaking out of the altercation. No one is a fool in their own estimation and they will believe the point they are making is a good one. In debate, concentrating on what you are going to say next means that you are not listening as carefully as you might to what is being said and there is a breakdown in communication.

Another technique is to give the listener positive 'strokes' – showing respect for them and their opinions. This can be done by emphasising points of agreement; the following graduation of 'degrees of agreement' is helpful in recognising not only whether you are for or against a proposal, but the degree of feeling you have for it either way:

- Sharing – 'I feel as committed as you do on this issue'.
- Supporting – 'I will help your efforts on this issue'.
- Sympathising – 'I applaud your efforts but do not feel obliged to help'.
- Acquiescence – 'I couldn't care either way'.
- Rejection – 'I cannot support you'.
- Opposition – 'I will act against you'.

It is useful to be clear where each of you stands on an issue by estimating where you are on the scale.

Of course, it is important to maintain your position if you do not agree with a proposal. It is not always possible to reach a satisfactory compromise. As one client remarked, 'I admire a consultant who makes different recommendations from those I wanted'.

Good news or bad news first?

Sometimes the question arises, 'Should I deal with the disadvantages of a proposal before its advantages, or vice versa?'

My rule of thumb, based on experience, is to start with the advantages of a proposal you want accepted, and start with the disadvantages of a proposal you want rejected. Experimental evidence tends to back this up (Handy, 1981); a group of subjects was told that an individual was intelligent, industrious, impulsive, critical, stubborn and envious. A second group was told the same, but the adjectives were read in the reverse order. Each group was then asked to characterise these individuals, and the first group (where the 'good news' came first) came up with a more favourable evaluation than the second.

Avoiding the answer 'No'

In the same way as the listener may wish to defer a decision to avoid the answer 'Yes', you may wish to do the same to avoid the answer 'No'. Once a decision is made, it is more difficult to undo; the listener, for example, will have made an emotional commitment to the decision once taken. (Happily, the same process, however, works in reverse. Having taken the decision in your favour, it is emotionally painful to undo it.)

So, if it looks as if your persuasion attempt is failing, and there is no satisfactory alternative to fall back on, then aim for a deferral. Taking the example of wanting to defer a progress review meeting, you might say, 'Well, obviously you're not very happy about this. Why don't I do some more sounding out and come back to you in a couple of days?' Although this sounds wishy-washy, it gives you a breathing space and allows you to continue to canvass support. This latter would be politically difficult to do if the decision had already been finally made not to defer.

This is but one aspect of negotiation.

Negotiation

Negotiating is not the same as persuasion in that:

- persuasion is between unequal parties – the persuadee can say no and that is it. In negotiation, the power is more evenly balanced as both parties have agreed that they want to reach an agreement;
- the roles are also more balanced on each side. The object is to find mutually satisfactory ground by bargaining. A process of movement rather than intransigence is expected on both sides.

Rational persuasion

Having pointed out the differences, however, it is worth summarising some of the more useful negotiating tactics.

The process of *adjournment* has already been described in the previous section. As well as avoiding the answer 'No', it can be used to allow tempers to cool or consultation with other parties to take place. (The latter may be apparent only; for example, a manager negotiating with a union may have given their 'final' offer; they cannot revise it further without losing credibility, but a pretence of consultation with his superiors may enable them to do so.)

There are problems when there is no common ground between opposite sides, i.e., there is no overlap between the least acceptable points in each side (see Figure 9.4). The consequence depends on the stakes involved (see Figure A2.4 in Appendix **2**). If the stakes are low you can simply agree to disagree, but if they are high, then each side will try to get the other to change its negotiating position. For example, a union may threaten strike action to encourage the management to increase a pay offer, the argument being it is worthwhile settling at the higher figure to avoid the potential disruption and loss.

Asking for more than you want can be useful in two ways. Firstly, if it is a matter of scale, then you can be negotiated down to what you wanted originally, whilst the opposite party will be satisfied too. (So, asking to defer the meeting by 10 days could result in a compromise of five days, which is certainly better than none at all.) Secondly, a number of minor proposals could be included amongst the major ones. The minor ones can be used to obscure the critical ones, or be sacrificed to secure the key results sought.

Sometimes experienced negotiators *make a large concession at the start* and use that to win a disproportionately more valuable number of smaller concessions from the other side by continually reminding them of the large concession made originally. (The counter to this is to insist that once a concession is made, it is no longer part of the negotiation.)

Listening is particularly important in negotiating, particularly reading between the lines to understand what is really being meant. If you and the other side are representatives who have often negotiated, you may have developed ways of communicating which the superficial observer would not notice. For example, both of you will know for certain when the other has truly reached his final offer. With a stranger it may be difficult to know whether the statement that the offer is final may be simply a strategic ploy.

Sometimes negotiators try to *upset* the other side in the hope that they may get some information or other advantage thereby. For example, there was a barrister who, when he wished to put witnesses off balance, called them by the wrong name.

A further variation to this is to introduce a *personal element* to the negotiation. The negotiator introduces emotion by (implicitly) claiming that tough negotiation is being tough with them as an individual. Do not fall into the trap of confusing the two – it is possible to carry out tough negotiation whilst still maintaining a pleasant personal relationship.

From the above, it will be seen that negotiation can be thought of as a form of 'game', with rules, rituals, specialised forms of words – and this is exemplified in the ritualised bargaining which goes on between employers and employee representatives.

Improving your persuasion skills

The same process applies to improving persuasion skills as with any other form of communication; preparation precedes action. After action, there is a review to see what lessons can be learned and applied to preparation on the next occasion.

You must therefore review each persuasion occasion to see what can be learned from it: what went well, what went poorly? How successful were you? Were you adequately prepared? It can be helpful to go back to the analysis stage and check out how well you did it. Did you assess the persuadee's objectives accurately? Did you remember all the arguments in favour of your proposal and had you anticipated all the objections that were raised?

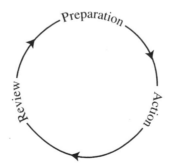

It is also sensible to review the persuasion session itself; how would you behave differently – for example, did you find yourself sidetracked onto an unimportant or irrelevant issue? Did the discussion degenerate into an argument?

Rational persuasion

The process of review should result in some clear lessons to be applied next time – to both preparation and action.

Try it. Success following trying out the techniques covered in this chapter will be even more persuasive than the text!

10 A career in consultancy

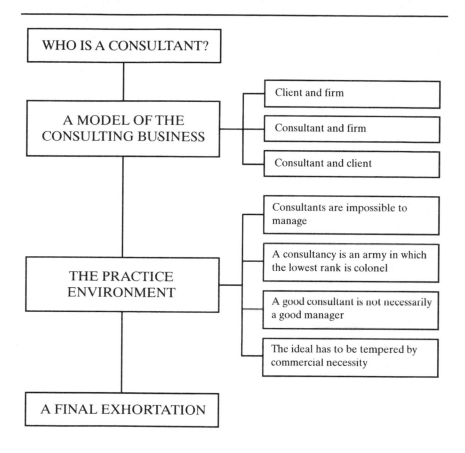

WHO IS A CONSULTANT?

A MODEL OF THE CONSULTING BUSINESS

Client and firm

Consultant and firm

Consultant and client

THE PRACTICE ENVIRONMENT

Consultants are impossible to manage

A consultancy is an army in which the lowest rank is colonel

A good consultant is not necessarily a good manager

The ideal has to be tempered by commercial necessity

A FINAL EXHORTATION

10   A career in consultancy

How can you expect to govern a country that has 246 kinds of cheese?

Charles de Gaulle

The pressure on organisations to cut costs has resulted over the last 10–20 years in a reduction in staff numbers. Increasingly this has meant that many projects have to be resourced – at least in part – from outside the organisation. This has resulted in the considerable growth in the number of consultants seen over recent years. This chapter is addressed to those who might be contemplating a career in consultancy or consultants who are reviewing their careers, and hopefully the thoughts presented will help in making career decisions.

Who is a consultant?

The nature of an individual consultant can vary; at one extreme is the guru. A guru is an individual who has achieved a substantial reputation for their expertise and is employed as a consultant because of this. They are sought in answer to the question, 'Who is the best person to help us on this problem?' They have an individual reputation which is largely independent of the institution to which they belong. In many instances gurus are academics who market themselves by presenting papers at conferences, writing books and so on.

At the other end of the scale is the 'management mercenary': people who enter consultancy early in their careers, often with a lot of knowledge but little experience, fall into this category. They will probably join a firm of consultants and grow in skill under the supervision of more experienced professionals. (This is similar to the training given in other professions in which, for example, solicitors or accountants have to serve out a period of articles.) Management mercenaries secure their work because they work in a firm of consultants rather than because of their own reputation, although this may change as they become more experienced. Internal consultants may well be in a similar position.

Between the two lie independent consultants. They will often work as associates or in small firms (as exemplified by Tom, Dick and Harriet Limited) and will get their work by means of networking – personal contacts, previous clients and the like.

The relationship between client and consultant also varies; the internal consultant is an employee, but sometimes former employees are retained on a 'consultancy' basis, so that their firm is able to continue to draw on their advice and experience.

This typology is illustrated in Figure 10.1.

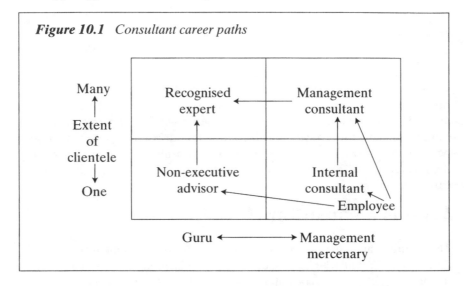

Figure 10.1   *Consultant career paths*

In the bottom right-hand corner is the label 'employee'; if you are employed you could be regarded as selling your services to one client – your employer.

From being an employee, you might proceed to become an external management consultant directly or do so from the position of internal consultant. Some management consulting firms do employ graduates in some specialities (e.g., in business analysis or computing science) without previous employment experience, but in most functions previous employment experience is required.

Beyond this, the management consultant might develop a specialism wherein they achieve individual recognition for their expertise. Alternatively, this might result from a career within a particular industry.

A model of the consulting business

One way to think about a consultancy is as a process in which there are exchanges of value. Figure 10.2 illustrates this in terms of the transactions between an individual consultant, their employing consultancy firm and the client.

The figure shows the exchanges of value which take place between the three parties, and these are described in more detail opposite.

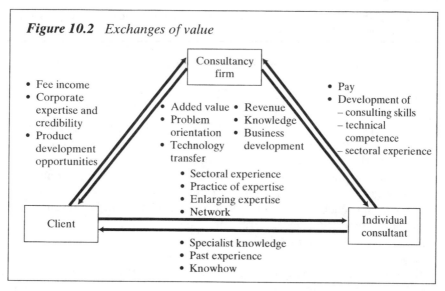

Figure 10.2 *Exchanges of value*

Between client and consultancy firm

It does not automatically follow that an external firm of consultants needs to be used on every project to be carried out: the client could use their own staff, or hire in the help required. The reasons why a client will turn to a firm of consultants are:

- They can *do the project better*. Better in this context need not mean only quality of output, but may also relate to timescale, risk, objectivity or a multitude of other factors.
- *Problem orientation*. A firm of consultants should have the breadth of resources to be able to provide consultants with the necessary skills required. The resources available within the client are usually limited and there is the risk that the problem may be tailored to match the available solutions.
- The firm of consultants may have a proprietary approach which is suitable but available only to clients. Alternatively, the consultancy may have a distinguished reputation in a particular specialist area in which the client needs help. In both these cases by working with the firm of consultants the client will have not only accomplished the project but also learned new approaches. The task of the consultancy firm in this respect is that of facilitating *technology transfer*. What a consultancy does is to take technology (i.e., knowledge or knowhow of limited or no availability in the client's organisation) and apply it to the client's problem. The consultancy therefore needs to plan its technology acquisition, whether it be through people (by recruitment), knowledge (by

training and contact with academia) or experience (from previous assignments).

What the consultancy firm gets from the client/consultant relationship is:

- *Fee income* – payment for services.
- *Corporate expertise and credibility*. A consultancy firm accumulates corporate experience from the projects carried out in the past and in quoting these underwrites its expertise. This expertise can be focussed on a particular market as well as on areas of specialisation.
- Consultancy should not be the mindless application of standard approaches; some innovation and flair are required on most assignments. Original approaches which are proven on a project may, however, be useful in applications elsewhere. For example, suppose a piece of computer software is developed on an assignment for administering and processing data from an attitude survey. The same software might be applicable on other assignments and, indeed, its availability could be a selling point in securing further work on attitude surveys. Assignment work therefore offers the consultancy firm scope for *developing new products and services*.

The exchanges between consultancy firm and client provide an insight to the personnel management and direction of consulting firms. The consultant is the medium whereby value is conveyed from consultancy to client; in fairly prosaic terms, the consultant is the product. Now, products have a life cycle and so do particular consultant specialisations. The consultancy offerings of today, for example, have only a little in common with those of 30 years ago. But 30 years could easily be the span of the career of a consultant. In that time they have to make sure they remain an attractive product to be marketed by their employer and bought by their clients. This means keeping up to date and maintaining special skills attractive to a market which has the funds to buy them. Consultancy is a profession where there can be individual obsolescence.

Between individual consultant and consultancy firm

All consultants or prospective consultants at some time or other consider whether they should work as sole practitioner or join a firm of consultants. This decision can be illuminated by considering the exchange of values between the consultant and consultancy firm.

What the individual gets out of joining a consultancy is more than remuneration. Many become consultants to obtain a practical post-graduate qualification in business and thereby hope to enhance their value and attractiveness to future employers.

Whilst employed as a consultant, the individual gains by developing the following:

- *Consulting skills*: as should be obvious from the contents of this book, consulting is a process which demands particular skills, and a period of work as a consultant develops these.
- *Technical competence*: larger consultancy practices may take individuals with little specialist knowledge or experience, but with high potential, and develop them. In all firms the individual should aim to develop their specialist ability. A former colleague who had recently left consultancy remarked that he had forgotten how much administration was involved in line management. Consultancy allows specialist skills to be built up by concentrated experience. An advantage of working in a group of consultants is that it exposes the consultant to other specialisations. Because of this it is possible in a firm of consultants to work on projects near the periphery of your expertise and thereby broaden it.
- *Sectoral experience*: a consultant will work with a variety of clients; they will thus experience a far wider range of business environments and commercial sectors than if they were to be employed as an executive over the same period.

It is worth noting that the character of consultancy in recent years has changed in respect of the length of time a consultant may spend working with any single client. It is a deliberate strategy amongst large consultancy practices nowadays to sell projects that require work years of consultancy input. This means that a consultant can be confined to a particular project for months, if not years. This does not provide the variety of experience that may have attracted the consultant into the profession. This phenomenon is not limited to large firms either; I recently met a consultant working in a 20 consultant practice, who had been engaged with the same client and project for more than three years.

More variety is available at senior levels, but even here, partners in large practices may find themselves wholly engaged with a single major client.

What the consultancy gets from the individual consultant is the following:

- The *fee income* they generate by working for clients.
- Their *knowledge*: this could be put to use among other consultants, through training and so on, thereby developing a greater in-house capability.
- Scope for *business development*: consultants with previous work experience will have their own network of contacts affording possible scope for promotion of the consultancy practice among them.

For individuals new to consultancy, there appear to be at least three stages in their career development within the firm:

A career in consultancy

(i)   *To do operating work.* At the start of their fee earning work, consul-
      tants will not be very choosy about the work they do – they will be
      happy to gain experience and learn their craft as a consultant.
(ii) *To do interesting operating work.* With increasing experience and
      growing confidence consultants will try to be more selective about the
      assignments they undertake.
(iii) *To develop into functions other than operating consultant.* A consul-
      tancy needs people to work in business development and managing the
      practice, and these tasks may take up a considerable amount of time
      of experienced consultants.

Not all consultants have the ability or desire to move on to stage (iii). This,
together with the remarks about individual obsolescence on p. 206 means
that *long-term careers in consultancy firms are the exception rather than the
rule*. The reasons are that firstly, many people enter consultancy with the
intention of leaving after three or four years, which they do. Secondly, for
economic reasons there is considerable pressure for individuals to move on
or move out. As people get older, their salary expectations become higher;
a 32-year-old consultant is cheaper than a 42-year-old one, and if both have
much the same value to the practice, there is the economic incentive to
replace expensive people with cheaper equivalents. The alternative is for the
longer-serving individual to increase their value, as a specialist, as a business
developer, or as a consultant manager, but this is not always possible.

A new consultant entering a consultancy firm should therefore carefully
consider what their next job might be, and when the 'exit windows' occur as
illustrated in Figure 10.3.

Lest all of this sounds very depressing, it is reassuring that many, if not most
of the top people in consultancy firms entered with the expectation that they
would spend only a short period in the profession.

The sole practitioner has the advantages of freedom of action and (potentially) making a lot more money than their employed counterpart. The
advantages of entering a firm of consultants, however, are:

- working with other professionals: it can be very lonely being a sole practitioner;
- training: if you are new to consultancy it may be better to understand how
  the business works in an environment where there is existing consultancy
  expertise;
- avoidance of administration: as a sole practitioner you need to do all your
  own administration;
- avoidance of feast or famine: a sole practitioner has to secure his contracts
  and then carry them out. This often leads to periods of alternate feast and

Figure 10.3 *Exit windows*

Exit window	Years after start	Comments
1	2–4	Will have learned basic craft of consultancy and reached point of diminishing returns in operating experience.
2	3–7	Should have taken on project management role, together with business development and internal management roles. Staying in consultancy beyond this point may make jobs outside consultancy more difficult to find.
3	7 +	Career options become fewer and may be limited to specialist or quasi-consultancy roles.

famine; whilst operating, he is not selling and thus when the present contract comes to an end, he has no income whilst he tries to secure the next one;
- scope for professional growth: the client is buying the reputation of a consulting firm as well as the individual consultant. As remarked above, this gives rather more scope for individuals to operate at the limits of their expertise or in new business sectors.

Between client and individual consultant

Although it may be the consultancy firm that wins a contract, it will be the individual consultant who carries it out. The client will form an opinion about the consultancy from the individual's performance of the project and it is the individual who is adding value to the client in exchange for the firm's fees. What the client will be looking for from its consultant is specialist knowledge, past experience and knowhow relevant to the issues being addressed. The client will rely on the consultancy firm to provide a consultant (or consultant team) who has these in the right areas.

It follows that if you want to be a consultant, you have to have something worth selling. It can thus be very difficult for generalists to enter the field of consultancy.

From the consultant's point of view, the value of being a consultant arises from doing projects for clients. This enables them to practise and enlarge their expertise in various sectors.

Even in the best managed consulting organisations there are periods when a consultant (like an actor) is occasionally 'resting' between projects. This can be very trying for new consultants and illustrates the importance of the point made above: notwithstanding all the internal virtues of a consultancy firm, the greatest benefit to consultants is drawn from the work they do for clients.

The idea of exchanges of value is thus very helpful in understanding consultancy and the role of the consultant in it. A summary of the key points relevant to a consultant's career is shown in Figure 10.4.

Figure 10.4 *Career considerations*

1 If you want to become a consultant, you must have an expertise prospective clients wish to buy. This may be focused on technical expertise or knowledge of a commercial sector, and will be embodied in your knowledge, experience and knowhow.
2 If you plan to join, or are in, a consulting firm, consider your long-term future. If you do not foresee your role developing as a renowned expert, business developer or manager, does the firm offer you a long-term career? If not, what are the appropriate exit points for you?
3 Decide what you want out of your consultancy experience to add value to you on the job market. What does it imply in terms of operating and other tasks?
4 What is the right environment to achieve these objectives? You need to decide whether you are able and wish to become a sole practitioner, or whether you should join a firm and if so, whether it should be large or small.

The practice environment

Management consultancy firms suffer from many of the shortcomings of professional practices in general and have a few specialised problems of their own, too. This section is addressed to all who are undergoing the culture shock of entering a consultancy firm. The difficulties are more apparent in large firms so I will concentrate on them, but the same issues will apply to some extent to the small firm. They are explained in the assertions below.

Consultants are impossible to manage

Or at least very difficult. This is because contrary behaviours are required from consultants:

- as consultants they are meant to be independent and make recommendations based on their own evaluations;
- by contrast, as members of a consulting firm, they need to follow the rules and guidelines established within the firm and to accept direction from the management.

The ideal therefore is a conforming individualist. In practice what happens is that in a firm of 100 consultants there will always be 99 prepared to question the decisions of the hundredth, and to tell them how things could be better.

A consultancy is an army in which the lowest rank is colonel

People entering consultancy generally do so from distinguished careers to date; they will have been outstanding in their previous positions. A consultancy firm, however is made up of people all of whom have similarly distinguished careers. Newcomers can have difficulty in adjusting to the fact that they are not the exceptional people they might have been in their previous employment. Furthermore, specialists whose advice has previously been unquestioned can be unsettled by the need to justify their conclusions or rewrite reports when subject to the quality assurance procedures in a consultancy firm.

A good consultant is not necessarily a good manager

As noted in Chapter **1**, the specialist tasks of a professional can easily crowd out the managerial ones. It is unusual, even at the most senior levels of any professional practice, to find individuals whose task is solely management; they will still have client relationships and perhaps operational responsibilities. Those charged with management will therefore not be as preoccupied with it as their counterparts outside the professions.

Moreover, the qualities of a first-class consultant are not the same as those of a first-class manager. Promotions into managerial positions therefore have to be handled with care, as in all professions; in larger practices, it is sensible to have scope for career advance without the requirement of taking on managerial responsibilities – perhaps by providing parallel specialist and managerial grades.

The ideal has to be tempered by commercial necessity

Consultants like to broaden their experience by enlarging the range of work they do and industries they work in. Conversely, clients are more attracted to individuals who already have experience of dealing with their problem in their industry.

Similarly, consultants like to select the assignments they take so as to achieve personal development goals. The incidence of sales rarely meets these needs, however, and there is a strong economic incentive for firms to keep consultants engaged in fee-earning work.

In both these cases compromise is necessary, and for the new consultant particularly it means that from time to time he has to do assignments which are far from his ideal. Happily, most find that once they have more experience and seniority they are able to be more selective.

A final exhortation

Consultants sell their time for a price; the price is determined by the value of what they can achieve in that time. The rarer and more in demand your specialist knowledge, the higher the price it can command. Therefore, never forget what it is as a consultant you are selling to your clients or to your employer. It may be your skills as a technical specialist or your knowledge of a particular market or industrial sector, or within a consultancy practice, it may be a particular strength in research, product development, business development or management. Whatever it is, take care to husband and enhance your value, by recognising where it lies and adding selectively to your knowledge and experience.

Afterword

As this edition appears only shortly before the year 2000, it seems appropriate to conclude with some millennial observations. Whilst this book is about the conduct and skills of consultancy, I conclude with some comments about its future context.

1 **The particular value of a practice will be judged according to how well it captures individual learning and makes it corporately available.** Knowledge management will become a key, explicit process within consultancy practices. The wide availability of suitable computer hardware and software means that all sizes of consultancy can and must, as a matter of course, collect, organise, and retrieve the learning they acquire from marketing, operational, and other activities. No longer will it be enough, therefore, simply to 'rebadge' somebody as a consultant and send them off to earn fees from day 1 of their joining a practice. Consultancy firms must add value to their consultants both through formal and informal training, and by having their own infrastructure (organisational and physical) that allows the synergies of consultants working together to be realised. The esteem in which firms are held, both by their clients and by their prospective employees, will depend on how well they do this.

2 **The current convergence of consultancy and services will reverse.** Services are pre-defined offerings (although in practice they will be tailored to the situation) whilst consultancy is problem orientated. Much of the work that is done by consultancy practices can be separated into a problem diagnosis phase (consultancy) followed by a service to address the problems diagnosed. Outsourcing activities in consultancy practices have also expanded, and these are of a service nature too. Similarly, many service organisations have sought to add consultancy to their portfolio of revenue earning activities – for instance, in engineering, IT and other similar sectors. But service provision is not the same as consultancy, and there will be a marked distinction between those who are 'service deliverers', and consultants. Service deliverers will be expert in their own specialist areas, whilst consultants will be skilled in making the link between business need, and the nature of the project or service required to meet it.

The distinction may become reflected organisationally in consultancy practices, with 'consultants' responsible for account management and diagnosis, bringing in teams of specialist service deliverers as their clients require them.

3 **Skills in implementation will be an increasingly important differentiator.**
Consultants are well known for being long on diagnosis, but short on
action. In part this is due to their role – by definition they rarely have the
executive power to command action in the client environment. But over
recent years, a facility to act quickly has become an important competitive quality in business, and a consultancy practice that can help clients
implement lasting change well will be increasingly valued.

The service deliverers referred to above will therefore need to have excellent implementation skills.

4 **Skills in putting together effective alliances will become more important.**
Organisational boundaries are increasingly permeable as we reach the
end of the century and, in the same way that organisations have sought
help from outside, consultants themselves will be faced with client
demands that they are unable to meet alone. The capacity to put together
alliances (of which, of course, the client is part) in an effective way will
become more important.

There are perhaps two comments about these predictions that can be made
with confidence. The first is that – like most predictions – in detail they are
almost certainly wrong. The second is, they show that consultancy is far from
mature. The world of consultancy will continue to change and I hope that
you and your clients, like me, will get not only great value but also enormous
fun from being part of it.

References and further reading

References

Beckhard, R. and Harris, R.T. *Organisation Transitions: Managing Complex Change* (1987 Addison Wesley).

Blake, R.R. and Mouton, J.S. *Managing Intergroup Conflict in Industry* (1964 Gulf Publishing).

Handy, C. *Understanding Organisations* (1981 Penguin Books).

Harrison, R. 'Understanding your organization's character' (*Harvard Business Review*, May–June 1972).

Hersey, P., K.H. Blanchard and Natemeyer, W.E. *Situational Leadership, Perception and the Impact of Power* (1978 Centre for Leadership Study).

Institute of Management Consultants *Code of Professional Conduct*.

Jay, A. 'Rate yourself as a client'. (*Harvard Business Review*, July–August 1977).

Schmidt, W. and Johnston, A. 'Continuum of Consultancy Styles' (1969 Occasional Paper of the University of Southern California Business Administration Department).

Further reading

Rather than provide a comprehensive bibliography, I thought it more useful to provide a focused guide to further reading.

Management Consulting: a Guide to the Profession edited by M. Kubr (1986 ILO). Provides a broad conceptual framework for management consultancy.

Ethical Business in Britain: Recommendations for Organisational Practice London Society of Chartered Accountants (1996).

Figuring Things Out: A Trainer's Guide to Needs and Task Analysis Zemke & Kramlinger (1982 Addison-Wesley). Do not be misled by the title; this is a first-class guide to data collection for many other purposes too.

What They Don't Teach You at Harvard Business School Mark M. McCormack (1986 Bantam Books). A deservedly popular guide to dealing with clients.

Organisational Behaviour: Its Data, First Principles and Applications; Kelly (1980 Richard D. Irwin). This is a well-written textbook which should be read to balance the views of those who have a predominantly economic view of organisation.

The Top Consultant Calvert Markham (1994 Kogan Page). I wrote this second book on consultancy for readers who wanted to explore issues of selling, operating and managing consultancy in more detail than covered here.

Economist Pocket Style Book (1986 Economist Publications)

Video films

Melrose Films has produced two videos which are particularly relevant to management consultants.

Client and Professional – Working Together (1989) is a drama concerning the service delivered by a professional to clients.

Managing Change (1991) is a fictional case study illustrating the issues involved in change in organisations.

Both are supplied with supporting material.

Appendices

Appendices

Appendix 1   The continuum of consultancy behaviours

Listening

The power of this seemingly simple – but too little used – skill is consider-able. Counsellors are themselves frequently baffled by clients who thank them profusely for their help, when the client has actually done all the work of sorting out the problem. The act of listening can make possible a quality and clarity of thought which enables one individual to bring their full experience to bear on the issue that troubles another.

Reflecting

Reflecting – or active listening – may involve the consultant's mirroring of the client's ideas so that the client views their own thoughts more freshly and objectively. Phrases like 'What you are saying ...', 'Let me see if I understand . . .' may signal this kind of consultant behaviour.

Clarifying

The consultant may go further by rephrasing some of the client's comments so that the issue is stated more sharply and precisely. Here the introductory phrases might be 'You seem to be saying that ...' or 'Is this what you mean?'

Interpreting

One step beyond clarification is the interpretation of what the client may mean. Here the consultant tries to express what may lie beneath the words themselves – or to put together the implications of several statements. It is expressing what may be the client's intentions clearly, but without evaluation.

Probing

Here the consultant may, through questions, direct the client's attention to aspects of their experience which they have not expressed as yet. This consultant behaviour again assumes that the client has the basic elements necessary to solve the problem. The consultant's function, therefore, is to help bring this experience to the front of the client's mind and focus their attention on it.

Providing new data

At this point the consultant begins to add ideas and information which are not in the client's direct experience. It may be data about new dimensions of the problem or its context. It may be information which the consultant has collected through a survey or research. The consultant's goal is clearly to expand the client's knowledge and view of the issues at stake and the boundaries within which those issues must be resolved.

Identifying options for action

Once the problem is clear – whether clarified by consultant or client – the task is to bring into focus the range of actions open to the client. It is the time when a consultant might say, 'It seems that you have the choice of doing this . . . or this . . . or this'. One of the consultant's most valuable contributions is often to expand the range of alternatives which a client considers. Here is one point where quite clearly two heads are better than one.

Proposing criteria for evaluation of alternatives

Sometimes a client has a clear picture of the problem and his possible courses of action – but he is not sure which is the best solution. Here the consultant can help by suggesting criteria to use in evaluation and to help the client arrange these criteria in some order of priority.

Recommending

There are times when a consultant's particular experience tells them that one of the client's potential actions is the right one. Having made certain that the client knows about all their options, the consultant may want to recommend one – and give reasons for doing so. The recommendation may be mild or forceful. In any case, however, the consultant must bear in mind the fact that the decision must be the client's – as it is the client who must live with the consequences.

Prescribing

This is an extreme form of recommending, in which the consultant assumes the role of expert. In effect saying to the client, 'If this is your problem, here is your solution'. The consultant may not even bother to list alternatives or go through the diagnostic stages with the client' acting as if his experience is so clearly more relevant than the client's that the weight of authority should clearly be his.

Planning the implementation

The ultimate use of consultant experience occurs when not only does the consultant prescribe what should be done, but develops the detailed action steps the client should take to carry out this prescribed solution to the problem.

This Appendix is taken from A Continuum of Consultancy Styles *by W. Schmidt and A. Johnston (1969), with kind permission of the University of Southern California.*

Appendix 2 Techniques for analysing change

Two techniques particularly useful in analysing change, because they help in deciding the action required to achieve it, are:

- force field analysis;
- Pareto's principle.

These can be used jointly and are described below, together with a further method which I call 'individual performance analysis'. Change also can create conflict, and a way of looking at this is discussed.

Force field analysis

Force field analysis (FFA) is a complicated name for a simple yet powerful technique. It presupposes that any situation is in a state of equilibrium at a given moment and that the forces for change balance those opposing change. This is illustrated in Figure A2.1.

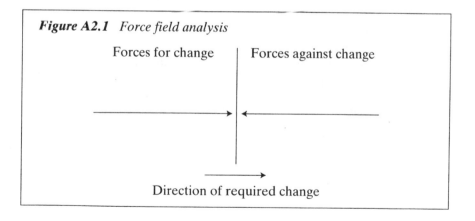

Figure A2.1 *Force field analysis*

Forces for change | Forces against change

Direction of required change

The steps involved in carrying out FFA are:

1 Define the nature of the change required. This needs to be done with care and may involve breaking down change into a number of factors. For example, the key change may be to make more profit, but there will be a large number of items which contribute to this, and it would be more helpful to analyse these. Thus, reducing reject rate, increasing selling price, increasing work rate, or reducing absenteeism could each be addressed using FFA, as each should contribute to increased profitability.

2 Identify what the forces are on each side. This is an activity which is probably best done with client staff, not only because of their knowledge of the situation but also because their participation should help in their recognising and accepting the need for specific changes.

At this stage it is important to identify all significant forces and some of these will be human as well as technical. For example, a significant restraining force on increasing selling prices may be the opposition of the managing director.

3 Determine the relative magnitude of the forces. Plainly, change can be more effectively accomplished by altering the more significant forces. Almost certainly, too, there will be a number of major forces about which you can do nothing, and it is necessary to recognise which they are.

4 Determine an action plan based on changing the balance of forces, i.e., increasing those which favour change and reducing those which oppose it. Increasing some forces for change may create a reaction, however, so avoid increasing those which make people feel threatened or pressured.

FFA helps to elicit the important factors influencing change and provides a basis for planning action. As an illustration, consider the case of a smoker who wants to reduce the number of cigarettes he smokes each day.

Step 1: Define the nature of the change required; this can be quantified – it might be, say, to cut from 50 to 10 cigarettes per day (but would probably be best to reduce to nil).

Step 2: Identify the forces on each side: Figure A2.2 lists the forces one group came up with.

Step 3: Identify significant forces you can do something about, and eliminate those you cannot. This step depends on who 'you' are: if you are the Government your capacity will be different from that if you are the subject yourself. So, if you are, say, a close friend or spouse of someone you wish to cut down smoking, you cannot do anything about advertising or the price of cigarettes.

Step 4: Determine an action plan. Increasing pressure to stop smoking may create increased resistance so you need to be more subtle. Much depends on whether the individual wants to reduce smoking, but finds it difficult, or whether he has no interest in it at all. Assuming the former, you might have a bet with him. 'I bet you £10 you cannot reduce your smoking to 10 per day for one month'. This could harness the desire to show self-control.

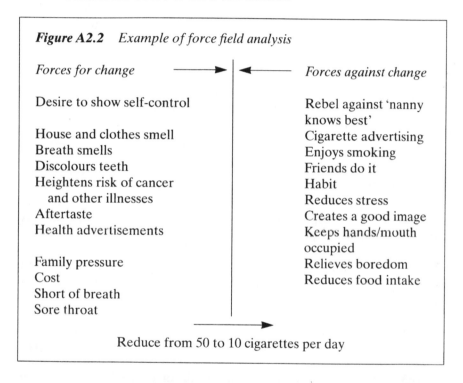

Figure A2.2   *Example of force field analysis*

Forces for change ⟶	◀ Forces against change
Desire to show self-control	Rebel against 'nanny knows best'
House and clothes smell	Cigarette advertising
Breath smells	Enjoys smoking
Discolours teeth	Friends do it
Heightens risk of cancer and other illnesses	Habit
Aftertaste	Reduces stress
Health advertisements	Creates a good image
	Keeps hands/mouth occupied
Family pressure	Relieves boredom
Cost	Reduces food intake
Short of breath	
Sore throat	

Reduce from 50 to 10 cigarettes per day

Reducing the forces against change might be achieved by using an anti-smoking chewing gum. This not only keeps your mouth occupied but reduces the pleasure from smoking.

If, on the other hand, the individual does not want to reduce the number of cigarettes smoked, the problem is not that of getting him to cut down, but getting him to *want* to cut down in the first place. This might involve a change of attitude, a topic covered in Chapter **4**.

Pareto's principle

Pareto was an Italian economist, who, examining the distribution of wealth, showed that a minority of the population owned most of the wealth. The graph in Figure A2.3 illustrates this distribution, plotting the cumulative proportion of wealth owned compared with the percentage of the population owning it, ranked from most to least wealthy.

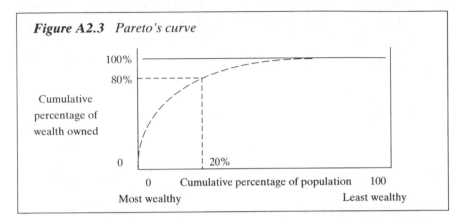

Figure A2.3 *Pareto's curve*

The curve, as drawn, shows that the 20 per cent of the most wealthy individuals own 80 per cent of the wealth. So, if the Government wished to raise a tax based on wealth, it would be more fruitful to concentrate its attention on the 20 per cent most wealthy than to put in a lot more effort to raise tax from the remaining 80 per cent.

This kind of distribution is replicated in many situations and can be defined as a general principle (which, for convenience, we will call Pareto's principle):

- *In any series of elements to be controlled, a selected small fraction, in terms of number of elements, always accounts for a large fraction, in terms of effect.*

The comments on wealth above also illustrate some other names by which this (rather complicated!) definition is known:

- the 80/20 rule;
- the law of diminishing returns.

Examples of Pareto's principle abound in everyday life. A small range of causes account for the majority of fatal road accidents. Addressing the major causes (e.g., drunken driving) will help in getting value for money in terms of road safety. A small number of brewing companies produce most of the beer drunk. A small range of faults will create the bulk of rejects through quality control. A small percentage of customers will account for the greatest proportion of sales, and so on. This principle is replicated in several management theories – for example:

- *Management by objectives*: managers are required to identify 'key result areas' – those areas of their work where high performance is going to have the greatest impact on their results.
- *Critical success factors*: selection of the information needed to support managerial activities should focus on success factors. In most industries there are usually three to six factors which determine success and these key jobs must be done exceedingly well for a company to be successful.

This latter example draws us to the relevance of Pareto's principle to the consultant; it could be restated thus:

- *In a consulting project there will be a small number of key factors which the consultant must heed and direct if it is to be successful.*

The consultant therefore needs to identify the key dynamics involved – those aspects which will have a disproportionate effect on the outcome; for example:

- those elements of production operations where the greatest savings can be made for given investment;
- the opinion leaders who have to be convinced of the recommendations;
- those tasks which, when well performed, will significantly increase the consultant's credibility.

Once the consultant has identified the key dynamics, he should use them to decide what needs to be done and to set his priorities.

Individual performance analysis

Force field analysis and Pareto's principle are generally applicable to situations of change, as they can be used to consider the technical aspects as well as the difficulties of dealing with people. Individual performance analysis combines a number of ideas to help in determining how the performance of an individual or group of individuals can be improved.

The analysis is based on two propositions:

(i) Individual or group performance is a function of how well a series of separate tasks is performed; as well as technical tasks these can also be process or managerial ones – for example, communicating with others, planning, motivating staff and so on.
(ii) The quality of performance of each task will be a function of:

- how clearly and well the task is defined;
- the individual's ability to do the task;
- the individual's motivation to do the task.

Change frequently involves new or different tasks, determining new priorities, learning new skills, doing things in a different way and so on. Individual performance analysis is helpful in situations in which performance is not reaching the standards required. Proposition (i) says that these new tasks and activities must first be identified, and proposition (ii) suggests that if satisfactory performance is not being achieved, it is because:

- people do not know what they have to do; or
- they are not able to do it; or
- they do not want to do it.

This can be rendered as an equation:

performance = direction $\times$ ability $\times$ motivation

All three components are required; however well motivated I am, it is improbable I shall win the Olympic high-jump championship. On the other hand, although I may be capable of preparing a first-class report on a particular topic, if I am not interested or have other priorities, the report may be barely adequate, or late. Finally, I can be willing and able to do the wrong jobs very efficiently, but that does not lead to effective performance. For example, a department may produce a comprehensive monthly report, putting in a lot of effort to produce it on time, but if none of the recipients reads it, the task is efficiently done but totally useless.

Problems of performance attributed to poor motivation are in practice often caused by deficiencies in ability or lack of clarity about the nature or priority of particular tasks.

- For example, some years ago I was invited to advise on a problem in a manufacturing plant. 'The difficulty', said the production director, 'is that although we have installed new processing equipment we simply are not reaching the levels of productivity we expected'. He wondered whether there was a problem with the first-line supervisors.

   I had a series of meetings with the supervisors, and it emerged that they were all concerned. What is more, they knew how productivity could be raised. The problem was not one of motivation or ability – it was that the important tasks of communication between supervisors and management were not being given the right priority.

   The assignment opened up channels of formal and informal communication between supervisors and management. Shortly afterwards productivity was 50 per cent higher than before the assignment.

Analysing conflict

There will be occasions when conflict arises – or at least is possible – as a result of a change project. Blake and Mouton (1964) suggested that when conflict occurs, people will believe that:

- conflict is inevitable and agreement is impossible; or
- conflict is not inevitable, yet agreement is impossible; or
- although there is conflict, agreement is possible.

These views will influence how people behave depending on the stakes involved, i.e., the importance they attach to the outcome. When the stakes are low, behaviour will be passive, but when they are high, behaviour will be very active. These types of behaviour are illustrated in Figure A2.4.

Figure A2.4 *Conflict analysis*

	Conflict inevitable, agreement impossible	Conflict not inevitable, yet agreement not possible	Although there is conflict, agreement is possible	Behaviour
High stakes	Win-lose power struggle	Withdrawal	Problem–solving	Active
Moderate stakes	Third-party judgement	Isolation	Splitting the difference	
Low stakes	Fate	Indifference or ignorance	Peaceful coexistence	Passive

The 'worst' outcome of conflict is the win-lose power struggle, which is energy-sapping to both sides and can for the winner be a pyrrhic victory anyhow.

A point of significance to note about the model is that, when faced by conflict, it is what people *think* to be the case which determines how they behave.

So, if participants *think* the stakes are high, and *believe* conflict is inevitable and agreement is impossible, then the result will be a win-lose power struggle. Similarly, you can infer these beliefs if a win-lose power struggle is taking place. If a win-lose power struggle is to be averted or stopped, then it is important that the beliefs of the participants about the nature of the conflict are changed – for example, that the stakes appear to be worth less, or that conflict is not inevitable or that agreement is possible. In this way the behaviours of the protagonists will become less destructive as they are modified as beliefs change.

Almost inevitably a consultant will be faced by conflict from time to time. Understanding the nature of the conflict as illustrated by the model can help in planning tactics to use to diminish disruptive consequences.

Appendix 3   Selected data collection and analysis techniques

This appendix includes some data collection and analysis techniques which I have found useful. They are:

- paired comparisons;
- repertory grid;
- critical incident;
- Delphi technique.

Paired comparisons

Paired comparisons is a means of producing a rank order of items. It involves comparing each item with each of the others in turn and assessing whether it is of more, equal, or less importance according to a predetermined scale. As an example, imagine you have to collect views on the relative importance of a number of consultancy skills – for example, for assessing consultants. These skills might be:

Technical knowledge
Project management
Report writing
Presenting
Persuasion
Data analysis
Commerciality.

Figure A3.1 shows a matrix for collecting this data which each judge completes. It is, in fact, half a matrix (because you do not have to compare B with A once you have compared A with B).

Figure A3.1 *Relative importance of consulting skills*

	PM	RW	Pre	Pers	DA	Comm	(d)	Total
Technical knowledge	2(a)	2	2	2	2	0(b)	10	10
Project management	(0)	2	2	2	2	0	8	8
Report writing	(0)	2	0	2	0		4	4
Presenting	(0)	0	2	0			2	2
Persuasion	(4)	2	1(c)				3	7
Data analysis	(0)	0					0	0
[Commerciality] (11)	X							11

Key points about the matrix are:

- Skills are written against each row leaving out the last skill. Then the same skills are written across the top in the same order as down the side, but starting with the second item. (In this way you avoid comparing a skill with itself.) Thus Figure A3.1 does not strictly need 'commerciality' at the bottom of the list, although it is included there for scoring purposes, and 'technical knowledge' is missed from the columns.
- Award a 2 if the row is more important than the column. Award 1 if they are equal and 0 if the column is more important than the row. Thus, because technical knowledge is ranked more important than project management, box (a) has a 2 in it, but because technical knowledge is ranked less important than commerciality, box (b) has a 0 in it. Further down, persuasion has been ranked equal with commerciality, so box (c) has 1 in it. Note that it is not necessary to be consistent; for example, although commerciality has been ranked *equal* to persuasion, project management has been ranked *more* important than persuasion and *less* important than commerciality.

- Scoring is as follows:

(i)   Add up the scores in each row (the sums are shown in column (d)).
(ii) Add up each column, but take the reverse of each score in a box— thus a 2 becomes a 0, 1 remains 1 and 0 becomes 2. These column scores are shown in brackets against the row they relate to.
(iii) Add the row and column scores together. The item with the highest score is ranked highest and so on.

The result in the example is therefore:

Most important   Commerciality
                  Technical knowledge

> Project management
> Persuasion
> Report writing
> Presenting

Least important Data analysis

Advantages

- It is easier to do than by trying to rank all items in one go.
- It allows judges to be inconsistent.
- It enables you to combine the views of several judges by adding their scores.

Disadvantages

- It looks complicated initially and needs careful selling to the client; sometimes the reaction may be that it is too complicated, but once they are familiar, clients seem very happy to use the charts.
- Take care to set up the chart correctly – one item out of place ruins it.
- The scoring is a little difficult to follow at first.

Operating hints

- Be on hand to help client staff to fill in the chart on the first occasion the use one.
- Do not let the client staff do the scoring unless they really want to.

Applications

Paired comparisons is a means of getting from a judge or judges not only a ranking but also a relative weighting of the elements under assessment.

One application is in job evaluation, where it can be used to rank whole jobs. A further application is to use paired comparisons for weighting factors. For example, in choosing the location of a new head office, a company may want to take into account the following factors:

- access to motorway systems and airport;
- access to mainline stations;
- secretarial and clerical staff locally available;
- office rents;
- close to chairman's country house;
- cheap housing for executives available;
- grants and other incentives available.

Not all these factors will be equally important, however, and a weighting can be attached by using the paired comparison method. Data on the relative merits of each prospective location could then be collected and compared for the more important locations.

Repertory grid

The repertory grid is a method of finding out how people look at things – the factors that they use in making judgements about significant differences between them. These factors are called 'constructs' and the objects to which they are applied are called 'elements'. One way in which constructs can be elicited is to invite judges to take three of the elements and to look for the similarities between two which distinguish them from the third. An example will illustrate this.

Suppose you want to learn about Harriet's views on public service; the elements you might take could be a number of jobs – say:

- Fireman
- Nurse
- Classical pianist
- Solicitor
- Dustman
- Carpenter.

Taking three of these elements – say, fireman, nurse and dustman – you would ask Harriet what two of these have in common which distinguishes them from the third. For these three she might make the constructs:

(i)   Works indoors – works outdoors.
(ii) Job held by mostly men – job held by mostly women.
(iii) Concerned with matters of life and death – not concerned with matters of life and death.
(iv) Long training required – little training required.
(v)   24 hours-a-day job – day work only.

And so on.

These differences, however, need to be ordered—they do not tell us much about Harriet's views on public service. So we might ask, 'In terms of their value to society, taking these jobs in groups of three, what distinguishes one job from the other two?'

Harriet, with some justice, might argue that her answers for these jobs would be the same as the list above. But you might want to penetrate a little further; you can do this by asking, 'Is this construct important and if so, why?' This could yield further constructs. So, applying this question to point (i) above – working indoors or outdoors – Harriet might comment, 'Working outdoors is less comfortable than working indoors', so another construct, the comfort of the working environment, has been generated.

Similarly, she may think that having to provide a service 24 hours a day results in having to work unsociable hours, which is another construct.

Another means of eliciting more constructs from those initially listed is to ask, 'Which construct is more important, and why?' Of those above, Harriet might select point (iii), because the preservation of life is of paramount importance.

All this is telling us a great deal about Harriet and her view of public service. Having an idea of the theory, how does the consultant use this method in practice?

Informal use

I use the repertory grid concept quite frequently in interviews when trying to find out about values in organisations. For example, if I want to know how managers judge their subordinates, I ask a question such as:

- 'Think about the best person in your team and the worst. Imagine them standing side by side and tell me about the differences between them in terms of their performance'.

The response to this question will explain quite a lot about how performance is judged in the organisation. The same question repeated at interviews with other members of top management should begin to show some consensus. This data can then be used, for example, to see if it is consistent with business objectives, or with the views of subordinates on the ways they are passed.

There are two key points in the phrasing of the question. The first is the choice of element, which in this case is the people in the manager's own team. The second is the context in which distinctions are being made – their performance. Changing either of these will affect the data elicited, as can be inferred from the table below.

Element	In terms of
People	Looks
Factory	Pollution
Product	Safety

Salesmen	Sales performance
Company	Quality of employee relations

Each of these combinations will give the views of the judge on different matters. People in terms of looks will yield different constructs from 'people in terms of safety'. Where you wish to combine views of different judges, a more analytical approach is better.

The analytical approach

The analytical approach uses the form illustrated in Figure A3.2, and its use is described by reference to the earlier example covering public services.

(i) Write each element (dustman, carpenter, etc.) on to a separate piece of card and number the cards (in this case 1 to 6).
(ii) Take three cards (either at random or in predetermined combinations of number, e.g., 123).
(iii) Ask the question, in terms of their social value, what characteristics do two of the jobs share which distinguishes them from the third?
(iv) These are written in the boxes at each end (as shown in Figure A3.2).

There are pitfalls in doing this:

- Double constructs – e.g., if the box on the left says 'works outdoors' and that on the right 'works with people'. These are separate constructs and should be on separate lines.
- Vagueness or ambiguity in the words used.
- Irrelevance – there are many similarities and differences, but the ones of interest are those in terms of their social value.

(v) Between the two constructs is a column to enter the score for each element, and the next step is to score all the elements for that construct. Shown is a five-point scale for each construct; the extreme described on the left-hand end scores 1 and that on the right scores 5. The score for each element depends where it lies between the two extremes, and the score is entered in the column for each element, for example, the first construct is 'works outdoors' – 'works indoors'. If element 1 is 'Fireman', it might score 2 as the work is mainly outdoors, and this score would be entered in column 1.

(If you are using this approach with a group, they may find it hard to understand the method of scoring. I simplify this by getting them to imagine the scale left to right on the table and laying out the cards with the elements written on them along it (see Figure A3.3). They can then simply transcribe the score from the card's position.)

Figure A3.2 *Repertory grid: form*

(Score 1)							*(Score 5)*
In terms of their social value what do the pair of jobs have in common?	1	2	3	4	5	6	In terms of social value what makes the single job different?
Works outdoors							Works indoors
Works primarily with people							Works primarily with things
Deals with matters of life or death							Deals with matters of little moment

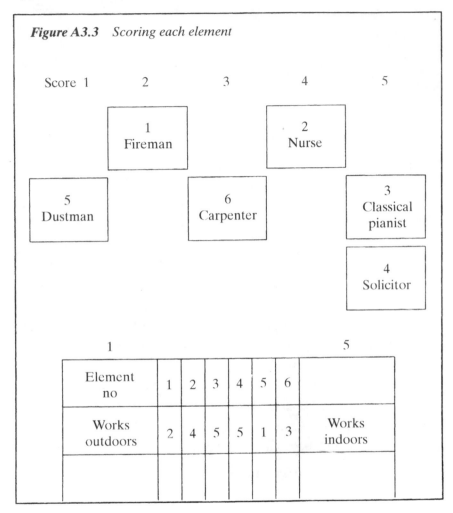

Figure A3.3 *Scoring each element*

Score 1   2   3   4   5

Element no	1	2	3	4	5	6	
Works outdoors	2	4	5	5	1	3	Works indoors

(vi) Finally, you need to assess which are the really important or relevant constructs. This can be done using the scoring, as follows:

  (a) Rate the elements according to overall assessment. In the example, therefore, Harriet would rate each job according to its social value, scoring 1 for low and 5 for high. (This ranking could be done by paired comparison if required.) The overall assessment is shown in the bottom row of Figure A3.4.

  (b) See how well the overall score correlates with the score for the elements under each construct. A simple way of doing this is to sum up the differences in score. The smaller the difference, the more relevant the construct. In Figure A3.4 the differences for each construct are shown in the row marked (a). In each case, there are quite large differences, so there does not appear to be a correlation.

(c) Some constructs will be written down in reverse order – i.e., the aspect of high social value will have been written on the left (e.g., 'deals with matters of life and death' in Figure A3.4), and this will have scored only 1. For constructs which have a very high score, reverse the scoring and repeat the process in (b) above. This has been done for the overall assessment in row (r); this ranks the overall assessment so that the highest score is 1 rather than 5. Again, the differences with the construct scores is shown for each in row (b). This shows that the construct 'deals with matters of life and death' correlates well (a low difference of a total of only 4). So Harriet believes that the social value of a job is strongly related to whether it deals with matters of life or death.

Applications of repertory grid

The repertory grid is a very powerful means of eliciting information from individuals about the way they look at things. Examples of its use are in:

- determining the factors to be used in a job evaluation system;
- carrying out attitude surveys;
- assessing the effectiveness of members of a public authority;
- training needs analysis;
- market research;
- quality control.

For example, it can be used to determine the core competencies required in consultants (mentioned under paired comparisons). Experienced consultant managers might be interviewed in a structured format, and asked to describe the contrast between high- and low-performing consultants. This would result in a series of defined key characteristics. The same group of consultant managers could then be asked to rank the characteristics in order of importance (using paired comparisons); this data would then be aggregated to form a view of the important skills for prospective consultants to have. The selection process would then be modified to take account of this; for example, if the ability to make effective presentations was deemed essential, prospective recruits might be required to make a presentation as part of the selection process. The appraisal system could also be modified to assess the key skills and training programmes developed to raise standards in the practice.

Critical incident technique

Like the repertory grid, this is a means of eliciting data from client staff about effective and ineffective behaviour. The data generated can be used in studies of job design, individual or group performance, selection and training and equipment design.

Figure A3.4 *Repretory grid: correlation*

(Score 1)   (Score 5)

In terms of their social value what do the pair of jobs have in common?		1	2	3	4	5	6	In terms of social value what makes the single job different?	Total Difference
Works outdoors	Element score	2	4	5	5	1	3	Works indoors	
	(a)	2	1	3	4	1	1		12
	(b)	–	3	1	–	3	1		8
Works primarily with people		4	1	2	1	4	5	Works primarily with things	
	(a)	–	4	–	–	2	3		9
	(b)	2	–	2	4	–	1		9
Deals with matters of life and death		1	1	5	4	5	4	Deals with matters of little moment	
	(a)	3	4	3	3	3	2		18
	(b)	1	–	1	1	1	–		4
Overall assessment		4	5	2	1	2	2		
	(r)	2	1	4	5	4	4		

It is most useful in situations when there is a lot of variety, ambiguity or flexibility and it is necessary to define what behaviour or circumstances lead to the best result.

The way this is done is to gather a number of 'experts' and collect data from them about critical incidents. A critical incident is an event which they observed as having a notably successful or unsuccessful outcome. It is best to describe the technique by means of an example.

Suppose a bank wishes to improve the quality of customer service amongst counter staff, the application of critical incident technique would be as follows:

(i) Gather together a group of counter staff, or their supervisors. It is important that the group have been able to observe ineffective and effective customer service and hence are 'experts' on it.
(ii) Collect information on critical incidents from them. These are descriptions of occasions they have observed effective or ineffective customer service, and you would ask for three pieces of information:

   • what the circumstances were;
   • what the member of counter staff did;
   • the outcome of what they did.

You can use a standard form to collect this data, and a completed example is shown in Figure A3.5.

Figure A3.5 *Critical incident form*

What were the circumstances?
A customer complained at the counter about the bank charges made to her account. She had become aware of them only when she had received her bank statement.

What did the member of counter staff do?
The teller explained the basis for charges, he looked at the bank statement and gave advice about how the customer might avoid them in future. He gave her a leaflet explaining bank charges and how to avoid them.

What was the outcome?
The customer was still unhappy about the unexpected bank charges but said, 'Thank you for your help, young man'.

Data on critical incidents does not have to encompass dramatic events – most of the events will be part of the routine of everyday work. The data will be collected in a discussion group (as in the present example) or you can ask the experts to note their observations down over a period. It is important, too, that effective and ineffective incidents are separated clearly.

(iii) The next step is to analyse the incidents. They provide a rich source of data and you could look for features under headings other than behaviour – for example:

Systems: bank charges levied without explanation or breakdown of their basis.

Behaviour: dealing with a complaint courteously, demonstrating knowledge of the basis of bank charges and how to avoid them.

In this case, both features might be relevant. The start of the analysis process is to write each feature of the incidents on to cards. (This helps in sorting them out later.) This is a task which can be done by the consultant either alone or in collaboration with the experts.

(iv) The cards can then be sorted into generically similar categories. This is a task that the experts should do. One method is to divide the experts into two groups which come up with different categories and then bring them together to combine their conclusions. In the example, therefore, customer service incidents might be categorised under:

- handling routine transactions;
- dealing with complaints;
- coping with failures in back-up systems;
- recognising when others need to get involved; and so on.

Figure A3.6 *Example of a behaviourally anchored rating system*

5	Demonstrates concern that customer has a complaint and energetically seeks to resolve it.
4	Listens sympathetically to complaint.
3	Listens passively to complaint.
2	Aggressive reaction to customer.
1	Gets into argument with customer.

(v) The behaviour in each of these categories can then be scaled according to their effectiveness. The scales created are sometimes called behaviourally anchored rating scales, or BARS. One such, on a five-point scale, is illustrated for 'dealing with complaints' in Figure A3.6.

The BARS or other scales are a major output of critical incident techniques. The example in Figure A3.6 could provide helpful input in assessing how well individual counter staff deal with complaints, or provide guidelines for training in handling complaints.

Delphi technique

The Delphi technique (named after the Oracle at Delphi renowned in classical times) was developed by the Rand Corporation in World War II. It is very useful in collecting data about complex or unclear situations from experts, who may have widely different viewpoints. It is therefore often used in planning, as a means of projecting the future. It has also been used as a method of problem solving. Examples of questions which might be addressed using the Delphi technique are:

- What will be the nature of customers' needs in retail banking in the next millenium?
- How will the transport choices of passengers change with increasing fuel costs?
- What education will be required to ensure a sufficient supply of knowledge scientists specialists in the next 15 years?

The approach is fairly laborious and should therefore be used only when the questions are of some moment.

In the Delphi technique the 'experts' are required to complete a series of questionnaires, each questionnaire being based on the responses to the previous one. There is thus no need for the experts to meet, and therefore it is possible to include experts from outside the client organisation or who are physically distant.

The technique consists of three stages, although each may involve more than one round of questionnaire:

(i) Establish the major responses to an initial open-ended question.
(ii) Determine the relative weighting of these responses.
(iii) Establish the reasons for experts' views which are significantly different from the norm.

A simple example illustrates how the technique works. Suppose you are planning a strategy for a food-processing company and you want to establish the impact of technology on food production over the next 10 to 20 years. First of all you would assemble a panel of experts – people who might reasonably be expected to have a view on this. Some of these will be in the client's firm, but there will be others, for example:

- customers of the client;
- manufacturers of processing and packaging equipment;
- competitors (who may of course take part only if they can share in the results of the study);
- food technologists;
- shippers.

The first questionnaire will be qualitative and ask questions around the theme:

- 'In your own area of business, what do you see to be the significant developments in technology which will affect food processing?'

Each member of the panel will give responses from their own viewpoint. For example:

- Customers (probably food distributors and retail outlets), will comment on consumer trends. For instance, the increased ownership of microwave ovens might result in increased demand for high-quality ready-made meals.
- Manufacturers of packaging equipment might predict that short batch runs will become cost-effective, thus allowing 'own label' brands to be produced for small customers.
- Food technologists could point to the use of genetic engineering in improving the production of synthetic food.
- Shippers might foresee new preservation techniques which make a greater variety of exotic fruit available.

And there will also be a host of other predictions.

The next questionnaire will seek the degree of agreement among experts in these matters. Figure A3.7 illustrates a portion of the questionnaire. At this stage the data collected is the degree of agreement with the statement. From this the strength of any prediction can be judged.

It is possible to have an intermediate stage which might categorise the statements and ask respondents to add others which might be prompted by this list. Next, you could ask for an assessment of the importance of each statement. The statements which were thought to be most important could then be assessed using the form in Figure A3.7.

Figure A3.7 *Example of extract from Delphi technique questionnaire (Part 1)*

Mark the following statements on a scale of 1–5 according to whether you agree strongly (1) or disagree strongly (5) with the statement. If you do not wish to comment, mark with zero.

4. Consumer trends	No comment	Strongly agree	Agree	Average	Disagree	Strongly disagree
4.1 Increasing demand for microwave oven ready meals	0	1	2	3	4	5
4.2 Trend to fresh food from frozen	0	1	2	3	4	5
4.3 Trend to frozen food from fresh	0	1	2	3	4	5
4.4	0	1	2	3	4	5

A popular marketing ploy for a consultancy is the use of a survey to create publicity for its services on a particular area. Surveys of this kind are frequently carried out using a technique based on the first two steps of Delphi technique as described above. For example, a firm selling consultancy in telecommunications may decide to get publicity by publishing a survey of trends in corporate telecommunications over the next 10 years. The firm will start off by taking a number of basic questions and (using stage (i) of the Delphi technique) get the major responses. The initial questions might include, 'How will inter-office communications change?' The responses could be:

- increasing use of facsimile transmission;
- greater use of electronic mail in large organisations;
- no change in telephone use.

The consultancy could then poll a large number of telecommunications equipment users to assess the degrees of agreement with these (or rather more narrowly defined) statements. The results could be presented in a statistical format which could be very useful to those involved in business planning in the telecommunications industry. For example, the results might show that:

- facsimile transmission usage will not supplant mail services;
- electronic mail usage will increase in all organisations, whatever their size, within five years;
- telephone usage is expected to remain static, but the number of people using them in business will increase.

Very often the surveys will show how responses to each question were split. For example, the responses to a different question is shown below:

- In which year do you foresee nuclear fusion becoming a practical source of domestic power?

2000–2005	3%
2005–2010	15%
2010–2015	27%
2015–2020	25%
After 2020	5%
Never	25%

The third questionnaire feeds back data to the experts on how their opinions compared with the averages for all those that commented. This is illustrated in Figure A3.8.

The request for explanatory comments at the end again enriches the data. In Figure A3.8, for example, the difference in opinions may be because the respondent believes that electronic mail will supplant telephone usage.

From the above it is obvious that the Delphi technique is hard work. It needs a lot of analysis work on the part of those administering it and time and effort from those responding. With large panels it also needs careful organisation. It is a useful technique for consultants to have in their kitbag, but one to be used sparingly.

Figure A3.8 *Extract of example of Delphi technique questionnaire (Part 2)*

The table below shows how your opinion compared with the average for all experts: (0 = average, □ = your opinion)

14. Growth Rates over the next 5 years in inter-office communication	Growth factors			
	0.75–1.0	1.0–1.25	1.25–1.5	1.5+
14.1 Facsimile	□0			
14.2 Electronic mail			0	□
14.3 Telephones		□	0	

Please comment below for those instances where your prediction differs from the average.

Appendix 4   Visual aids

Experiments indicate that people remember what they see rather better than what they hear. Visual aids are therefore used in a presentation to aid understanding and increase retention, as well as to help make it more interesting.

There are many types of visual aids, and the pros and cons of those mainly used by consultants are described below, but first some general rules on their use are provided.

1   A visual aid should be for the benefit of the audience: it is to help you to communicate your message. It should be kept simple. I once saw a presenter use 50 complex slides covered with writing to illustrate a 30-minute presentation. It was disastrous: the slides confused rather than clarified what was said.
2   Make sure that your visual aids are visible to everybody in the audience. If you have the chance, check visibility beforehand. Remember not to get in the way yourself.
3   Remember to talk to the audience and not your visual aids. (This particularly applies if a projection screen is behind you.)
4   Notwithstanding the previous point, do check the visual aids from time to time; slides, for example, do get out of sequence or upside down, and you should check that what you expect is actually appearing on the screen.
5   Remember that, the more complicated the visual aid, the more likely it is to go wrong. Of presentation horror stories, 90 per cent involve a failure to do with visual aids.
6   Never forget that visual aids are meant to complement, not substitute for, a presentation. I have seen superb visual aids supporting appalling presentations; the presenters had thought the quality of the visual aids would hide the overall low standard. They didn't. Do not let the medium become a substitute for the message.

Blackboard

Blackboard and chalk are probably the simplest visual aid medium around, but are rarely used in business. Where I have come across them, the blackboard and easel have been used to support a flip chart.
Pros: very simple. Drawing/writing can be done during the presentation.
Cons: chalk is dirty to use. Black is not a particularly suitable background colour. If preparing beforehand, only one 'picture' is possible.

Verdict: avoid using it if you can. Apart from the disadvantages noted above, it is old-fashioned and smacks of school.

Whiteboard

Special coloured pens are used to write on the whiteboard.
Pros: as for the blackboards, but it shows up better.
Cons: if preparing beforehand, only one 'picture' is possible. Whiteboards can be difficult to clean.
Verdict: useful for illustrating points at a meeting in an office, but do not use them for more formal presentations.

Flip charts

Flip charts with felt-tip markers are very commonly used nowadays.
Pros: can be prepared beforehand or can be used 'live'. Sheets can be retained on pad or displayed by pinning up round the room (e.g., in a training session).
Cons: freehand lettering and drawing can look amateurish and be hard to read. Difficult to use without a flip chart stand as well.
Verdict: excellent for discussions, meetings of small groups and training courses. Less good for formal presentations, but a useful fallback if the screen-based visual aids are not appropriate or cannot be used.

Flock-backed or magnetic boards

These are specially prepared boards which adhere to a felt or magnetic surface.
Pros: visually interesting to watch the presenter put the picture together. Very useful for a 'build up' type of presentation.
Cons: require considerable work to prepare. Materials can get scruffy.
Verdict: probably best used to illustrate presentations which will be repeated (e.g., a standard training session).

Overhead projection

Transparencies, transpaques, viewfoils or acetates (as they are variously known) can be easily prepared and displayed on an overhead projector.
Pros: unlike most other projection methods, this can be used in daylight. Drawing/writing can be done 'live'. Under the presenter's control. Computer software and printers are available to produce transparencies to a high standard.
Cons: overhead projectors seem very fault-prone; cooling fans can be noisy and the bulbs seem to break at the least opportune times. Difficult to produce multi-coloured transparencies.

Verdict: good for formal presentations as a medium, but take care with preparation of the transparencies. In particular, avoid using a standard typewriter for lettering – it looks amateurish.

Slide projector

Slides should be used with large audiences in preferance to transparencies.
Pros: commands visual attention. Photographs can be shown if necessary.
Cons: slides may be more expensive to prepare than transparencies. Have to show slides in semi-darkness at least, with attendant problems for audience.
Verdict: slides now seem to be a common medium for formal presentations by management consultants. Common pitfall is that they 'say' rather than 'show' things.

Films

Films can be shown using a film projector or video.
Pros: very good for putting across a message in a consistent way. Commands attention.
Cons: everything else stops whilst the film is running. Costly to prepare, and it has to be prepared professionally, otherwise unfavourable comparisons will be made with television.
Verdict: useful in disseminating a message consistently (e.g., throughout a chain of 500 shops) during the course of a project. Not often used for consultancy presentations, but there are many films commercially available for training purposes.

Video projection

Video projection is useful not just for the projection of videotape; it can be used to display computer output, and there is software available which enables you to pre-programme a series of pictures.
Pros: the advantage of slides or transparencies, but more flexibility (e.g., allows moving images).
Cons: at the time of writing, the equipment is not commonly in use and you will have to transport your own.
Verdict: the most complicated type of visual aid, but it is impressive to see. Risk that the medium may get in the way of the message.

Appendix 5 The IMC code of professional conduct and ethical guidelines

The institute of Management Consultants (IMC) is the recognised professional institute for management consultants in the UK. It has a long-established code of professional conduct, to which its members are subject. This code, however, is valuable for all management consultants, and is therefore reproduced in full below.

Principle 1

Meeting the client's requirements

A member shall regard the client's requirements and interests as paramount at all times.

Rules:

Competence
1.1   A member will only accept work that the member is qualified to perform and in which the client can be served effectively; a member will not make any misleading claims and will provide references from other clients if requested.

Agreement on deliverables and fees
1.2   A member shall agree formally with the client the scope, nature and deliverables of the services to be provided and the basis of remuneration, in advance of commencing work; any subsequent revisions will be subject to prior discussion and agreement with the client.

Sub-contracting
1.3   A member shall sub-contract work only with the prior agreement of the client, and, except where otherwise agreed, will remain responsible for the performance of the work.

Confidentiality
1.4   A member will hold all information concerning the affairs of clients in the strictest confidence and will not disclose proprietary information obtained during the course of assignments.

Non-poaching

1.5   A member will not invite or encourage any employee of a client for whom the member is working to consider alternative employment, unless it is the purpose of the assignment.

Due care

1.6   A member will make certain that advice, solutions and recommendations are based on thorough, impartial consideration and analysis of all available pertinent facts and relevant experience and are realistic, practicable and clearly understood by the client.

Communication

1.7   A member will ensure that the client is kept fully informed about the progress of the assignment.

1.8   A member will encourage and take note of any feedback provided by the client on the performance of the member's services.

Respect

1.9   A member will act with courtesy and consideration toward the individuals contacted in the course of undertaking assignments.

Principle 2

Integrity, independence, objectivity

A member shall avoid any action or situation inconsistent with the member's professional obligations or which in any way might be seen to impair the member's integrity. In formulating advice and recommendations the member will be guided solely by the member's objective view of the client's best interests.

Rules:

Disclosure

2.1   A member will disclose at the earliest opportunity any special relationships, circumstances or business interests which might influence or impair, or could be seen by the client or others to influence or impair, the member's judgement or objectivity on a particular assignment.

2.1.1   *Rule 2.1 requires the prior disclosure of all relevant personal, financial or other business interests which could not be inferred from the description of the services offered. In particular this relates to:*

- *any directorship or controlling interest in any business in competition with the client*
- *any financial interest in goods or services recommended or supplied to the client*
- *any personal relationship with any individual in the client's employ*
- *any personal investment in the client organisation or in its parent or any subsidiary companies*
- *any recent or current engagements in sensitive areas of work with directly competitive clients*
- *any work for a third party on the opposite side of a transaction e.g. bid defence, acquisitions, work for the regulator and the regulated, assessing the products of an existing client.*

Conflicts of interest

2.2   A member shall not serve a client under circumstances which are inconsistent with the member's professional obligations or which in any way might be seen to impair the member's integrity; wherever a conflict or potential conflict of interest arises, the member shall, as the circumstances require, either withdraw from the assignment, remove the source of conflict or disclose and obtain the agreement of the parties concerned to the performance or continuance of the engagement.

2.2.1   *It should be noted that the Institute may, depending on the circumstances, be one of the 'parties concerned'. For example, if a member is under pressure to act in a way which would bring the member into non-compliance with the Code of Professional Conduct, in addition to any other declaration which it might be appropriate to make, the facts should be declared to the Institute.*

Inducements

2.3   A member shall not accept discounts, hospitality, commissions or gifts as an inducement to show favour to any person or body, nor attempt to obtain advantage by giving financial inducements to clients or client staff.

2.3.1   *Payment for legitimate ,marketing activity may be made, and national laws should be respected.*

Privacy of information

2.4   A member shall not use any confidential information about a client's affairs, elicited during the course of an assignment for personal benefit or for the benefit of others outside the client organisation: there shall be no insider dealing or trading as legally defined or understood.

2.5   When required or appropriate a member will establish specific methods of working which preserve the privacy of the client's information.

Objectivity

2.6   A member will advise the client of any significant reservations the member may have about the client's expectation of benefits from an engagement.

2.7   A member will not indicate any short-term benefits at the expense of the long-term welfare of the client without advising the client of the implications.

Principle 3

Responsibility to the Profession and to the Institute

A member's conduct shall at all times endeavour to enhance the standing and public recognition of the profession and the Institute.

Rules:

Annual affirmation

3.1   A member will provide the Institute with annual affirmation of adherence to the Code of Professional Conduct.

Continuing Professional Development

3.2   A member will comply with the Institute's requirements on Continuing Professional Development in order to ensure that the knowledge and skills the member offers to clients are kept up to date.

3.3   A member will encourage management consultants for whom the member is responsible to maintain and advance their competence by participating in Continuing Professional Development and to obtain membership of the Institute.

Professional obligations to others

3.4   A member shall have respect for the professional obligations and qualifications of all others with whom the member works.

3.5   A member referring a client to another management consultant will not misrepresent the qualifications of the other management consultants, nor make any commitments for the other management consultant.

3.6   A member accepting an assignment for a client knowing that another management consultant is serving the client will ensure that any potential conflict between assignments is brought to the attention of the client.

3.7   When asked by a client to review the work of another professional, a member will exercise the objectivity, integrity and sensitivity required in all technical and advisory conclusions communicated to the client.

Fees

3.8   A member will negotiate agreements and charges for professional services only in a manner approved as ethical and professional by the Institute.

3.8.1   *Members are referred to the Institute's 'Guidelines on Charging for Management Consulting Services'.*

Publicity

3.9   A member, in publicising work or making representations to a client, shall ensure that the information given:

–   is factual and relevant
–   is neither misleading nor unfair to others
–   is not otherwise discreditable to the profession.

3.9.1   *Accepted methods of making experience and/or availability known include:*

–   *publication of work (with the consent of the client)*
–   *direct approaches to potential clients*
–   *entries in any relevant directory*
–   *advertisement (in printed publication, or on radio or television)*
–   *public speaking engagements.*

Members are referred to the Institute's 'Guidelines on the Promotion of Management Consulting Services'.

Personal Conduct

3.10   A member shall be a fit and proper person to carry on the profession of management consultancy.

3.10.1 *A member shall at all times be of good reputation and character. Particular matters for concern might include:*

- *conviction of a criminal offence or committal under bankruptcy p* *-*
  ceedings
- *censure or disciplining by a court or regulatory authority*
- *unethical or improper behaviour towards employees or the general public.*

3.11 A member shall not wilfully give the Institute false, inaccurate, misleading or incomplete information.

More recently the IMC has established ethical guidelines for its members. An abridged version of their guidance document is given below.

The Institute has published these guidelines to assist members and to provide some tests which can be used to gauge the extent or otherwise of members' ethical behaviour.

In addition to the three Principles in the Code of Conduct (shown above) this guidance describes two additional principles which should attach to an ethical decision, and sets out a number of questions designed to assist consultants to gain an objective insight to their quandary.

Basic guidelines

A consultant should consider, with these guidelines, the interests of a wider number and range of 'stakeholders'. 'Stakeholders' has become common usage in ethical circles to refer to those individuals or organisations who have an interest or stake in the situation. Stakeholders may include the general public and the national interest.

Two basic touchstones or tests to use are *transparency* and *vulnerability*

Transparency means the degree to which there is openness in the situation, that is, how much knowledge or information has been made available to the stakeholders. If there is not full and complete openness the reason for such lack of transparency should be carefully examined by the member.

Vulnerability refers to the extent to which each of the stakeholder's interests are at risk as a result of the proposed action (or inaction). It may be that a client or a third party is vulnerable because of ignorance, incompetence or financial weakness. A consultant must give due weight to stakeholder's interests before acting. However, the client comes first, and a consultant's ethical concerns and any resulting actions must be explained to the client.

Some questions for testing possible ethical dilemmas

Below are some questions designed to assist in considering how to deal with an ethical problem. They are not equally applicable to every situation and discretion should be exercised in selecting those that are relevant.

The background

It is important to try to place dilemmas in context, and the initial questions are designed to obtain facts about the situation.

1 Have you defined the circumstances accurately?

2 How did this situation occur?

3 What is your role in this situation?

4 How does your intention compare with the probable results?

5 Are you confident that your position is as valid over a long period of time, as it seems now?

6 Under what conditions would you allow exceptions to your stand?

This process itself may bring a different perspective to a matter, which may result in the potential dilemma dissolving without further action. The very act of seeking objective facts may expose the core of the problem and thus its potential resolution. Some consultants may find that progressing each of these questions with a trusted colleague or associate may help to clarify the answers and make the action to be taken easier to identify.

However, the clearer understanding obtained as a result of your self-questioning may serve to heighten the dilemma and expose a difficult challenge. The following questions are suggested to help you formulate a solution.

Vulnerabilities

1 What options do you have? As an adviser?

2 What opportunities do you have to discuss the issue with a colleague or third party?

3 What are the consequences for each stakeholder of your action – or equally important - inaction?

4 To whom and to what, do you give your loyalty as a person and as a member of the organisation?

5 Could your actions withstand cross-examination in court by an eminent barrister?
(This question is proposed as the strictest of all public credibility tests.)

This second group of questions is aimed at helping individual members to formulate an objective understanding of their quandary and to understand where the vulnerabilities lie.

The next few questions are focused differently, and are concerned with transparency. If you feel uncomfortable about any of the answers, you should probe more deeply into the reason(s) for this.

Transparency

1 Can you discuss the problem with the client before you make the decision?

2 Would you feel coomfortable explaining your behaviour to your family? Your friends? Your fellow workers?

3 Would you feel comfortable if your actions were announced on television or printed in a newspaper?

4 Would you feel confident that the action you propose to take (or not to take) would be viewed as proper by your peers?

Conclusion

These testing questions are offered as guidance for consultants to help in forming their own opinion. The questions are not exhaustive or exclusive, and other questions may suggest themselves during the course of working through the process.

Full details of these guidelines, together with a commentary on the questions raised, are available from the IMC.

Coventry University